FILM AFTER FILM

FILM AFTER FILM

Or, What Became of 21st-Century Cinema?

J. Hoberman

VERSO
London • New York

This paperback edition first published by Verso 2013
First published by Verso 2012
© J. Hoberman 2012, 2013

1 3 5 7 9 10 8 6 4 2

Verso
UK: 6 Meard Street, London W1F 0EG
US: 20 Jay Street, Suite 1010, Brooklyn, NY 11201
www.versobooks.com

Verso is the imprint of New Left Books

ISBN-13: 978-1-78168-143-5

British Library Cataloguing in Publication Data
A catalogue record for this book is available from the British Library

Library of Congress Has Cataloged the Hardcover Edition as Follows

Hoberman, J.
  Film after film : or, what became of 21st-century cinema? / J. Hoberman.
      p. cm.
  Includes bibliographical references and index.
  ISBN 978-1-84467-751-1 (hardback : alk. paper)
  1. Motion pictures—History—21st century. 2. Motion pictures—Reviews. 3. Digital
media—Philosophy. I. Title.
  PN1993.5.A1H58 2012
  791.43009'05—dc23
                                      2012015580

Typeset in Minion by MJ Gavan, Cornwall
Printed in the US by Maple Vail

CONTENTS

PREFACE

It may seem absurd, barely a decade into the millennium, to speak of a distinctly "twenty-first-century cinema." Despite the universal predilection for organizing trends by decades, it's obvious that cultural development is neither determined by a timetable nor bound to an arbitrary calendar. And yet, in the case of the cinema there are two—or even two and a half—reasons to consider the possibility that, since 2001, the nature and development of the motion picture medium has become irrevocably altered.

This new situation, which was accompanied by the oft-articulated perception that motion pictures, as they had existed in the century following the Lumière brothers' first demonstration of their *cinématographe*, had entered a period of irreversible decline, arises from a technological shift in the basic motion picture apparatus—namely, the shift from the photographic to the digital that began tentatively in the 1980s, and gathered momentum from the mid '90s onward. The digital turn occurred in the midst of and was amplified by pre-millennial jitters, not unlike the fantasy that the world's computers would crash when the date shifted from December 31, 1999 to January 1, 2000. The second, more unexpected and less rational, reason for the new situation occurred barely nine months into the twenty-first century. This was a world-historical happening, namely the events of September 11, 2001. As watched by millions "live" and in heavy rotation on TV—which is to say, as a form of cinema—these events could not help but challenge, mystify, and provoke filmmakers as individuals while, at the same time, dramatizing their medium directly in an impersonal way. No less than *Titanic* or *The Lord of the Rings* trilogy or the saga of *Harry Potter* (and actually, a good deal more so), the events of 9/11 were a show of cinematic might.

This is not to say that twentieth-century cinema no longer exists—even nineteenth-century cinema is with us still. But the digital turn, accompanied by a free-floating anxiety regarding the change in cinema's essential nature and a cataclysmic jolt out of the clear blue sky that, for the vast majority of the world's population, was apprehended as a manmade cinematic event, have all combined—perhaps conspired—to create something new. That new thing is the subject of this book.

Film After Film is a direct outgrowth of my work as both a lecturer on cinema history and a professional journalist who reviewed (or reported on) current movies on a weekly basis. Like many twenty-first-century films which fuse the digital and the photographic, *Film After Film* is also something of a cyborg entity, combining analysis and reportage. The book is divided into three parts. The first, titled "A Post-Photographic Cinema" (Film After Film) and greatly expanded from an essay first published in *Artforum*, proposes the notion of twenty-first-century cinema and attempts to characterize, theorize and historicize it. Part II, "A Chronicle of the Bush Years" (Film After Film After Film …), culls the 400 or so weekly reports and occasional cover stories I published in the *Village Voice* between September 2001 and November 2008 to revisit the early twenty-first century as it unfolded—or, put another way, to write the first draft of its film history.

The 750-word weekly film review is a specific journalistic form: over a period of months and years, these topical short pieces document a writer's attempt to make sense of the ongoing flux of movies amid the ongoing flux of events. Thus, part II is a chronicle of the George W. Bush presidency, a reign defined not only by the events of 9/11 but by continuous foreign wars, the much-publicized threat of additional terror attacks, and further disasters—both natural and manmade—as viewed from a screening room. The movies discussed are nearly all American and, while not necessarily the strongest of the period (some of those may be found in other sections) are nevertheless the ones that seemed most directly responsive to or reflective of the post-9/11 climate. Chronologically arranged, these journalistic reports have been somewhat edited but never updated. Rather than rewrite them in light of subsequent events (which include the movies' receptions), thus contaminating the spontaneity of an original impression, I have chosen to annotate and historically contextualize my original response in bold type.

As already noted, one impetus for *Film After Film* came from a series of university courses I taught on the nature of twenty-first-century cinema. This book is very much intended as a resource, if not a text, for similar courses. By way of an addendum (or an extended footnote to part I), part III, "Notes Toward a Syllabus" (Some Films After Film), offers twenty-one short essays on programs of work that I showed (or would have liked to have shown) in class. For a number of reasons—sometimes technical, at others thematic or aesthetic—these seem to me to be quintessentially twenty-first-century motion pictures. Reworked from class lectures and/or reviews—most of which were originally published in the *Village Voice*, though several versions of pieces first appeared elsewhere, including *Artforum* (*Battle in Heaven*, *The World*, and *The Strange Case of Angelica*), *Film Comment* (*Russian Ark* and *Carlos*, as well as the essay on Arnold Schwarzenegger), and *Sight and Sound* (*Dogville*)—these film notes focus on international production in a variety of cinematic modes (albeit work characterized by a certain historical self-consciousness).

Many, though not all, of the cinema-objects discussed here are available on DVD. In addition to providing practical suggestions for a survey of twenty-first-century cinema, this selection should serve to demonstrate that, hardly the arid desert some have imagined, the century's first decade abounded with significant and radically innovative cinema.

J. Hoberman
New York, March 2012

PART I:
A POST-PHOTOGRAPHIC CINEMA

I predict that all movies will be animated or computer-generated within fifteen years.

—Bruce Goldstein, "Flashback: The Year in Movies," *Village Voice* (December 28, 1999)

It is in the nature of analogical worlds to provoke a yearning for the past ... The digital will wants to change the world.

—D. N. Rodowick, *The Virtual Life of Film* (2007)

CHAPTER ONE

THE MYTH OF "THE MYTH OF TOTAL CINEMA"

Can we speak of a twenty-first-century cinema? And if so, on what basis?[1]

In the immediate aftermath of World War II, the French film critic André Bazin offered a narrative in opposition to a then current notion that cinema developed in the spirit of scientific inquiry. Bazin characterized cinema as an idealistic phenomenon and cinema-making as an intrinsically irrational enterprise—namely, the obsessive quest for that complete representation of reality that he termed Total Cinema.

"There was not a single inventor who did not try to combine sound and relief with animation of the image," Bazin maintained in "The Myth of Total Cinema." Each and every new technological development—synchronous sound, full-color, stereoscopic or 3-D movies, Smell-O-Vision—served to take the cinema nearer to its imagined essence, which is to say that "cinema has not yet been invented!" Moreover, once true cinema was achieved, the medium itself would disappear—just like the state under true communism. Writing in 1946, Bazin believed that this could happen

---

1   In the context of this discussion, I will use *cinema* to mean a form of recorded and hence repeatable moving image and, for the most part, synchronized recorded sound. Television kinescopes and TV since videotape are *cinematic*; so is YouTube. The terms *motion pictures* or *movies* imply a projected image; *film* refers to movies that are produced on or projected as celluloid (or its derivatives) and hence have some basis in photography.

by 2000. In fact, something else occurred: the development of digital computer-generated imagery (CGI) broke the special relationship that existed between photography and the world.

The Myth of Total Cinema, the "recreation of the world in its own image," was for Bazin a factor of cinema's essence: the medium's integral realism was predicated on the camera's impartial gaze (the French word for lens is *objectif*), as well as the chemical reaction by which light left an authentic trace on photographic emulsion. In "The Ontology of the Photographic Image," an essay published in 1945, Bazin had noted that "photography affects us like a phenomenon in nature … The photograph as such and the object in itself share a common being." Because of this impartial, indexical connection between the photograph and that which was photographed (the profilmic subject or event), motion pictures produced an all-but-automatic image "unburdened" by artistic interpretation. Like a shadow or a bullet hole, a photograph was a form of evidence—a "hallucination that is also a fact." Moreover, each photograph was derived from its own material evidence in the form of the negative image produced by the initial photo-chemical reaction. Such negatives might be altered, cropped in the course of printing, or even destroyed but, at least initially, the image existed as a recognizable physical entity—unlike the infinitely malleable binary code produced, however indexically, by a digital camera.[2]

The divorce between photography and the world was initially experienced as a crisis in photography. Thanks to Photoshop, the image editing program first introduced in 1990, as well as other forms of digital manipulation, the photographic became an element or subset of the graphic. Previously, as art historian Julian Stallabrass observed in the mid 1990s, "forging ordinary photographs involved great skill and, if all variants and the original negatives were not destroyed, could always be unmasked." Digitalization, which made image manipulation easily accessible, was "a technique which lends itself to the production of useful lies." Photography might retain "its powers of resemblance," but it would lose "its veracity."[3]

---

2 Both "The Myth of Total Cinema" and "The Ontology of the Photographic Image" are included in Bazin's *What Is Cinema?*, ed. and trans. Hugh Gray, Los Angeles: University of California Press, 1967.

3 Julian Stallabrass, *Gargantua: Manufactured Mass Culture*, London: Verso, 1996.

As the digitally manipulable photograph superseded the world as raw material for image-making, the existential crisis for motion pictures was even more intense: Bazin had imagined cinema as the objective "recreation of the world." Yet digital image-making precludes the necessity of having the world, or even a really existing subject, before the camera—let alone the need for a camera. Photography had been superseded, if not the desire to produce images that moved. Chaplin was perhaps but a footnote to Mickey Mouse; what were *The Birth of a Nation* and *Battleship Potemkin* compared to *Toy Story 3*? With the advent of CGI, the history of motion pictures was now, in effect, the history of animation.[4]

---

4   Although hardly the most expensive, the most radical use of photographic motion pictures as visual data to be digitally sweetened may be found in Richard Linklater's feature animations *Waking Life* (2001) and *A Scanner Darkly* (2006), both of which were originally shot and edited as ordinary motion pictures. Many animations, most famously Disney's *Snow White* (1937), made use of a rotoscope to trace the motion of filmed performers; Linklater employed a digital rotoscope, using a program created by art director Bob Sabiston, that logarithmically transformed his original footage into animation. (Faces are abstracted, although their expressions remain remarkably precise; landscape is rendered as swaths of color characterized by shifting paint-by-numbers highlights. Outlines are unstable, with a woozy Soutine-like flow. The earth heaves and shudders; space bobs and weaves.) *Waking Life* includes an ironic discourse on André Bazin's ontology of the photographic image, playfully dramatizing the Bazinian notion of motion pictures as tied to reality and intrinsic to a specific time-space, while the title of *A Scanner Darkly*, from Philip K. Dick's novel, takes on additional meaning as reality is refracted through an alternate form of photography.

CHAPTER TWO

THE MATRIX: "A PRISON FOR YOUR MIND"

The process began in the early 1980s with two expensive and much-publicized Hollywood features—both of which, like certain animated cartoons of the 1920s, inserted "live actors" into virtual environments. *One From the Heart* (1982), Francis Ford Coppola's experiment in electronic image-making, returned but $1 million on a $26-million investment and effectively destroyed his studio, while Disney's *Tron* (1982) the first sustained exercise in computer-generated imagery, was a movie whose costly special effects and mediocre box-office returns would be credited with (or blamed for) delaying CGI-based cinema for a decade.[1]

---

1   This is not true. *Tron* was not a fiasco, nor was the progress of CGI cinema halted. For the first time, however, the digital tail wagged the analogic dog: *Tron* was out-grossed by the coin-operated arcade video-game released in conjunction with the movie. A second game, *Discs of Tron*, appeared in 1983; the computer game *Tron 2.0* was released in 2003, following the movie's appearance on DVD. The 2011 3-D "reboot," *Tron: Legacy*, essentially recapitulated the earlier film by being set almost entirely inside a computer with characters who are anthropomorphized bits of computer code. However ridiculously literal-minded the premise, the idea of a game programmer vanishing into his creation is still an apposite allegory, and the setting is more than appropriate, as just about everything worthwhile about *Tron: Legacy* is computer-generated.

In a 2003 essay, British producer Keith Griffith enumerated the landmarks of Hollywood digital cinema, going back nearly twenty years:

Tron's literalist representation of cyberspace predated William Gibson's *Neuromancer* by several years, although the movie was actually closer to *Alice in Wonderland* or *The Wizard of Oz* in supposedly taking place inside a computer where all the characters, except the hacker Flynn (Jeff Bridges), were—in a longstanding Disney tradition—anthropomorphized computer code. As such, *Tron* might be considered a founding example of cyborg cinema, combining digital and photographic imagery. The movie's most dramatic effect was the virtual tracking shot, in which a non-existent camera seemed to move through an imaginary landscape. More advanced and popular cyborgs, Steven Spielberg's *Jurassic Park* (1993) and George Lucas's *The Phantom Menace* (1999), seamlessly fused photography and CGI imagery to have real people interact convincingly onscreen with non-existent creatures, offering early clues to the new direction. So did the numerous popular discussions surrounding the production of digital personalities like Lara Croft, who made her first appearance in the 1996 video game *Tomb Raider*, or the resurrection of dead film stars, as in the 1995 episode of HBO's aptly titled *Tales from the Crypt*, featuring "Humphrey Bogart," or the Super Bowl

---

Barry Levinson's *Young Sherlock Holmes* (1985) was the first film to feature a computer-generated character in the form of a stained-glass knight; in *Star Trek IV* (1986) the heads of the principal cast were scanned to create a time-travel effect. Three-dimensional computer-generated imagery made its debut in James Cameron's *The Abyss* (1989), and he then carried forward his experiments in morphing to create the first human-based computer character in *Terminator 2* (1992).

Applied in a more naturalistic fashion, this technique is referred to as "motion capture" and was commonly used in video games from the mid 1990s onward.

In *Death Becomes Her* (1992), Robert Zemickis digitally cosmeticised both Meryl Streep and Goldie Hawn, while in Spielberg's *Jurassic Park* (1993), with its realistic marauding prehistoric animals, audiences were reportedly driven to edge of their seats. *Forrest Gump* (1994), *The Mask* (1994), *Casper* (1995), and *Species* (1995), were all landmark, mega-budget films from the front line of a digital cinema movement, which was to lead to *Toy Story* (1995), the first 100-percent computer-generated animation motion picture. Since then the technological process has accelerated phenomenally and *Titanic* (1997), *Antz* (1998), *A Bug's Life* (1998), *The Phantom Menace* (1999), *The Matrix* (1999), and *Gladiator* (2000), all "pushed the digital envelope" further than most people could have dreamt was possible a decade earlier.

XXXI commercial in which "Fred Astaire" danced with a Broom Vac.[2]

Both *Jurassic Park* and *The Phantom Menace* also engaged in a particular form of naturalization by inscribing CGI into prehistory, whether that of planet Earth or of the *Star Wars* saga. In his 2001 book, *The Language of New Media*, Lev Manovich made the provocative observation that the aesthetic underlying *Jurassic Park* is akin to Socialist Realism, which strove to project the radiant future socialist society into the familiar world of the present. *Jurassic Park* strives "to show the future of sight itself."

> Just as Socialist Realist paintings blended the perfect future with imperfect reality, *Jurassic Park* blends the future supervision of computer graphics with the familiar vision of the film image ... The dinosaurs are present to tell us that computer images belong safely to a past long gone— even though we have every reason to believe that they are messengers from a future still to come.

The Phantom Menace, which was also projected digitally in some theaters, not only evoked but embodied the future of cinema. So, in another way, did Douglas Gordon's 1993 video installation, *24 Hour Psycho*—in which, wrenched from its natural context and re-presented as a re-animated (or perhaps, de-animated), glacially slow-motion digital image of itself, requiring a full day to watch, Hitchcock's old-fashioned analog motion picture became an extreme object of contemplation.[3]

---

2 Television commercials aside, this form of reanimation has remained largely hypothetical, despite the projects starring Bruce Lee and George Burns announced in the wake of *Jurassic Park* (Katharine Stalter and Ted Johnson, "H'wood cyber dweebs are raising the dead," *Variety*, 11/4/1996). In 1998, Universal Pictures announced an "all-digital" feature that would bring back Boris Karloff's Frankenstein monster in a new sequel to the studio's 1931 *Frankenstein*; the project was never realized.

3 Gus Van Sant's 1998 shot-by-shot remake of *Psycho* is an analog analog. Everything about the personal relations in the original *Psycho* suggests a present dominated by the dead hand of the past. So, too, Van Sant's movie. How well-made it seems! How powerful the music, economical the staging, creepy the premise, clever the mise-en-scène, crisp and confident the editing ... how unfashionably leisurely the pace! Who needs actors?

The most paradoxical aspect of Van Sant's recreation is its timid fidelity to a movie that smashed the commercial conventions of its day. Thus, this new *Psycho* is often surprisingly OK. It is, after all, still *Psycho*—just a superfluous and inferior version.

A cyborg production like *24 Hour Psycho* further induces what some experience as a loss of temporal indexicality. Cinematographer and film-maker Babette Mangolte has argued that digital image-making may be distinguished from photographic cinema in its intrinsic inability to embody temporal duration or a sense of "real time," and that this is true even when photographic motion pictures are projected in digital form: "Why," she wonders,

> is the brightness of the LCD screen, the relentless glare of the digital image with no shutter reprieve, no back and forth between one forty-eighth of a second of dark followed by one forty-eighth of projected images, with no repetitive pattern as regular as your own heartbeat, unable to establish and construct an experiential sense of time passing and why could the projected image do it so effortlessly in the past and still can?

Mangolte's question, posed in the 2003 anthology *Camera Obscura, Camera Lucida*, suggests that, for some, the essence of film—if not cinema—is not so much a matter of the photographic indexical as the presence of a material flicker; film may be defined by the rhythm of the motion picture projector, which is to say the sense of motion pictures as an apparatus or machine. In this sense, the Austrian avant-garde filmmaker Peter Kubelka's 1958 *Arnulf Rainer* which, made without a camera, alternates clear and opaque 16mm footage, may be considered cinema's Ground Zero and the series of frame-by-frame painted films with which Stan Brakhage ended his career an assertion of film's material, a-photographic essence.[4]

Rather than indexicality of the photographic image, the new essence of cinema might be found in Andrei Tarkovsky's notion of "imprinted time" or duration. Writing on the significance of the first Lumière *actualités*, Tarkovsky observed that

> for the first time in the history of the arts, in the history of culture, man found the means to *take an impression of time*. And simultaneously the possibility of reproducing that time on screen as often as he wanted, to repeat it and go back to it. He acquired a matrix for *actual time*. Once

---

4   In the radiant future of 2000, Brakhage's painted cinema, along with the simulated 3-D projection pieces that Ken Jacobs called "The Impossible," Luis Recoder's projection of two films through a single projector, and even the enthusiastic audiences for the Museum of Modern Art's ongoing series of 8mm and super-8 cinema, seemed to be examples of "film outliving its death."

seen and recorded, time could now be preserved in metal boxes over a long period (theoretically for ever) … *Time, printed in its factual forms and manifestations*: such is the supreme idea of cinema as an art.

It has often been observed that, with its absence of flicker and greater sense of continuity, the video image seems eternally "present." What then is one to make of Christian Marclay's 2010 installation *The Clock*, a digitally-projected assemblage of photographic motion pictures that, in its perfectly chronological, minute-to-minute temporal references, functions as a twenty-four-hour timekeeper? (*The Clock's* thousands of clips include everything from *High Noon* and *Easy Rider* to *Back to the Future* and *Pulp Fiction*. No list can possibly do it justice.) In London, New York, Los Angeles, and elsewhere, *The Clock* demonstrated Tarkovsky's assertion—albeit in a vulgar sense—as it held an audience spellbound and hyper-aware of time passing.[5]

Although the suspense inherent in many of the original clips undoubtedly contributed to *The Clock's* power to fascinate the spectator, one might also observe that the heightened awareness of time, as well as *The Clock's* utilitarian capacity to tell time in real time, provided a new sort of indexicality: The experience of watching a movie is forcibly literalized as the experience of watching a movie and this is further emphasized by the presence of so much familiar material. For many, much of *The Clock* is pre-saturated in personal memory or nostalgia.[6]

5   See Randy Kennedy and Ben Ratliff, "Flock Around 'The Clock,'" *New York Times*, 2/17/2011. Klaus Biesenbach reports a similar experience when Douglas Gordon's *24 Hour Psycho* was first shown at Kunst-Werke in Berlin in 1993 (*Douglas Gordon: Timeline*, New York: The Museum of Modern Art, 2006, 14). Among the many salient observations regarding Marclay's editing, sources and sleight of hand, documentary filmmaker Thom Andersen noted, in *The Clock's* wittiest, most erudite early appreciation, that the installation "takes time away, and then gives it back … It is a very generous movie [*sic*]" ("Random notes on a Projection of The Clock by Christian Marclay at the Los Angeles County Museum of Art, 4:32 PM, July 28, 2011–5:02 PM, July 29, 2011," *Cinema Scope*, Fall 2011).

6   As noted by Rodowick, "If photography and film are the matrix from which time-based spatial media evolve, then an ontological examination of the medium, no matter how variable or unfinished, leads to the surprising conclusion that what we have valued in film are our confrontations with time and time's passing" (*The Virtual Life of Film*, Cambridge, Mass.: Harvard University Press, 2007, 73).

It may be argued that, as fashioned from pre-existing, often well-known movie and television clips and thus employing many beloved stars, *The Clock* was in fact a traditional motion picture or, at the very least, a celebration of motion pictures and their undying appeal. (It was praised by several New York art critics specifically for its presumed love for movies.) Nevertheless this epic projection was, of course, digital, and—like *24 Hour Psycho* or other Gordon installations—only possible as a form of digital image-making. *The Clock*'s occasional cropping and stretching of the original material is a factor of the high-definition video format which demands a 16:9 aspect ratio. (Marclay employed further digital manipulation in making *The Clock*, sweetening some footage by removing voiceovers that implied a past tense, eliminating overly emphatic music, and creating new sound effects where necessary.)

In short, whether as a source of visual data or as a delivery system, computer-generated imagery has introduced a radical impurity into the motion picture apparatus that was developed at the turn of the twentieth century and which, save for the introduction of synchronous sound, remained markedly consistent for 100 years. Thus, *The Matrix* (1999), written and directed by the brothers Larry and Andy Wachowski, represents a landmark hybrid in its combination of live action with frame-by-frame digital manipulation. No previous animated film had so naturalistically represented the physical world. "Once you have seen a movie like *The Matrix*, you can't unsee it," a Los Angeles exhibitor told the *New York Times* in 2002, referring to the ways in which CGI had altered the action film, in part by allowing serious actors to perform impossible stunts. *The Matrix*, as film critic David Edelstein would note the following year, "changed not only the way we look at movies but movies themselves." *The Matrix* "cut us loose from the laws of physics in

---

Not only does *The Clock* preserve analogic cinema but also the idea of time-keeping paraphernalia, a technology that is also being rendered anachronistic—in this case by cell and smart phones. Something of this pleasure could be seen in the enthusiastic response to two overtly revivalist and cinephilic (as well as extremely successful) movies released in the same year *The Clock* appeared, namely Michel Hazanavicius' *The Artist*, a faux silent-era movie, shot in black and white and an old-fashioned 1:33 screen ratio, and Martin Scorsese's *Hugo*, a 3-D extravaganza celebrating cinema pioneer Georges Méliès. Striking in my experience of both movies was the evident delight that audiences took in their anachronistic attractions—exaggerated silent cinema acting and primitive, hand-painted trick films.

ways that no live-action film had ever done, exploding our ideas of time and space on screen."[7]

In addition to vaulting the gap between photographed humans and computer-generated humanoids known as the "uncanny valley," *The Matrix* provided an irresistible ruling metaphor that was heightened in its force by the approaching millennium—humanity lives in simulation, in a computer-generated illusion created to conceal the terrifying Desert of the Real. "There's something wrong with the world, but you don't know what it is," the most informed character told the movie's computer-nerd protagonist, articulating the loss of photographic certainty in a digital world even while offering the red pill that will allow the protagonist to see things as they actually are.

As with *Tron*, the hacker was the hero but, to a far more sophisticated degree, cyberspace was the place. Despite its fantastic premise, *The Matrix* evoked and identified a recognizable world—a new social reality in which freedom and social control had merged, while information, entertainment, fantasy, advertising, and communication seemed indistinguishable. This was reinforced by the movie's incidental social realism—the narrative was not just dependent on computers but cell phones and instant messages. At the same time, *The Matrix*'s own matrix of self-referential film sequels and websites, as well as participatory fan sites and video games, suggest an entire virtual environment.[8]

Media theorist Henry Jenkins considers *The Matrix* to be the quintessential "entertainment for the age of media convergence … a narrative

---

7   Rick Lyman, "Job Openings in Hollywood: Heroes Wanted," *New York Times*, 8/4/2002; David Edelstein, "Bullet Time Again: The Wachowskis Reload," *New York Times*, 5/11/2003.

8   *Enter the Matrix* cost $20 million to produce, the most expensive such game up until that time, while *The Matrix* further distinguished itself from traditional movies in its adapting computer gaming as a basis for narrative. David Cronenberg's *eXistenZ* (1999), released a few months before, explored the same idea. But where *The Matrix* was predicated on a demonic computer program, *eXistenZ* played with the notion of a virtual-reality game in which there is no real world to which one can return. (There is no red pill in *eXistenZ*—it's all fun and games, complete with the Freudian notion of a "game urge.") Other non-linear, game- or web-driven movies released in 1998 and 1999 include *The Truman Show*, *The Blair Witch Project*, *Fight Club*, *Run Lola Run*, and *Being John Malkovich*. In the summer of 2001, Paramount opened *Lara Croft: Tomb Raider*, eventually to become the top-grossing movie ever based on a video game.

so large that it cannot be contained within a single medium." *The Matrix* further benefited from and made use of DVD technology which, introduced in 1996, came into its own as a consumer product in the late 1990s (and soon began to provide the movie industry's margin of profit), not least because of the extras the new format permitted, including commentary and self-promoting production documentaries. In August 2000, Time Warner announced that a record-setting 3 million *Matrix* DVDs had been sold. What's more, in addition to promoting itself, *The Matrix* also popularized certain ideas associated with French philosopher Jean Baudrillard—namely the notion of the Hyperreal, "a real without origin or reality," which might be one way to characterize CGI, as well as *The Matrix* itself.[9]

In short, *The Matrix* (now hopelessly dated) was understood in its moment as an historical event. Shortly before millennial New Year, *Entertainment Weekly* made Jeff Gordinier's "1999: The Year That Changed the Movies" its cover story. "Films of the new guard dart and weave," Gordinier wrote, "they reflect the cut-and-paste sensibility of videogames, the Internet, and hip-hop," as well as the MTV-conditioned sensibility of the audience. "You don't 'watch' a film like *Fight Club*," Gordinier explained, "you mainline a deluge of visual and sonic information (including a hefty chunk of the IKEA catalog) straight into your cranium." Speaking for his audience, David Fincher had reassured the movie's producers: "Don't worry, the audience will be able to follow this. This is not unspooling your tale. This is downloading."

Released at the height of the dot.com bubble, during a period in which computers saturated the home entertainment market in the manner that television did in the 1950s, *The Matrix* was an idea whose time had clearly come. In January 2000, less than a year after the movie's release, Time Warner—the world's largest media conglomerate as well as the studio that produced *The Matrix*—merged with the world's largest internet-service provider, America Online (AOL), in a deal which involved the transfer of $182 billion in stocks and debts and was the largest in history.

---

9   As Herbert Muschamp wrote of *The Matrix*, shortly after its release, one is "never entirely certain what is real photography, what is computer-generated imagery, what is a location, what is a set, what actions are performed by actors, what by stand-ins" ("If the Cityscape Is Only a Dream," *New York Times*, 5/2/1999).

Evoking "a prison that you cannot smell or taste or touch ... a prison for your mind," *The Matrix* premise invited allegory. For architecture critic Herbert Muschamp, the Matrix suggested "the monoculture of shopping malls, theme parks, edge cities, suburban subdivisions, convention centers and hotels." It might also be AOL Time Warner or Hollywood or the National Entertainment State. The main thing is this: one cannot stand outside it. Thus, in the universe of *The Matrix*, Bazin's dream arrived as a nightmare, in the form of a virtual cyber existence: Total Cinema as a total dissociation from reality.[10]

---

10   The familiarity of this trope may be deduced from the bored disappointment that characterizes the critical reception accorded *The Matrix Reloaded* and *The Matrix Revolutions* (both 2003). However these movies elaborated on the original *Matrix* mythology, they were understood as banal recapitulations.

CHAPTER THREE

THE NEW REALNESS

"If the plastic arts were put under psychoanalysis," Bazin begins his "Ontology of the Photographic Image," then "the practice of embalming the dead might turn out to be a fundamental factor in their creation." If the motion pictures of the twenty-first century were placed under psychoanalysis, their symptoms might reveal two types of anxiety—one objective, the other hysterical.

Objective anxiety is manifested both in a recognition that the motion picture *medium*, as it has more or less existed since 1896, is in an apparently irreversible decline—the mass audience is eroded, national film industries have been defunded, film labs are shuttered, film stocks terminated and formats rendered obsolete, parts for broken 16mm-projectors are irreplaceable, laptop computers have been introduced as a delivery system—and then in a feeling among cinema-oriented intellectuals that film *culture* is disappearing. The latter may be seen in the increased marginalization of movie criticism as a journalistic practice and the experience of a more general lost love of movies (or cinephilia), as most eloquently and pessimistically articulated by Susan Sontag in her widely read centennial essay, "The Decay of Cinema."

"Each art breeds its fanatics," Sontag declared. "The love that cinema inspired, however, was special.

It was born of the conviction that cinema was an art unlike any other: quintessentially modern; distinctively accessible; poetic and mysterious and erotic and moral—all at the same time. Cinema had apostles. (It was like religion.) Cinema was a crusade. For cinephiles, the movies encapsulated everything. Cinema was both the book of art and the book of life.[1]

This objective anxiety is also a factor of what film theorist David Rodowick has termed the "digital will"—namely the sense that CGI technology inherently strives to remake the world while motion pictures (as we knew them), having surrendered their privileged relationship with the real, are in some sense obsolete. It is this anxiety that underscores the *neo*-neo-realist position of the Danish Dogma '95 group despite, or perhaps because of, its use of digital video. The most important motion pictures produced according to Dogma's ten commandments were Lars von Trier's *Idiots* (1997) and Jesper Jargil's *The Humiliated*, a 1998 documentary on the making of *Idiots*, precisely because of their emphasis on "life-acting," namely the staging and documenting of authentic transgressive behavior.[2]

---

1   Not insignificantly, Sontag linked the medium's decline to the approaching millennium: "Cinema, once heralded as the art of the twentieth century, seems now, as the century closes numerically, to be a decadent art" ("The Decay of Cinema," *New York Times Magazine*, 2/25/1996).

2   The original Dogma restrictions were as follows:

1. Filming must be done on location. Props and sets must not be brought in (if a particular prop is necessary for the story, a location must be chosen where this prop is to be found).
2. No background music. The sound must never be produced apart from the images or vice versa. (Music must not be used unless it occurs within the scene being filmed, i.e., diegetic.)
3. No tripod. The camera must be a hand-held camera. Any movement or immobility attainable in the hand is permitted. (The film must not take place where the camera is standing; filming must take place where the action takes place.)
4. The film must be in color. Special lighting is not acceptable. (If there is too little light for exposure the scene must be cut or a single lamp be attached to the camera).
5. No f/x. Optical work and filters are forbidden.
6. The film must not contain superficial action. (Murders, weapons, etc. must not occur.)

The key expression of objective anxiety, however, is Jean-Luc Godard's magisterial *In Praise of Love* (2001) which, no less than Godard's first feature *Breathless*—albeit with somewhat less jouissance—responds to a new situation in cinema history.

Two-thirds shot on black-and-white 35mm and the rest on luridly synthesized digital video, *In Praise of Love* mourns the loss of photographic cinema, as well as the memory and history that, more than an indexical trace, photography makes material. Studied as they are, Godard's unprepossessing, sometimes harsh images of the city and its inhabitants—many of them dispossessed—feel as newly minted as the earliest Lumière brothers views; they evoke the thrill of light becoming emulsion. Much of the movie is a voluptuous urban nocturne with particular emphasis on the transitory sensations that were the essence of the first motion pictures. (*Pace* Bazin, there are passages where *In Praise of Love* appears like a fact of nature while Hollywood movies, exemplified by *Schindler's List* and *The Matrix*—which are, at least by association, digital—are rather, Godard insists, a substitute for history.)

Such cinematic eulogies were not uncommon in the early twenty-first century. These twilight movies include Tsai Ming-liang's *Goodbye, Dragon Inn* (2003), a lament for vanished popular cinema, its audience, and its means of presentation, in a specifically Taiwanese context, as well as several notable avant-garde films such as Pat O'Neill's *Decay*

---

7. Temporal and geographical alienation are forbidden. (That is to say that the film takes place here and now.)
8. Genre movies are not acceptable.
9. The final picture must be transferred to the Academy 35mm film with an aspect ratio of 4:3, that is, not widescreen. [A requirement stipulating that the film be *filmed* on Academy 35mm was relaxed to allow digital video productions.]
10. The director must not be credited.

The tenth commandment may be taken as a joke.

The main thing distinguishing Dogma's realism from *cinéma vérité* was the presence of actors. Thus *Idiots* (1998) is a movie about acting … out: Operating under some obscure philosophical imperative, the youthful members of a Copenhagen commune confound the local bourgeoisie with a form of dada guerrilla theater, engaging in wildly regressive, sometimes disgusting behavior in public places—what they call "spassing"—and thus making a tragicomic spectacle of adult normals drooling, thrashing, disrobing, otherwise mimicking extreme agitation of the mentally disabled.

of Fiction, Bill Morrison's *Decasia,* and Ernie Gehr's *Cotton Candy* (all released in 2002). As Tsai presented the ghost-ridden movie theater, so *Decay of Fiction* evokes a haunted movie set. O'Neill spectrally populated the abandoned Ambassador Hotel, an old-time movie-star hangout and frequent movie location, with transparent actors dressed according to period styles.[3]

In a 2011 roundtable on experimental digital cinema, filmmaker Lynne Sachs identified a nostalgic "fetishism of decay," noting digital effects designed to simulate film scratches and dust: "We don't want things to age. Nevertheless, we miss the chemical reactions, the fact that physical things change, so we simulate decay." Each in its way, *Decasia* and *Cotton Candy* savor photographic disintegration even as they are overtly preservationist in intent. Rather than a moldering hotel, Morrison documents decomposing 35mm nitrate footage culled from a number of film archives, while Gehr records the ancient pre-cinematic toys in San Francisco's Musée Mécanique, notably the sort of hand-cranked photographic flip-book known as mutoscopes and most particularly (so it seems) those with photographs that are torn, faded or damaged.[4]

We may not, per Babette Mangolte, experience time according to the rhythm of twenty-four frames per second, but we are watching change. That *Decasia* and *The Decay of Fiction* have been largely exhibited in digital form while *Cotton Candy* was digitally produced infuses their pragmatism with a measure of rueful, guilty digital ambivalence. (The abandonment of the old medium is similarly acknowledged in Linkletter's *Waking Life* which, shot and edited as an ordinary motion picture, yet proposes a new sort of indexicality.) At the same time, however, several distinguished film artists created digital works which in their use of real

---

3   *The Decay of Fiction* exemplifies a particular cinematic uncanny, in which historically self-conscious ghost movies are set in places haunted by movies. The founding example is Billy Wilder's 1950 *Sunset Boulevard,* a noirish Hollywood story made in the late afternoon—the magic hour—of the studio system. Wilder brought back a silent star Gloria Swanson to play her aged self thus satirizing while attesting to the power of motion pictures to reanimate past and raise dead. (See my "'A Bright, Guilty World': Daylight Ghosts and Sunshine Noir," *Artforum*: February 2007.)

4   Roundtable on Digital Experimental Filmmaking, *October* 137 (Summer 2011). Ironically, images preserved as digital data have a far shorter life than images preserved on polyester safety film. See John Belton, "Digital Film: A False Revolution," *October* 100 (Spring 2002).

time and duration, could be said to make the motion picture medium *more itself*. However dissimilar, Abbas Kiarostami's "undirected" Warholian tracking film and acting vehicle *Ten* and Aleksandr Sokurov's ninety-five-minute single take *Russian Ark* amplified each other for both premiering in competition at the 2002 Cannes Film Festival. (Neither won any awards.)

Russian Ark, in which Sokurov's camera tours Petersburg's Hermitage Museum in one choreographed movement, was distinguished by a number of historical achievements—as the first unedited single-screen, single-take full-length feature film; as the longest single SteadiCam sequence; and as the first uncompressed High Definition movie recorded onto a portable hard disc. And yet, as pointed out by Rodowick, who insists that "digitally acquired information has no ontological distinctiveness from digitally synthesized outputs that construct virtual worlds," the certainty of watching absolute, unmediated continuity is gone. Rodowick does not address the possibility of an automatically printed time code, assuming perhaps that it could be easily forged. *Russian Ark* has significant post-production manipulation. In some instances, the frame has been resized to eliminate unwanted objects, the camera speed adjusted, the lighting modified, and the color temperatures conformed. In one scene the perspective of a wide-angle lens is simulated, while the movie ends with a swirl of digitally-created snow and fog. No less than *The Matrix*, then, *Russian Ark* is an animated movie created from photographic material.[5]

---

5   A parallel instance may be found in Alfonso Cuarón's 2006 science-fiction film *Children of Men*. Although cinematographer Emmanuel Lubezki insisted on shooting the movie's climactic seven-and-a-half-minute tracking shot—Clive Owen cradling a newborn baby in a mad dash from a nightmare prison camp through an urban free-fire zone—in a single take, other apparent instances of virtuoso choreographed continuous motion were actually series of short shots digitally combined.

By comparison to *Russian Ark*, Rodowick praises Eric Rohmer's period film *The Lady and the Duke* (2002) for its authentic use of digital technology. To evoke late-eighteenth-century Paris, Rohmer commissioned a series of paintings based on contemporary engravings. Actors were filmed before a green screen and keyed into these virtual locations, moving through revolutionary Paris like solid, yet shadowless, phantoms. In a way, *The Lady and the Duke* elides film altogether in vaulting from the pre- to the post-photographic. "You could say I'm faithful to Bazin's teachings," the director told an interviewer. "I do think that resorting to a highly visible artifice gives me truth"

And yet, *Russian Ark*'s single take is what Tarkovsky would have called the "impression of time" and the movie is essentially Bazinian, most radically in its performative aspect—that is, in the orchestration of the camera and profilmic event. The same is true for *Ten*, for which the filmmaker placed his mini-camera on an automobile dashboard to document the conversations of the car's driver and passengers as they drove through Tehran. Each in its own way, these digitally created "film objects" confound the distinction between staged fiction and documented "truth." In both cases, the directors have made something happen in life. While these motion pictures may be considered as a form of canned theater, both employ digital technology in order make quintessential motion pictures.

Elsewhere, the loss of indexicality has promoted a new, compensatory "real-ness," emphasizing film as an object (if only an object in decay). *In Praise of Love*, which begins *in media res* and ends with a prolonged flashback, can be understood as a continuous loop—and hence, as a film installation. *Goodbye, Dragon Inn*—a sort of superimposed double-feature with the older movie "inserted" inside or framed by the newer one—also suggests an installation, perhaps one designed to be projected in the since-demolished Taipei theater where the movie is set. Both *Decay of Fiction* and Michael Snow's 2002 perceptual vaudeville show **Corpus Callosum* (which, like *Decay of Fiction* or Eric Rohmer's *The Lady and the Duke*, is a twenty-first-century Méliès trick-film to Kiarostami and Sokurov's digital *actualités*) were exhibited as gallery installations.

History doubles back on itself. **Corpus Callosum* ends in a screening room with the presentation of Snow's crude cartoon of a weirdly elastic, waving human with a twisty foot kick. Rigorously predicated on irreducible cinematic facts, Snow's structuralist epics—*Wavelength* (1967) and *La Région Centrale* (1971)—announced the imminent passing of the film era. Rich with new possibilities, **Corpus Callosum*'s self-described "tableau of transformation," largely set in a generic fun-house office and featuring wackily distorted "information workers," heralds the advent of the next. Snow and Gehr were at one point in the late 1960s and early 70s considered to be part of the "structural" tendency in avant-garde filmmaking, heavily invested in the specific properties of the film medium.

(Aurélien Ferenzi, "Interview with Eric Rohmer," *Senses of Cinema*: archive. sensesofcinema.com/contents/01/16/rohmer.html).

In switching to digital technology, they had demonstrated a comparable concern with the nature of this new medium.

So too, Guy Maddin's confessional narrative *Cowards Bend the Knee* (2003), which was initially shown as a ten-part peep show installed on a battery of mutoscopes. *Cowards Bend the Knee* employed the conventions of silent cinema with transitions marked by irises and intertitles standing in for dialogue; when projected, the action was accompanied by a combination of classical and program music, as well as sound effects. Such gratuitous anachronism is something other (and nuttier) than mere nostalgia. Artisanal puppet animations like Trey Parker's *Team America: World Police* (2004) and particularly Henry Selick's 3-D *Coraline* (2009), with its perverse, although not absolute, refusal of CGI, are further instances of what might be called the New Realness; related, albeit disparate, examples of willful, neo-retro primitivism would include Maddin's deliberately silent feature *Brand Upon the Brain!* (2006), Neil Young's post-dubbed super-8 protest opera *Greendale* (2003), and Ken Jacob's reworked 1903 *actualité Razzle Dazzle* (2006) which, like Gehr's *Cotton Candy*, programmatically fuses ancient photographic and modern digital technology.

The cinema of international film festivals has showcased many successors to the short-lived Dogma movement in the form of modestly produced motion pictures, digital or analog, which, like Kiarostami's *Ten*, purposefully blur the distinction between staged fiction and recorded reality. Neither pseudo nor mock documentaries, these movies might be characterized as "situation documentaries," asserting their media specific realness through the use of long takes, minimal editing, behavioral performances, and leisurely contemplation of their subjects or setting. Drama is subsumed in observation. Landscape trumps performance.

Pedro Costa's *Ossos* (1997), *In Vanda's Room* (2000), and *Colossal Youth* (2006) allow Lisbon slum-dwellers to dramatize their lives or, at least, play themselves talking before the camera. With their deliberate compositions and purposeful lighting, Costa's features have the feel of staged documentaries—as do certain works by China's Jia Zhangke or the Austrian filmmaker Ulrich Seidl. More radical and less stylized are those unprepossessing, minimalist narratives which are shot like documentaries, notably Kiarostami's *Ten* and those of Argentine director Lisandro Alonso—*La Libertad* (2000), *Los Muertos* (2004), and *Liverpool* (2008). Related artists include Spanish filmmaker Albert Serra and the

Portuguese director Miguel Gomes; a quintessential example of this rudi-mentary, rock-hard ultra-literalism is Paz Encina's *Paraguayan Hammock* (2006) in which, rather than coaxing a narrative from a documentary situation, simply uses voiceover and editing to impose one. The first 35mm all-Paraguayan feature produced since the 1970s, Encina's willfully primitive movie could have been made a century ago—albeit in black and white, with a pair of actors behind the screen presenting the movie's asynchronous dialogue. It opens with a lengthy, static long shot in which an elderly couple emerges from the woods to hang their hammock in a clearing. "What is wrong with you?" one asks the other. Their words—like all of the movie's dialogue—are obvi-ously post-dubbed and delivered in the indigenous Guaraní language. From their conversation, it gradually becomes apparent that their son is a soldier fighting in a war. The day goes on. The couple performs their separate chores as each remembers or imagines a conversation with the absent boy. With their repetitive discourse, the protagonists suggest a pair of Beckett characters. Inevitably, the movie comes full circle. As day ends, the old couple returns to their hammock—once more seen in long shot. In the fading light, they expand their three topics of conversation (the dog, the weather, their son) to acknowledge death and even each other. Then the old man lights a lamp, and the two shuffle off back into the woods. Encino holds the blank screen for a minute or two, ending with the sound of rain.

Such "situation documentaries" operate in the gap between non-fiction and fiction recognized by Italian neo-realist films like Visconti's *La Terra Trema* (1948), with its cast of non-actors dramatizing their lives *in situ*, and further refined (or perhaps de-refined) in the Warhol Factory features of the mid 1960s, most notably those starring Edie Sedgwick as herself. Movies like *La Libertad* and *Paraguayan Hammock* are predi-cated on and assert film's indexical relation to the real even when, as with *Ten*, they are produced with digital technology.[6]

6 Bazin anticipated this aspect of the situation documentary when he approvingly wrote of Roberto Rossellini's *Paisan* (1947) that the film's "unit of cinematic narrative" was "not the 'shot', an abstract view of reality which is being analyzed, but the 'fact'." Specifically, he cites *Paisan's* final section which is obliquely edited from relatively long takes, often shot with a mobile camera, and characterized by an emphasis on landscape: "The partisans surrounded in the marshlands, the muddy waters of the Po Delta, the reeds stretching away to the horizon, just sufficiently tall to hide the man crouching down in

The great performance artist of the mode is Sasha Baron Cohen who first introduced his alter-egos Borat and Brüno as television personalities. Indeed, in some ways, the partially-staged situation documentary is analogous to the international phenomenon known as "reality television," anticipated in the US by MTV's long-running *The Real World* (1992–), precipitated by the network-produced *Survivor* series (2000–), and continuing through various editions and iterations of *American Idol* (2002–), *The Bachelor* (2002–), *The Apprentice* (2004–), *The Biggest Loser* (2004–), *Dancing With the Stars* (2005–), *Jersey Shore* (2009–), etc., as well as Jennifer Ringley's twenty-four-hour dorm room website JenniCAM (1996–2003). Indeed, as demonstrated by the aftermath of the 2008 presidential campaign and the run-up to the 2012 election, reality television has become the template for American politics.

From a philosophical point of view, the most paradoxical exercise in New Realness is Lars von Trier's post-Dogma *Dogville* (2003). At once abstract and concrete, *Dogville* plays out on an obvious, if schematically organized, soundstage and thus, in addition to providing a narrative, documents the scaffolding on which a narrative is conventionally constructed. This soundstage world, in which all the actors on the set are at all times potentially visible, meets the Dogma requirement that "filming must be done on location"—call it Dogmaville. Filled with close-ups and jump-cuts, *Dogville* was shot on digital video—a format that not only allows for a greater sense of spontaneity than 35mm but in its immediacy effectively precludes any nostalgia inherent in the movie's period setting.

On the eve of the Anglo-American invasion of Iraq, scarcely two months before *Dogville*'s Cannes premiere, Robert C. Byrd of West Virginia rose on the floor of the US Senate to announce that he wept for his country:

> I have watched the events of recent months with a heavy, heavy heart. No more is the image of America one of a strong, yet benevolent peace-keeper. The image of America has changed. Around the globe, our friends

---

the little flat-bottomed boat, the lapping of the waves against the wood, all occupy a place of equal importance with the men." ("An Aesthetic of Reality: Neorealism," *What Is Cinema? Volume II*, Los Angeles: University of California Press, 1971). Perhaps inspired by Rossellini's example, Robert Bresson's use of non-actors in *Diary of a Country Priest* (1951) and subsequent films also presages the situation documentary.

mistrust us, our word is disputed, our intentions are questioned ... We flaunt our superpower status with arrogance.

Von Trier's Rocky Mountain town may be a superpower writ small, but it is explicitly a realm of self-righteous fantasy and proud delusion. In one sense a two-hour-plus build-up to the end credit montage, *Dogville* saves catharsis for its final moments. The town's hitherto unseen dog turns "real"—that is, photographic—and so does von Trier's abstract "America." What we have previously witnessed was simply a play, as well as a representation. Von Trier's documentary realness, recording actors on a set in a way that they can never be imagined to be anything else, is ruptured by a greater realness—namely a montage of photographic evidence, wrenching images of human misery in America, set to a disco beat.

It's a nasty prank, but who could possibly laugh at these indexical images of naked distress? Or readily turn their back, as encouraged to do, by leaving the theater? Is the audience ignoring reality and returning to their Dogville? Or is it vice versa?[7]

---

7   *Dogville*'s final sequence draws heavily on Jacob Holdt's *American Pictures*, a multi-media presentation that is an unsettling mix of *The Lower Depths*, *On the Road* and the biblical Book of Revelations. A minister's son (from a family whose first-born sons have been ministers for the last 300 years), Holdt came to the US during the waning days of the counterculture and stayed through the 1970s, hitchhiking back and forth across the country, supporting himself by selling his blood, staying with the poorest of the poor and documenting his adventures with a $30 pawnshop camera. First a slide show, then a movie and a book, and currently a website—and thus an early example of so-called convergence cinema—Holdt's magnum opus is at once travelogue and exposé, hippie masterpiece and brimstone homily. The movie *American Pictures* (1984) played continuously for years in Copenhagen; the published version remains the best-selling Danish book ever written about the US. No Dane of von Trier's generation or background could have been unaware of Holdt's visceral sense of America as an unjust, racist, violent society—blighted by the primeval curse of slavery and defined by its black underclass. Holdt's critique lurks beneath *Dogville*'s surface to explode with maximum force after the movie is over.

CHAPTER FOUR

QUID EST VERITAS:
THE REALITY OF
UNSPEAKABLE SUFFERING

Objective anxiety became manifest at the height of the dot.com bubble in the late 1990s and the panicky anticipation of the Y2K "virus," the period Rodowick calls "the summer of digital paranoia," when (as he paraphrased Marx) *The Matrix*, et al. suggested that "all that was chemical and photographic [was] disappearing into the electronic and digital."

Hysterical anxiety can be even more precisely dated. For many, and not just those in Hollywood, the events of September 11, 2001 provided the ultimate movie experience—spectacular destruction predicated on fantastic conspiracy, broadcast live, as well as repeatedly (and even recorded by some participants on their cell phones), and watched by an audience, more or less simultaneously, of billions. This surely is what the composer Karl Stockhausen, among others, meant when, in the course of a press conference at the Hamburg Music Festival on September 16, 2001, he undiplomatically referring to the events of 9/11 as "the greatest work of art imaginable for the whole cosmos."[1]

These events—or rather, this Event—established a new cinematic

---

1 Stockhausen continued, "Minds achieving something in an act that we couldn't even dream of in music, people rehearsing like mad for 10 years, preparing fanatically for a concert, and then dying, just imagine what happened there. You have people who are that focused on a performance and then 5,000 people are dispatched to the afterlife, in a single moment. I couldn't do that. By comparison, we composers are nothing" (Julia Spinola, "Monstrous Art," *Frankfurter Allgemeine Zeitung*, 9/25/2001, English edition).

paradigm and Hollywood's response was fascinating, particularly in that magical thinking is what movies are all about. Only days after the Event, the studios eagerly reported that the FBI had informed them they could be the terrorists' next target. On September 21, rumors of an impending attack swept Los Angeles. The industry felt somehow guilty and even responsible, although not everyone was as blunt (or innocent in his megalomania) as Robert Altman, who told the Associated Press that, "These people have copied the movies. Nobody would have thought to commit an atrocity like that unless they'd seen it in a movie ... We created this atmosphere and taught them how to do it."[2]

Did the history-changing shock of this cinematic event plunge the nascent twenty-first century into an alternative universe, one in which motion picture fairy tales actually did come true? Or was it rather a red pill that parted the veil on a new reality that already existed? The 9/11 Event was understood by some filmmakers as a horrible unintended consequence of their medium and taken by others as a challenge to the notion of the movies as a medium with a privileged relationship to the real.[3]

---

2 The catastrophe was not only anticipated by the blockbuster disaster films of the 1990s but also by the globalist melodramas of which Michael Haneke's *Code Unknown* (2000) may be considered the first and most successful example—mapping the ways in which a chance encounter on a Paris street links all manner of individuals and suggesting that the movement of immigrants throughout Europe is not an abstract issue but one with intimate consequences. Lesser, post-9/11 examples of this we-are-the-world middlebrow mode—in which a geographically dispersed ensemble is mystically conjoined—include Alejandro González Iñárritu's *40 Grams* (2003) and *Babel* (2006), Barbara Albert's *Free Radicals* (2003) and *Falling* (2006), and Paul Haggis's 2005 Oscar-winning *Crash*.

3 Slavoj Žižek seems to have been the first to connect *The Matrix* and 9/11: "'The shattering impact of the bombings can only be accounted for against the background of the borderline which today separates the digitalized First World from the Third World's 'desert of the real'" (*Welcome to the Desert of the Real*, New York: The Wooster Press, 2001).

Similarly, when *Dogville* premiered in Cannes in May 2003, only weeks after president George W. Bush had declared America's "mission accomplished" in Iraq, it was taken by some American critics as a personal affront. With a defensive bitterness verging on panic, *Variety*'s Todd McCarthy wrote that "Von Trier indicts as being unfit to inhabit the earth a country that has surely attracted, and given opportunity to, more people on to its shores than any other in the history of the world."

This was not necessarily conscious as when, during the course of an on-set press conference, Steven Spielberg would describe his fantastic *War of the Worlds* (2005), the first Hollywood movie to allegorize 9/11, as an exercise in realism, even insisting upon a key concept of the New Realness: "The whole thing is very experiential [*sic*]." *War of the Worlds*, Spielberg maintained, was not simply entertainment, like such earlier fantasies of interplanetary warfare as *Independence Day* (1996) or *Starship Troopers* (1997): "We take it much more seriously than that." The movie, he promised reporters, would be "as ultra-realistic as I've ever attempted to make a movie, in terms of its documentary style ..." Spielberg, like Altman, was speaking on behalf of his medium. Cinema itself would insure that the post 9/11 disaster film would be experiential, communal and above all naturalistic.[4]

Although the mayhem in *War of the Worlds* references 9/11 in every instance, the most brutal New Realness is manifest in Mel Gibson's *The Passion of the Christ* (2004), a movie that seemingly stands opposed to all entertainment values and which, in fact, aspired to be far more than a movie by representing and, in a sense, identifying with a unique instance of divine intervention—and hence, proposing itself as a cinematic event to trump even 9/11. For a true believer, *The Passion of the Christ* is not a narrative but an icon—an object through which to meditate upon the spectacle of a defenseless man beaten, stomped, and tortured to death so that he might redeem the sins of all humanity since the beginning of time!

As a subject, Gibson's Jesus Christ has less in common with any previous movie protagonist than with the greenish-purplish, pustulent, putrifying subject of Grünewald's Isenheim Altarpiece. As a movie, *The Passion* passes the point of no return with the eleven-minute chastisement sequence in which Jesus is lacerated, first with rods and then studded whips, until his back resembles a side of raw beef. The crux of *The Passion* is the experience of a crucifixion; the near continuous violence

4   It seems highly appropriate that Steven Soderbergh's *Contagion* (2011), an "ultra-realistic" account of a worldwide epidemic, would have been the number one US box-office attraction on the tenth anniversary of 9/11. The Events of September 11 and the images it produced are inevitably invoked in any cinematic visualization of catastrophe. The prologue to Lars von Trier's doomsday drama *Melancholia* (2011) features a small rogue planet colliding with earth in an unmistakable reference to a plane entering the World Trade Center.

and gore is meant to excruciate the viewer. Using numerous overhead shots, Gibson assumes a fallen world and projects an essentially medieval worldview. (The crucifixion only emerged as a subject for artists with the first millennium; passion plays didn't exist before the twelfth century.)

As detailed by art historian Mitchell B. Merback in *The Thief, the Cross and the Wheel: Pain and the Spectacle of Punishment in Medieval and Renaissance Europe* (Chicago, 1999), medieval Christian devotion required immersion in the Passion's "grisly details," while other devotional practices centered on the experience of a tortured, pain-racked body. (Merback finds analogies in medieval Europe's contemporaneous fascination with martyrdom, flagellation, extravagant forms of punishment, and public executions.) The antithesis of a film like Robert Bresson's *Diary of a Country Priest* (1951), Gibson's atavistic Christian art goes for shock rather than sublimity. The filmmaker employs extreme, even gross, horror movie tropes, as well as blatant digital effects—the Roman whip and Christ's wounds in the chastisement sequence, as well as the final shot of 3-D stigmata.[5]

From the silent era on, movies drew power from their affinity to religious ritual; *The Passion* inverts this equation, and redeems moviegoing. The cinema is transformed from a questionable, possibly sinful activity into a source of collective identity as well as a communal rite. Entire congregations rented theaters in order to the share the experience, often bringing young children. For these religious audiences, *The Passion* functioned as a sermon but, unlike a sermon, the end of the screening was greeted with applause—or so I've been told. However gruesome its presentation, *The Passion* was taken as a gift from God. Evangelical leader and child psychologist James C. Dobson was not alone in welcoming this redemption of a debased popular culture: "In any other context, I could not in good conscience recommend a movie containing this degree of violent content. However, in this case, the violence is intended not to titillate or entertain, but to emphasize the reality of the unspeakable suffering that our Savior endured on our behalf."[6]

---

5 Writing in *Film Quarterly*, Stephen Prince has pointed out that these digital effects would seem to contradict the film's vaunted basis in realism: "Among its other significant attributes, *The Passion of the Christ* gives us perhaps the first really striking demonstration of digital wizardry used to create images that viewers deem truthful and authentic."

6 Dobson, widely considered the most influential evangelical minister in the

As *The Passion*'s sanctified violence and horror impressed a devout audience with the reality of "unspeakable suffering", so the real-ness of Gibson's extreme filmmaking intrigued more secular artists. Not everyone was as honest as Quentin Tarantino who, when asked by interviewer John Powers if he'd seen Gibson's *Passion*, replied that he "loved it … I think it actually is one of the most brilliant visual storytelling movies I've seen since the talkies."

> It has the power of a silent movie … It is pretty violent, I must say. At a certain point, it was like a Takashi Miike film. It got so fucked up it was funny … I was into the seriousness of the story, of course, but in the crucifixion scene, when they turned the cross over, you had to laugh.

Tarantino would subsequently lend his imprimatur to exploitation director Eli Roth, author of the quasi-pornographic torture-based horror films *Cabin Fever* (2002) and *Hostel* (2005), low-budget DV productions with stylistic affinities to the New Realness, by employing Roth to contribute a trailer to his compilation film *Grindhouse* and by producing *Hostel II* (both 2007).[7]

Gibson's blockbuster stimulated other filmmakers—but not simply because of its mayhem. Movies as varied as Gus Van Sant's crypto-Kurt Cobain ode *Last Days* (2005), Cristi Puiu's black comedy *The Death of Mr. Lazarescu* (2005), Julia Loktev's structural suspense film *Day Night Day Night* (2006), Paul Greengrass's 9/11 docudrama *United 93* (2006), Julian Schnabel's medical case history *The Diving Bell and the Butterfly* (2006), Steve McQueen's prison story *Hunger* (2008), Filipino director Brilliante Mendoza's true-crime *Kinatay* (2009), Jerzy Skolomowski's existential chase film *Essential Killing* (2010), and Danny Boyle's self-amputation ordeal *127 Hours* (2010)—many based on or inspired by true stories, and all built around a discreet experience—are examples of post-*Passion*

US, made news a year later in early 2005 when he and his organization Focus on the Family criticized the TV cartoon character SpongeBob SquarePants for appearing in a music video designed to teach children about multiculturalism, that the group deemed "pro-homosexual."

7   In addition to torture porn, the New Realness has found popular expression in the revival of zombie films. Perhaps the problematic distinction between dead and undead allegorizes, among other things, the ambiguous relation between analog and digital image-making.

anti-entertainment, aspiring to a visceral realness and being additionally "experiential" in their emphasis on real-time duration.[8]

Noting their over-determined endings, film critic Nathan Lee bracketed several such movies with *The Passion of the Christ*, as "death trips." No less crucial is their interest in constructing an ordeal—both on the screen and for the audience. *Last Days* was immediately recognized as analogous to Gibson's project. *Washington Post* reviewer Anna Hornaday called it "the grunge generation *Passion of the Christ*," predicting (erroneously) that it might prove "as powerful a communal and spiritual experience." Van Sant's suicidal rock star is only the most obvious martyr. Others include an alcoholic non-entity who dies on a hospital gurney, a would-be suicide bomber, the passengers and crew of a hijacked plane, a French fashion writer sentenced to a living death, an Irish revolutionary who embarks on a fatal hunger strike, and a Filipino hooker. In every case, their passion is presented as an object of contemplation.

United 93, which more or less demands that its audience live through a doomed flight from take-off to crash, is the most therapeutic of these movies. The quintessential new disaster film, *United 93* is explicit in its

---

8   It's worth noting that three of these were made by gallery artists who might be expected to have a more developed sense of cinema as installation and that *Hostel*, originally advertised as "A place where your darkest, sickest fantasies are possible, where you can experience anything you desire," has an experiential aspect as well. Roth has repeatedly cast himself as a historically determined filmmaker, maintaining that he is making entertainments for the children of 9/11; he claims to have drawn inspiration from terrorist videos such as the one showing the decapitation of journalist Daniel Pearl, and favorably compared his imaginary torture to the actual torture approved by former Vice-President Dick Cheney.

If *Hostel*, *Hostel II*, and such other examples of so-called torture porn as *Saw* (2004) and its sequels arise from the same fear and desire for vengeance that inspired the torture of prisoners at Guantánamo and Abu Ghraib, so, in some respects, does their sacred analogue—which shows Roman soldiers running amok and all but bludgeoning Christ to death. While *Day Night Day Night*, *Hunger*, and, to a lesser degree *United 93*, allow the audience to identify with terrorists—as to several, aesthetically more naïve movies like Hany Abu-Assad's *Paradise Now* (2005), this should not be confused with a filmmaker like Roth's identification. His highbrow equivalent is Michael Haneke, a serious guy out to destroy the matrix of bourgeois complacency, overtly punishing the audience in his two versions of *Funny Games* (1997 and 2008), and an audience surrogate in *Caché*.

use of real time and designed for audience participation. New disaster is experiential and communal. Just as the now notorious trailer distilled the movie's narrative arc (albeit without offering the final catharsis), audiences mimicked the action: having paid to see *Inside Man*, unsuspecting viewers had their attention "hijacked." According to some descriptions in the press, the angry patrons at AMC Loews Lincoln Square banded together to yank the trailer.

Kinatay (the title means "slaughter" in Tagalog) is the most radical of these films. The movie is crudely shot from the perspective of a twenty-year-old police trainee who, moonlighting for extra money, finds himself trapped on behalf of the spectator, in a hellish world. Over the course of a forty-five-minute, more or less real-time sequence, and before his eyes, a young prostitute is abducted, beaten, tortured, raped, sodomized, murdered, and matter-of-factly dismembered. That these atrocities are murkily rendered on HD, more often heard than seen, serves to add insult to injury, even as Mendoza's anti-technique amplifies the horrifying spectacle of relentless degradation. *Kinatay* is not a movie to be lightly recommended but it is something that must be endured to be understood.[9]

---

9   *Kinatay* was by far the least entertaining and most loathed example of cine-brutalism found in a 2009 Cannes competition which, notable for its extreme New Realness violence, included Lars von Trier's quasi-pornographic *Antichrist* and the punishing first-person subjective camera of Gaspar Noé's "psychedelic melodrama" *Enter the Void*—both examples of post-*Passion* experiential cinematic ordeals. (It may not be coincidental that Willem Dafoe, the male star of *Antichrist*, had his first Hollywood starring role as Jesus in Martin Scorsese's 1988 *Last Temptation of Christ*.)

Variety all but called Mendoza a fraud, predicting that his supporters would dwindle in the face of so gratuitous and "vile" a movie. The *Hollywood Reporter* objected to *Kinatay*'s "forced voyeurism" and "deliberately ugly" cinematography. While *Screen*'s international critic's jury awarded *Antichrist* a pathetic 1.6 out of a possible four stars, four of the same ten film journalists marked *Kinatay* zero; in total, Mendoza's film scored an unbelievably low 1.2. Roger Ebert blogged that Vincent Gallo's *Brown Bunny* had been surpassed as the worst film ever shown at Cannes; jury president Isabelle Huppert's announcement of Mendoza's prize for best director was greeted by the press with incredulous gasps and a chorus of boos.

What was Mendoza's sin and why was it greater than von Trier's? While von Trier, who taunted the press by calling himself the "world's greatest director," is a showman and an ironist, Mendoza offers no such thrills. Although *Kinatay*'s most favorable notice compared the movie to the minimalist procedural *Henry: Portrait of a Serial Killer* (1986), the most obvious analogy, and one Mendoza was hardly subtle in suggesting, went unmentioned. Not only is the movie's sacrificial victim named Madonna, but images of Jesus can be spotted in several locations (including the gangster's abattoir).

CHAPTER FIVE

SOCIAL NETWORK

Like *The Passion*, *Kinatay* draws on the lowest horror movie tropes in its grimly experiential representation of human suffering and depraved indifference. At a higher level of aspiration one finds a variety of self-reflexive attempts that use genre conventions to represent a new "social-real" of existential terror, cyber-globalism, viral images, digital will, and social networking.[1]

Further examples of this new social-real would include George Romero's horror films *Land of the Dead* (2005) and *Diary of the Dead* (2007), and Matt Reeves's *Cloverfield* (2008)—the last of which, purporting to be a subjective camcorder documentation of a cataclysmic disaster, is notable for integrating the two poles of digital image-making: expensive CGI and amateur DV. More specifically, although each in its own way, Antonio Campo's Haneke-influenced youth film, *Afterschool* (2008), Brian De Palma's anti-war *Redacted* (2007) and Errol Morris's

---

1 These include Olivier Assayas's exercise in globalizing videogame cyber-pornographic simulation *demonlover* (2002); Mamoru Oshii's anime *Innocence* (2004); the parody puppet-animation action flick *Team America: World Police* (2004); Stephen Chow's globalizing post-*Matrix* CGI live-animated cartoon *Kung Fu Hustle* (2004); Michael Haneke's surveillance cam, digital-vs.-analogic art-thriller *Caché* (2005); Alfonso Cuarón's post-apocalyptic science fiction *Children of Men* (2006); James McTeigue's terrorist burlesque *V for Vendetta* (2007); and, admirably indifferent to audience expectations, Richard Kelly's sci-fi split-screen *Saturday Night Live* mash-up *Southland Tales* (2007).

investigative documentary *Standard Operating Procedure* (2008) explore the implications of YouTube—of self-produced movies being uploaded to the web for a potential audience of tens of thousands.[2] Jia Zhangke's theme-park set *The World* (2004) and Joe Swanberg's humorously scaled-down exercise in social networking, *LOL* (2006), are both revisionist versions of the globalistic melodrama, as is the more widely seen and highly praised David Fincher–Aaron Sorkin "Facebook" movie, *The Social Network* (2010). At once a form of neo-neo-realism and an attempt to make a contemporary new wave film, Swanberg's low-budget production is characterized by primitive jump cuts and all manner of sound/image disjunction, as when a panicky voicemail message is heard over a montage of faces or when email messages function as silent movie intertitles.

Utterly classical in its film language, *The Social Network* addresses the origin and appeal of the motion picture's latest rival. Like any form of entertainment, social networking succeeds to the degree that it successfully compensates people for something missing in their lives—a lost sense of neighborhood or extended family or workplace fraternity or class solidarity or even self-importance. As dramatized in *The Social Network*, the story of Facebook's creation is not unlike that of any large corporation—megalomania rewarded, sweethearts trampled, partners buggered. Shoring up its own historical bona fides, the movie explicitly compares Facebook's youthful founder Mark Zuckerberg to the media-mogul protagonist of Orson Welles's *Citizen Kane*. Zuckerberg's real achievement, however, was something more mysterious than founding a newspaper or a twenty-first-century MGM or Standard Oil; his

---

2   The first YouTube video was uploaded in April 2005; by the end of the year, a hilarious meme that started in the UK swept the internet, re-subtitling a key tantrum from Oliver Hirschbiegel's 2005 portrait of Hitler in the bunker *Downfall*, so that Bruno Ganz's disheveled, ranting Führer was made to browbeat his dumbfounded generals about everything from his lost Xbox to his difficulty using Microsoft's Vista operating system to the 2007 Super Bowl upset to (supposedly speaking for Hillary Clinton) Barack Obama's primary victories, denouncing "those fainting sissies over at MoveOn.org choking on their tofu because I voted for the Iraq War." By late 2008, the *New York Times* reported, there were over a hundred versions on the web: "The lesson of the parodies seems to be that *Downfall* was a closeted Hitler comedy" (Virginia Heffernan, "The Hitler Meme," *New York Times Magazine*, 10/26/2008).

genius was to manufacture intimacy through the creation of a parallel, personalized internet: offering an ongoing second life in a virtual gated community.[3]

For its users, Facebook offers a sort of post-cinematic Total Cinema—it is the cyberspace equivalent of super-8 or video home movies, giving anyone the opportunity to be the star of their own ongoing online situation documentary. Objectively, however, Facebook creates a new sort of reification—a sphere in which everyone is a potential database self-defined by consumption. (In early 2011, certain movie studios—or rather media conglomerates—were studying the possibility of using Facebook as a platform by which users could rent movie downloads, a suggestive way of reconstituting the lost motion picture audience.) True to its moment however, *The Social Network* is less interested in mapping this new system of human interaction than in psychoanalyzing it as the projection of its quintessential user: Mark Zuckerberg. The key insight in *The Social Network* is that its imagined Zuckerberg—who is not particularly friendly and not at all prone to sharing—created his virtual community to address his specific situation.[4]

As Kafka's self-starved Hunger Artist found his métier in his idiosyncratic nature (there just wasn't any food he liked to eat) so *The Social Network*'s anti-hero invented Facebook in response to the psychic pressure of an individual quirk or character flaw, globalizing his own inability to connect with actual people. Ostensibly critical of Zuckerberg, *The Social Network* nonetheless proved to be a priceless advertisement for Facebook. As 2010 ended, the investment bank Goldman Sachs valued the worth of Zuckerman's business at $50 billion; the firm invested $500

---

3   It was perhaps this sense of a new reality that inspired *New York Times* critic Manohla Dargis to ironically propose *The Social Network* as a double bill with *The Matrix*. It is also tempting to imagine *The Social Network* as a film-installation embedded in or framed by *Avatar*. The juxtaposition would combine process with product: feverishly working at his laptop, the visionary artist "Mark Zuckerberg" (a stand-in for James Cameron) conjures up an outlandish virtual world; he is surrounded by the fantastic cyber-creatures of virtual jungle, as well as dreams of world salvation and love in the arms of a blue giantess.

4   The equation between Zuckerberg and Kane was echoed after a fashion, a year later, by the fantastic eulogizing around the death of Apple founder Steve Jobs—hailed an industrial genius and visionary on par with early twentieth-century hero Thomas Alva Edison.

million in Facebook and was preparing to raise another $1.5 billion from their clients.[5]

The protagonists of Swanberg's all but homemade *LOL* (its title is the online abbreviation for "laugh out loud") are dutiful citizens of Zuckerberg's world (even though, as the movie was made in 2006 and was thus all but instantly anachronistic, Facebook is not their social network of choice). Close to psychodrama, *LOL* stars its three main creators and was largely improvised by them. According to an explanatory extra included in the DVD release, the movie was "born out of ideas batted back and forth via computer, cell phone, etc., and then filmed in the same manner that people use webcams or their cell phones"—which is another way of describing its narrative. The opening shot is a computer screen with a moving mouse clicking on a file. Someone has posted his girlfriend's private striptease on line. Her dance is cross-cut with close-ups of a dozen or more transfixed spectators, each occupying his own personal space and staring dumbfounded (and pants down?) at his own personal screen.[6]

LOL, in which every dysfunctional or imaginary romantic relationship is mediated by social networks, might have been titled, after Marshall McLuhan, *The Mechanical Bride*. So too, Pixar's even more alienated, mega-million dollar, state of the art CGI spectacular *WALL-E* (2008), directed by Andrew Stanton. An unaccountably optimistic vision of human extinction, and thus a dialectical response to the new disaster film, *WALL-E* successfully vaults the uncanny valley that precludes audience identification with humanoid simulations to enlist as its protagonist a solitary robot trash-compactor who (or which) is single-mindedly organizing the endless detritus of an abandoned, implicitly analog world. (Whereas the ruined heart of a great city would once have invoked the specter of World War II, it now carries an unmistakable sense of New York City's Ground Zero.) The spectacle of this devoted dingbot working

5   In early 2011, Facebook received even better press, recognized as a political force and credited as an organizing tool (along with YouTube and Twitter) used by young activists to bring down the governments of Egypt and Tunisia; the company was somewhat ambivalent about its revolutionary role, having shut down a page co-started by Google executive Wael Ghonim because he violated Facebook policy in using a pseudonym.

6   This representation of the cyber-audience may be compared to the cyber-auction early in *Hostel*, with would-be killers bidding on fresh, unsuspecting victims …

alone to fashion a Grand Canyon out of neatly compacted garbage provides a breathtaking sense of eternity.

For much of *WALL-E*, its endearing, Chaplinesque hero—part Sisyphus, part Third World scavenger—is the earth's last vestige of humanity. (A single plant and the trash-compactor's cockroach sidekick are Earth's only signs of life.) Utterly superfluous, the descendants of the planet's former inhabitants drift through space in a giant, robot-controlled shopping mall known as the Axiom, too bloated to do more than slurp down Happy Meals and watch TV.

Pixar's computer animation represents the epitome, thus far, of digital will. Even the indexical presence of a drawing or painted cel has vanished. Is this universally acclaimed motion picture then part of the problem or part of the solution? *WALL-E* satirizes the technology it deploys; it bemoans yet celebrates the death of analog image-making, consigns old-fashioned movies to the trash heap, even while worshipping their fragments. Although Kubrick's 1968 *2001* is ruthlessly parodied throughout, a Hollywood movie made the very same year serves as *WALL-E*'s privileged artifact. An ancient VHS tape of *Hello Dolly* (once the epitome of elephantine, retrograde movie-making), seen solely in terms of a back lot musical number, is the robot's most prized possession. This fetish serves to instruct the (male-coded) machine on the nature of the human, providing a synecdoche for the entire cultural heritage of the pre-apocalyptic Earth.[7]

Celebrating (or embalming) an obsolete technology, *WALL-E* is the *2001* of 2008—a post-photographic film set in a post-human universe. The movie's single human actor is the designated special effect. A clip of cheerful prancing on a long-lost Hollywood soundstage signifies the Desert of the Real, as glimpsed from within the Matrix of Total Cinema. In the context of *WALL-E*, the tape of *Hello Dolly* functions as an installation, the equivalent of *24 Hour Psycho*. The movie includes one other

---

7   Christopher Nolan's 2010 *Inception* offered another, more material and most likely inadvertent criticism of CGI-driven cinema. Although the movie's premise—trained "dream invaders" entering and mucking about with individual psyches—is entirely based on constructing imaginary subjective worlds, *Inception*'s narrative excitement is largely derived from a climax that suggests nothing so much as D. W. Griffith's 1916 *Intolerance*, with Nolan building suspense through parallel action by cutting back and forth between four or five "levels" of reality. The primitive special-effect "editing" trumps the image-conjuring splendor of the digital world.

example of analog cinema—the holographic image of the Buy 'n' Large Corporation's long-dead CEO whose pre-recorded instructions are periodically delivered to the Axiom's captain.[8]

At once avant and pop, horrendously bleak and cheerfully cute, WALL-E may be considered the twenty-first century's quintessential motion picture to date. It is not, however, the most elaborate evidence of the New Realness. That, along with the furthest advance of Total Cinema, may be found in the revival of 3-D movies that began in the mid 1990s with a series of documentaries to which IMAX projection added the dimension of size, notably James Cameron's underwater, digitally shot *Ghosts of the Abyss* (2003).

Cameron's voyage to the bottom of the sea was also something else— namely, the avatar of his 3-D *Avatar*. Announcing the advent of digital 3-D, it was produced shortly before the director embarked on a motion picture which, as the highest-grossing movie in history, would rival *The Passion of the Christ* as the early twenty-first century's most influential commercial release.[9]

---

8   Another 2008 fantasy (or fantasy about fantasy), Michel Gondry's gently outlandish *Be Kind Rewind* pondered the death of cinema—or at least the death of home video. When all the VHS tapes in the rundown Be Kind Rewind video store are inadvertently erased, an employee and his friend begin producing new fifteen-minute videocorder versions of 1980s and '90s blockbusters— beginning with *Ghostbusters*. Reducing movies to their most infantile level, these ridiculously low-tech little movies are exercises in junkyard whimsy, serious examples of the grassroots "imperfect cinema" imagined by Cuban cultural theorist Julio García Espinosa back in the days of '68. From another perspective, Harmony Korine's 2009 quasi-underground movie *Trash Humpers* similarly revels in the instability of the digital image.

9   Assayas's *demonlover* is partially predicated on an industrial battle to develop 3-D pornographic animes. Released in Hong Kong on April 14, 2011, the 3-D soft-core sex comedy *3D Sex and Zen: Extreme Ecstasy* broke the opening-day record previously set by *Avatar*, in part because of the number of patrons who travelled from mainland China where censorship precludes the movie's release.

CHAPTER SIX

POSTSCRIPT: TOTAL CINEMA REDUX

The most seamless cyber-fantasy is, of course, James Cameron's prodigiously successful *Avatar* (2009), a technological wonder that is essentially a 3-D science-fictionalized cavalry Western along the lines of Kevin Costner's 1993 hit *Dances With Wolves*.

After fifteen years percolating in producer-writer-director Cameron's imagination, *Avatar* shows earthlings on a mission from their own despoiled world to strip-mine the lushly verdant planet Pandora and, not coincidentally, subjugate its materially primitive but spiritually advanced inhabitants, the Na'vis—cyborg creatures that, thanks to extremely sophisticated "image capture," are played by recognizable, if distorted, human actors. As preparation for taking control of the planet, the Sky People, as the Na'vis call them, attempt to infiltrate the Na'vis by linking human consciousness to Pandoran avatars. The movie is, in effect, a metaphor for its own computer game. *Avatar*'s hitherto disabled protagonist finds himself inside a twelve-foot-tall, blue-striped, yellow-eyed, flat-nosed humanoid—and he can walk! Ensconced in his game self (or avatar), our hero explores a mad jungle populated by six-armed neon tetra lemurs, flying purple people eaters, hammer-headed triceratopses and leathery demon dogs—as does the spectator, experiencing this CGI fantasy world in total depth.

Although Cameron was a prophet, the idea of stereoscopic cinema is as old as the medium. Motion-picture pioneers Thomas Alva Edison and the Lumière brothers mulled the possibility of 3-D; in 1915, Edison's erstwhile employee Edwin Porter developed an anaglyphic system based on superimposed green and orange images. In November 1921, a few weeks after Harry K. Fairall showed the first anaglyphic feature *The Power of Love*, and less than two months before Dr. Hugo Riesenfeld demonstrated a rival 3-D system, D. W. Griffith told the *New York Times* that "motion pictures will never realize their ideal effectiveness until they are stereoscopic."

Sergei Eisenstein advanced a similar position in celebrating the 1946 part-color Stereokino production, Aleksandr Andriyevsky's *Robinzon Kruzo*, a feature motion picture shot entirely in 3-D (and, as it was initially projected on a lenticular screen, the first 3-D movie to dispense with anaglyphic glasses). *Robinzon Kruzo* anticipates *Avatar* not only in its technological ambitions but in its immersive mise-en-scène. The first (and stronger) half of the movie is devoted to the protagonist's solitary exploration of 3-D space in the form of a wondrous, verdant jungle populated by exotic tree-dwelling creatures.

Eisenstein deemed 3-D to be inherently progressive ("Mankind has for centuries been moving toward stereoscopic cinema") and hence, naturally, Soviet: "The bourgeois West is either indifferent or even hostilely ironical toward the problems of stereoscopic cinema." Indeed, when bourgeois Hollywood turned its attention to stereoscopic cinema—along with widescreen formats and enhanced sound—it was not for art's sake but rather to follow the logic of the capitalist system, an effort to regain its technological edge and reverse declining market shares in the post-TV era.[1]

---

1   Eisenstein noted stereo's two most evident tendencies—its capacity to pierce "the depth of the screen," and alternately, its ability to create a "palpably three-dimensional" image that "pours out of the screen." He naturally thought the latter was stereo's "most devastating effect," although it's the deep focus that allows for the more rarefied spatial experience. The beauty of photographically produced 3-D arises from its novel stylization of that world; a succession of paper-thin, pop-out book planes, stereo-photographic depth is a thing in itself. Bazin was disappointed, writing in his 1953 essay "Will Cinemascope Save the Film Industry" that "stereoscopic relief" created not a heightened sense of reality, but its opposite, "the impression of an unreal, unapproachable world far more than does the flatness of black-and-white film ... The unreality of his universe, which seems strangely spun out of a hole on the screen, would be enough to condemn it."

Seven years after the appearance of "The Myth of Total Cinema," Bazin

In the early twenty-first century, Hollywood is again compelled to compete with new forms of home entertainment (even as DVD sales dwindled from their 2004 peak). During the summer of 2010, some sixty 3-D features were reported in various stages of production. As pointed out by Dave Kehr in *Film Comment*, the studios acted as though 3-D were the equivalent of talking pictures, using the latest development in Total Cinema to sell exhibitors an expensive new delivery system and—not exactly an afterthought—to slap a hefty surcharge on ticket prices.[2]

Six of 2010's ten top-grossing movies—*Toy Story 3, Alice in Wonderland, Despicable Me, Shrek Forever After, How to Train Your Dragon*, and *Tangled*—were released in 3-D. All of these, save *Alice in Wonderland* (which was shot flat and subsequently converted to 3-D to catch the stereo wave), were examples of Pixar-style CGI "solid animation" and thus of post-photographic *Matrix* cinema. Not total cinema but digital will. A movie like *Toy Story 3* is essentially redundant in imbuing virtual depth with virtual depth.[3]

---

appears to have lost faith in the medium's advance toward the Real. Not only was stereoscopic cinema problematic but color photography as well, bringing "a whole set of new conventions that, all things considered, may make film look more like painting than reality." But in fact, stereo photography created a new sort of naturalism. 3-D is an attraction that has little to do with, and may even detract from, narrative. As in the first motion pictures, small sensations dominate. Where 2-D movies privilege action, 3-D movies induce optical awareness.

2   It's by no means clear that 3-D is not, as it was in the 1950s, a transitory novelty. "Ripples of fear spread across Hollywood" after the 2011 Memorial Day weekend, with the disappointing box office grosses registered for two 3-D movies, Walt Disney Studio's $400-million 3-D production *Pirates of the Caribbean: On Stranger Tides* and Paramount's digital animation *Kung Fu Panda 2* (Brooks Barnes and Michael Cieply, "3-D Starts to Fizzle, and Hollywood Frets," *New York Times*, 5/30/2011).

3   Whereas 3-D digital animation normalizes the fantastic, the "unreal" depth of photographic 3-D defamiliarizes the ordinary. As a result, 3-D CGI animation has little investment in the dialectic between actual flatness and reconstituted depth (which one is more "real"?) that underwrites 3-D's visual drama. Unlike flat, cel animation, solid animation already provides the illusion of deep space. That is why, although digitally sweetened, the animation of *Coraline* has a tension beyond that of even the most visually dynamic computer animations. Something actually happened in depth, in the world, in front of the camera—3-D restores the dimension that Selick's puppets actually possessed.

Avatar, described by many reviewers as "immersive" or "trippy," is by contrast a cinematic experience that seamlessly synthesizes live action, animation, performance-capture, and CGI to create what is essentially a non-participatory video game: *Jurassic Park*'s menagerie running wild in *The Matrix*'s double *eXistenZ*. The game structure is operative throughout: the earthling Sky People are divided into hawks and doves, with the protagonist Jake as a sort of double double-agent, simultaneously reporting back to the base's most militant Marine as well as acting as a tough but tender biologist. The former wants him to find out "what the blue monkeys want." The latter knows that the Na'vi are ultra-green—a New Age matriarchal eco-friendly culture which, as demonstrated in a mass-swaying transubstantiation ceremony held several times beneath a cosmic weeping willow, is spiritually connected to Every Living Thing.

As *WALL-E* makes a fetish of the photographic cinema that it has displaced, so *Avatar* presents itself as a critique of the system it embodies. This most global of cinematic triumphs is a blunt attack on rapacious globalization. More specifically, *Avatar*'s utopian vision is founded on an implacable repudiation of America's history—as well as its present. The Sky People are not only heirs to the white settlers and conquistadors who crossed the Atlantic to colonize the new world but are explicitly associated with the Bush administration. They chortle over the failure of diplomacy, wage what is referred to as "some sort of shock-and-awe campaign" against the Na'vis, and goad each other with bellicose one-liners like, "We will blast a crater in their racial memory so deep they won't come within a thousand clicks of here ever again!" Moreover, the viewer is encouraged to cheer when uniformed American soldiers are blown out of the sky and to root for a bunch of naked, tree-hugging aborigines led by a renegade white man on a humongous orange polka-dot bat.

Thus, *Avatar* is an unusually robust, even blatant, example of Marcuse's repressive desublimation, appealing to the public with images that are "irreconcilable with the established Reality Principle" and even at apparent odds with its manufacturer's class interests. How could the Hollywood matrix—let alone 20th Century Fox, the studio affiliated with Rupert Murdoch's rightwing News Corp—permit such a vision? The real question is: given cinema's mandate to create a better world, how could it not?

Not surprisingly, *Avatar* was criticized by conservatives as anticapitalist, anti-militarist, or anti-American eco-propaganda, and by religious groups (including the Vatican) as anti-monotheist. Correspondingly, the *Avatar* scenario was passionately embraced by groups who experienced their own marginality. A widespread meme in which Photoshop-savvy fans recruited celebrities and pop icons into the Na'vi tribe peaked in mid-February 2010 with the poignant, real-world spectacle of Palestinian activists in blue body paint and full Na'vi drag protesting the Israeli barrier that had been erected around their village. More than any movie in memory, *Avatar* seemed to offer a hallucination that was also a fact, and some spectators responded as though they were players who had graduated to the higher levels of the computer game so vividly represented in Mamoru Oshii's 2001 movie, *Avalon*.[4]

Waking up back in the lab where his disabled body reposes in a metal box, Jake realizes that "out there [in Pandora] is the true world and in here is the dream." Although it has been suggested that *Avatar* represented a paradigm shift away from the dystopia of *The Matrix*, it is only in the sense of presenting *The Matrix* in reverse. Pandora is a utopia—even a global network—in which, just as the protagonist is able to transmit his consciousness into a Na'vi body, so the pantheist Na'vis are able to plug into plants and animals using an umbilical cord that critics were pleased to compare to a USB cable.[5]

The cable news network CNN coined the term "Post *Avatar* Depression" to describe the condition of those frustrated individuals who flooded online fan sites with posts that detailed their despondent, in some cases near-suicidal, state at not being able to continue to live in Pandora. Even allowing for the possibility of prankish exaggeration, these confessions attest to the continuing power exerted by what Bazin

---

4   This identification with Pandora's oppressed inhabitants is far more existential than the appropriation of the Guy Fawkes mask used in *V for Vendetta* as the marker of political protest. The mask-wearers are mimicking the movie's strategy; the Na'vi impersonators are marking themselves as *Avatar* citizens.

5   Writing on *Avatar* in *The Nation*, Stuart Klawans was disturbed by recurring images of Jake in his metal box, noting that Jake "as a stand-in for the gamer, ought to be doing something, if only with his thumbs." Released the same day as *Avatar* and reviewed with it on the same page by the *New York Times*, James Cameron's *Avatar: The Game* was less rhapsodically received: "It is extremely easy on the eyes and is certainly well put-together, but it is also thoroughly vapid, wholly generic in its sensibility and utterly devoid of any emotional or intellectual engagement."

called "the recreation of the world in its own image," and the attraction of that world, however fantastic. With *Avatar*, the tantalizing promise of Total Cinema—now decisively post-photographic—was viscerally experienced: Unbearably distant, yet overwhelming near.

PART II:
A CHRONICLE OF
THE BUSH YEARS

CHAPTER SEVEN

2001: AFTER SEPTEMBER 11

NEW YORK, SEPTEMBER 18, 2001

Last Tuesday's terror attacks on the World Trade Center and the Pentagon blew a hole in the Toronto International Film Festival as well. Hundreds of journalists emerged from early-morning screenings to chaotic first reports (a publicist hysterically screaming "they bombed the Pentagon"), rushing from the insular world of round-the-clock movies to a total immersion in the big CNN picture and the hours of redial required to get a New York phone connection.

All screenings were canceled (at least for a day). So far as the press was concerned, the festival's 300-odd movies had already been abandoned in favor of a phantasmagoria of urban disaster, mind-boggling cartoon explosions, digicam special effects, world-obliterating violence, and incomprehensible conspiracy. In my case, the catastrophe was actually occurring a few blocks from home, but recurring "live" TV images of my neighborhood grocer, subway stop, and daughter's public school didn't in themselves account for the awful familiarity of the images.

"He who imagines disasters in some ways desires them," Theodor Adorno noted in the middle of the last century. Imagining this disaster is what the movies are all about. It was as though a message had bounced back from outer space. The giant dinosaurs, rogue meteors, and implacable insect-aliens that had destroyed movie-set Manhattans over the past few years were now revealed as occult attempts to represent the logic of inevitable catastrophe. Jerry Bruckheimer's justly maligned big-budget re-creation of Pearl Harbor in particular seemed to have emerged from some parallel time-space continuum to provide an explanation for what was even now occurring. (Wednesday's news that Warner Bros. was postponing much of its fall slate—including *Collateral Damage*, the Arnold Schwarzenegger movie whose West Side Highway poster was already an anti-landmark, visually footnoting the fallen towers—only served to confirm that terrorist warnings were no longer necessary.)

Screenings did resume during the restless thirty-six hours before the first packed, New York-bound trains were able to cross the US border. But there was a clear distinction between the films one saw prior to Tuesday morning and the films one saw while killing time in the big waiting room that Toronto became after Tuesday. Seen on September 12, the tragic beauty of Jean-Luc Godard's cinema eulogy *In Praise of Love* was all the more piercing; the callow posturing of its rote anti-Americanism was now impossible to shrug aside ...[1]

---

1   Actually, there was one movie in Toronto appropriate to the occasion. Press screened on the festival's opening, opposite the party, Peter Watkins's six-hour projected video piece *La Commune (Paris, 1871)* made for (and largely buried by) French TV, was as much immersion as narrative—complicated yet lucid and contagiously exciting, unfashionably intended to change the lives of its participants as well as its viewers.

"The Commune as test of the revolutionary legend," reads one of Walter Benjamin's notes for his Arcade Project—and it is also the test of Watkins's radical film practice. Over the course of his fiercely independent career, Watkins has more or less reinvented historical filmmaking. *La Commune* makes a historical feature in the form of an experimental documentary. This visually spare and conceptually rich re-creation of a doomed political utopia, entirely filmed in a derelict factory with a large cast of non-professionals, begins with a few of the actors introducing themselves and touring the abandoned, debris-strewn set. Thereafter, *La Commune* is filmed, literally, in the present tense—mainly in direct address delivered by the actors, for the camera of the guerrilla media enthusiasts of "Commune TV." The reporters, meanwhile, interrogate their own points of view, and the action is frequently interrupted by bulletins from the government's Versailles Television, which has its own suitably foppish newsreader as well as a resident pundit (a royalist historian Watkins recruited through an ad in *Le Figaro*). The director, who used a similar strategy of interpolated TV reporting in his first feature, *Culloden* (1964), knows his newsroom clichés. Indeed, the rise of a media monolith has long been one of his major issues.

Sustained over a period of hours, this impassioned hubbub conveys

The events of September 11 were a cinema event, the most immediately and extensively documented catastrophe in human history.

In the days following the cataclysm, the *Los Angeles Times* reported entertainment industry concern that "the public appetite for plots involving disasters and terrorism has vanished." Thus, Warner Bros. postponed *Collateral Damage*, and the screenwriters, David and Peter Griffiths, suffered another setback when Fox suspended their top-secret project, *Deadline*, a hijack drama written for James Cameron. Jerry Bruckheimer decided that the time might not be right for *World War III*, which called for nuclear attacks on Seattle and San Diego. Even comedies suffered collateral damage. Disney put off the release of the Tim Allen vehicle *Big Trouble*, which involves a nuclear bomb smuggled aboard a jet plane; MGM shelved *Nose Bleed*, with Jackie Chan starring as a window washer who foils a terrorist plot to blow up the WTC. Scheduled telecasts of the *X-Files* movie and *Independence Day* were canceled, along with a *Law and Order* episode about bioterrorism in NYC.

The CBS show *The Agency* dropped a reference to Osama bin Laden. (Concerned about bin Laden's charisma, the Bush administration contrived to have his video removed from heavy TV rotation and his subsequent US tele-appearances curtailed—except in the context

---

tremendous immediacy. This remarkable ensemble piece is a portrait of the public; the actors are always in some sense talking as themselves. Discussion of the issues that beset the Commune regularly segues into references to present-day concerns. *La Commune* is meant to evoke the unfamiliar sensation of revolutionary euphoria, of living (and dying) in a sacred time. Watkins's 210 actors researched their characters as much as they learned their lines; their performances are less a matter of acting than role-playing. Discussion of 1871 easily segues to present-day concerns—there are even meetings to discuss the film.

In their 1962 "Theses on the Paris Commune," the French Situationists noted that those who examine history from "the omniscient viewpoint of God [or] the classical novelist … can easily prove that the Commune was objectively doomed … They forget that for those who really lived it, the fulfillment was already there." And so it is here. Focused on process and profoundly anachronistic, *La Commune* is a syncretic work of left-wing modernism—evoking not only Brecht and Dziga Vertov but Soviet mass spectacle and the didactic Godard—is at once immediate and self-reflexive. Watkins restages history in its own ruins, uses the media as a frame, and even so, manages to imbue his narrative with amazing presence.

of the Fox show *America's Most Wanted*.) *Sex and the City* trimmed views of the twin towers; Paramount airbrushed them from the poster for *Sidewalks of New York*. Sony yanked their *Spider Man* trailer so as to eliminate images of the WTC and similarly ordered retakes on *Men in Black II* that would replace the WTC with the Chrysler Building. DreamWorks changed the end of *The Time Machine*, which rained moon fragments down on New York.

A prominent TV executive assured *The New York Times* that post-9/11 entertainment would be "much more wholesome" and that "we are definitely moving into a kinder, gentler time" (presumably 1988 when candidate George H. W. Bush introduced that phrase). A DreamWorks producer explained that the present atmosphere precluded his studio from bankrolling any more movies like *The Peacemaker* and *Deep Impact*. What then would movies be about?

Hollywood expected to be punished. Instead, it was drafted. Only days after the terror attacks, the Pentagon-funded Institute for Creative Technologies at the University of Southern California convened several meetings with filmmakers—including screenwriter Steven E. De Souza (*Die Hard, Die Hard 2*), director Joseph Zito (*Delta Force One, Missing in Action*), and wackier creative types like directors David Fincher, Spike Jonze, and Mary Lambert. The proceedings were chaired by Brigadier General Kenneth Bergquist; the idea was for the talent to "brainstorm" possible terrorist scenarios and then offer solutions. (Why not? Did we not live in a country where Steven Spielberg had been called upon by Congress to offer insight into hate crimes and Tom Clancy was interviewed by CNN as an expert on terrorism?)

For the first time since Ronald Reagan left office, it became all but impossible to criticize the movie industry. After George Bush's late September suggestion that Americans fight terrorism by taking their families to Disney World, Disney chief Michael Eisner sent an e-mail praising the president as "our newest cheerleader." One leader cheers the other. In Congress, conservative Republican Henry Hyde requested Hollywood's help in addressing the "hearts and minds" of the Arab world. Unable to ignore the similarity between their religious fundamentalism and ours—thanks to the reverends Jerry Falwell and Pat Robertson's suggestion that the events of 9/11 might be God's punishment for America's sinful behavior—the administration sought to promote the patriotic values of "tolerance" and entertainment.

On the other hand, according to the October 3 *Washington Post*, video stores were enjoying "huge rentals of heroic combat movies" with *Rambo* and *Die Hard With a Vengeance* "flying off Blockbuster shelves." Four days later, in retaliation for the Afghani Taliban's refusal to surrender Osama bin Laden, US and British forces launched Operation Enduring Freedom. The studios moved up military films like *Behind Enemy Lines* (which tested even better post-9/11) and the Somalia combat film *Black Hawk Down*. Warner Bros., supposedly out beating the bushes for a new Rambo, could only regret having so hastily yanked *Collateral Damage*—surely the season's perfect movie.

In the weeks following September 11, New York saw a number of notable openings, including David Lynch's *Mulholland Drive*, Catherine Breillat's *Fat Girl*, Richard Linklater's *Waking Life*, and Wes Anderson's *The Royal Tenenbaums*, not to mention the first installments of the Harry Potter saga and *Lord of the Rings*.[2]

---

2   The work closest to me, physically as well as emotionally, was my friend and neighbor Ken Jacobs's *Circling Zero: We See Absence*, a digital video home movie focusing less on the attack than its aftermath. A resident of Chambers Street with a loft formerly in the shadow, literally, of Trades, as well as a cinephilosopher whose continually innovative and richly eccentric movies mix heady formalism with deeply intuited film-historical and social concerns, Jacobs was out of town the day the buildings fell. Consequently, much of *Circling Zero* concerns his and his wife Flo's attempt to slip past the police and National Guard barricades that marked the militarized forbidden zone a few blocks up from Ground Zero, and re-enter their home. Amazingly, they get through. Pasted on a neighbor's door is the scrawled note, "I Just Started Walking North." As a sort of flashback to this adventure, Jacobs interpolates footage of the WTC aflame shot by his daughter Nisi from the building's roof. Particularly striking is the number of other people on their roofs similarly documenting the unfolding disaster. *Circling Zero* is intensely personal— in visual terms, it's totally first-person—but it's also a portrait of the body politic. The crowds of cops, volunteers, vendors, and tourists that circle the absence are as organic as antibodies surrounding a wound. The tape's last half explores another fact of nature: the Sargasso Sea of flowers, votive candles, and handmade placards that would consume Union Square throughout the fall of 2001. Jacobs's fascination with the fantastic assemblage around the new public space is evident. The impromptu performances and metaphysical debates of this spontaneous agora are, in every sense, signs of life.

The December 2001 press screening for *The Lord of the Rings* was the first I ever attended where critics were frisked with a hand-wand metal detector and asked to check their cell phones. Although this was clearly a response to the possibility of the movie being pirated, these precautions were explained as necessary in view of a presumed terrorist threat.

Ten years later, the Harry Potter franchise had grossed over $2 billion and *Mulholland Drive* would top several critics' polls as the decade's best movie but, in late October 2001, the commercially released movie to most fully manifest the post-9/11 mood, at least in New York, was the first feature by twenty-six-year-old writer-director Richard Kelly.

NEW YORK, OCTOBER 30, 2001

A moodily self-involved piece of work, part comic book, part case study, *Donnie Darko* employs *X-Files* magic realism to galvanize what might have been a routine tale of suburban teen angst—or borderline schizophrenia. Kelly begins fiddling with normality from the opening scene, the evening of the 1988 presidential debate between then vice-president George H. W. Bush and Massachusetts governor Michael Dukakis, wherein a sitcom family—tense mom, supercilious dad, two smirking teens, and an annoying little sister—gathers in the dining room to partake of a delivered pizza. "I'm voting for Dukakis," announces the oldest Darko sister (Maggie Gyllenhaal), causing her father (Holmes Osborne) to choke on his slice. A discussion regarding the candidates' respective economic policies quickly degenerates into vulgar abortion jokes and the revelation that middle child Donnie (Maggie's actual brother Jake) is off his medication and receiving messages from outer space.

Clearly we are dealing with an advanced life form. The mysterious forces of the universe demonstrate their power most vividly in the snoozy aftermath of the Bush-Dukakis dustup, when Donnie is summoned from his bedroom out into the night. Waking the next morning somewhere in the middle of the local golf course, he returns home to discover that a plane engine has inexplicably fallen from the sky and crashed through his bedroom ceiling. Convinced that the world will end in twenty-eight days, Donnie continues to experience alien visitations in the form of a monstrous toothy rabbit named Frank.

Signs of a parallel universe abound. An unhappy fat girl roams through Donnie's high school, an institution fronted by a bronze statue of a squatting mastiff. His gym class impassively watches a videotape on "fear management." A beatnik English teacher (Drew Barrymore) assigns her students to read "The Destructors," Graham Greene's jaundiced story of teenage nihilism. Smiling and mumbling to himself, socially maladroit Donnie manages to hook up with a new girl (Jena Malone) who has the Grimm name of Gretchen and a lurid family story to match. "You're weird," she tells him, adding, "That was a compliment." Meanwhile the town suffers a few curious plagues: the school is flooded, a home burns down. Donnie's shrink ups his meds and embarks on a regimen of hypnosis. (The first session comes to an abrupt end when the spellbound patient begins fondling his crotch.)

With Barrymore (*E.T.*) as Donnie's English teacher, Katharine Ross (*The Graduate*) as his therapist, and Patrick Swayze (*Dirty Dancing*) as a demonic motivational speaker, the movie's casting is both showy and inspired. Holmes Osborne is a sympathetically smooth and spineless Darko paterfamilias; Mary McDonnell, his wife, full of false cheer, carries hilarious intimations of early 1991 and the Gulf War, through her status as Stands With a Fist, Kevin Costner's righteous mate in *Dances With Wolves*. But the movie rests on the hunched shoulders of its spaced-out protagonist. Jake Gyllenhaal refuses to make direct contact with the camera. Goofy, poignant, frozen and shambolic, he convincingly portrays Donnie's eccentric genius—riffing on the sex life of the Smurfs, arguing with his science teacher on the nature of time travel. Gyllenhaal's sidelong performance allows him to take spectacular delusion in stride— he tries to kill Frank when the rabbit appears in his malleable bathroom mirror, and hallucinates ectoplasm emanating from his father's chest.

Although the big influence on Kelly seemed to be Paul Thomas Anderson's wildly ambitious and similarly apocalyptic *Magnolia*, released in time for the millennium, *Donnie Darko* is steeped in Reagan-era '80s pop culture. The movie's metaphysics are largely derived from *Back to the Future*, there's a particularly strange and funny allusion to *E.T.*, and in one of the most haunting scenes, Donnie and Gretchen watch Sam Raimi's 1987 *Evil Dead II* in an empty theater. The sub-Toni Basil MTV-style routine performed by Donnie's kid sister and her dance group, Sparkle Motion, is as lovingly choreographed as the soundtrack has been assembled.

Premiered in January 2001 at Sundance, *Donnie Darko* received a mixed response. While *Village Voice* critic Amy Taubin praised it as her favorite film of the festival, others appeared to resent its ostentation (big stars and special effects) or complained about its hubristic shifts in register. No less than Donnie, the movie has its awkward moments. Kelly makes too much of Beth Grant's uptight New Age gym teacher, and there are more than enough sinister cloud formations racing across the sky. But the writer-director has a surefooted sense of his own narrative, skillfully guiding the movie through its climactic *Walpurgisnacht*—or, should we say, carnival of souls.

The events of September 11 rendered most movies inconsequential; the heartbreaking *Donnie Darko*, by contrast, felt weirdly consoling. Period piece though it is, Kelly's high-school gothic was perfectly attuned to the present moment. A splendid debut under any circumstances, as released for Halloween 2001, it had an uncanny gravitas.[3]

Donnie Darko was not a hit. By mid November, after weeks of US air strikes, Taliban fighters abandoned Kabul; on December 7 (the

---

3   Grossing a mere $600,000 in its mayfly initial run, *Donnie Darko* would become the millennium's first cult film. In January 2002, the Two Boots Pioneer Theater, a hundred-seat venue attached to a pizza parlor in New York's East Village, began weekend midnight screenings that, enjoying scarcely more than word-of-mouth publicity among the disaffected young, would continue for twenty-six months through March 2004. (According to the Pioneer's co-owner Phil Hartman, it was his teenage son who first brought the movie to his attention.) By spring, the Landmark chain, acting on patron requests, had begun midnight screenings in other American cities, starting with Denver, and opening in London in late 2002, and *Donnie Darko* had its first successful commercial run. Meanwhile, Kelly started a website devoted to and elaborating on the movie; this in turn inspired fan-driven message boards.

Released in early 2002, the *Donnie Darko* DVD was filled with cryptic material addressed to devotees; it sold over 750,000 copies and, by some estimates, grossed fifteen times the money the movie made in its North American theatrical release. In July 2004, Kelly premiered his director's cut at the Seattle International Film Festival—some twenty minutes longer than the original, the revised *Donnie Darko* was released nationally that summer. (For simultaneous mainstream recognition see John Hartl, "Why 'Donnie Darko' gained a following, got second chance," *Seattle Times*, 6/2/04; Mark Olsen, "Movies: Time-traveling to success," *Los Angeles Times*, 7/14/2004; Robert Levine, "The Resurrection of 'Donnie Darko,'" *New York Times*, 7/18/2004; and Nathan Lee, "How 'Donnie Darko' Refused to Die," *New York Sun*, 7/20/2004.)

sixtieth anniversary of Pearl Harbor), Kandahar fell to the US-led coalition, although bin Laden and Taliban leader Mullah Mohammed Omar eluded capture. Rushed into theaters in late December 2002, the great box-office beneficiary of what was called the new bellicosity (and another movie predicated on a fallen aircraft), Ridley Scott's *Black Hawk Down* proved perfectly attuned to the present moment in its tone of aggrieved injury. Adapted from Mark Bowden's bestselling minute by minute account of the Battle of the Bakara Market in Mogadishu, the worst incident in the ill-fated US humanitarian mission to Somalia and the most costly firefight to involve American troops since Vietnam, *Black Hawk Down* originally ended with a specific reference to 9/11. A print screened for select journalists in mid November 2001 had a closing crawl listing events that followed the Mogadishu mission that the movie depicts, ending with terror attacks on the World Trade Center and Pentagon.[4]

The events of September 11 allowed Americans to feel like victims and act like bullies—just like the hapless soldiers of the 1993 Somalia mission. (There were eighteen American casualties and more than ten times as many Somalis killed.) It's difficult to construe *Black Hawk Down* as a pro-war movie, but to question its representation of us-versus-them is the next worst thing to being an American Taliban. My own less-than-enthusiastic review prompted an instant invitation to spar with cable TV's preeminent right-wing gasbag, Bill O'Reilly. I declined.

Rereading my review I'm not sure what prompted O'Reilly's interest. It's possible that he might have seen me as a useful foil against which he might praise the movie. I made no mention of the movie's patriotic core of revealed truth, rather suggesting that "American soldiers don't seem to know exactly what they doing here" and that *Black Hawk Down* was possibly "the most extravagantly aestheticized combat movie ever made," which is to say—a movie. "Very little

---

4   "In the end, I just felt that it was obvious," Scott told one journalist, explaining why the reference was dropped. (Rick Lyman, "An Action Film Hits Close, But How Close?," *New York Times*, 12/26/2001.) Once the war against Iraq began, US military-intelligence officials told the press that, before the war, the Iraqi military command had circulated copies of *Black Hawk Down* as an illustration of how America might be defeated ("Sticking to His Guns," *Time*, 4/7/2003).

emotional capital is invested in the characters, and as the various choppers, tanks, and snipers converge in the bloody vortex of downtown Mogadishu, *Black Hawk Down* becomes pure sensation ... Scott's ambition is to trump Steven Spielberg's D-Day landing and Francis Coppola's aerial assault." Although I made a closing reference to the film's "racial color-coding," others, notably *New York Times* critic Elvis Mitchell were blunter in accusing Scott of "glumly staged racism" in depicting the Somalis as "a pack of dark-skinned beasts."

Arnold Schwarzenegger's long-awaited, well-advertised *Collateral Damage* succeeded *Black Hawk Down* as the nation's premier (and most-protested) box-office attraction. Its release tastefully postponed after September 11, this once routine tale of an LA firefighter's revenge on the Colombian terrorists who blew up his wife and child was reborn as an Event—endorsed by no less an authority than former New York mayor Rudolph Giuliani and subject to demonstrations a week before its opening.[5]

---

5   Warner Bros. invited Giuliani and the staff of the Twin Towers Fund he set up to aid the families of the New York firefighters and police officers lost in the 9/11 attacks, to attend a preview. Speaking at the preview, Giuliani revealed that Schwarzenegger had personally donated $1 million to the fund and helped raise an additional $4 million, adding, "I'm very supportive of Arnold Schwarzenegger" ("Giuliani: Film Criticism Is Premature," *New York Times*, 2/7/2002).

Protests against *Collateral Damage* were led by the Rev. Brian Jordan, a Franciscan priest who ministered to workers at Ground Zero, and who—although he had not yet seen the movie—maintained that it was insulting to both Colombians and firefighters. (Carolyn Feibel, "Colombia activists protest new Schwarzenegger film," AP Online, 2/4/2002.) *Black Hawk Down* was widely protested, largely sight-unseen, by Act Now to Stop War and End Racism (ANSWER) and the Somali Justice Advocacy Center. One of the actors in the movie, Brandon Sexton III, criticized the movie to a student group at Columbia University for portraying Somalis as "savages without any reason to oppose the US military presence in Somalia." (See Geoffrey Gray, "Activists Protest No.1 Movie: 'Black Hawk' Damned," *Village Voice*, 2/6/2002; and Adrian Brune, "Protesting *Black Hawk Down*," *The Nation*, 2/21/2002.)

CHAPTER EIGHT

2002: THE WAR ON TERROR BEGINS

NEW YORK, FEBRUARY 19, 2002

An embarrassment on September 12, a patriotic vision five months later: Warner Bros. evidently began testing, and perhaps tweaking, the Arnold Schwarzenegger vehicle *Collateral Damage* back in November, discovering, to no one's surprise, that audiences were far more responsive to the scenario than before the terror attacks. (The intra-studio paper trail would doubtless provide a crash course in emergency marketing.) Thus the movie's release version begins as if in the fiery heart of the World Trade Center holocaust, with Arnold and his fellow smoke-eaters saving lives. "Heads up—let's do it!" the star cries, as if anticipating the signal for passenger rebellion given on the fourth hijacked plane, *Let's roll!*

One scene later, Arnold's central-casting wife and son are vaporized before his eyes when a bomb detonates outside the Colombian consulate. Small by WTC standards, the explosion reportedly leaves nine dead and twenty-four injured, but it is more than sufficient to light the fuse of Arnold's one-man war on the El Lobo terrorist cadre. Perhaps newly added to the film is the scene wherein the hooded guerrilla leader sends a videotape blaming "American war criminals" for provoking his group's action. Even more key to the movie's emotional thermostat is the Colombian leftist who openly sympathizes with the terrorists, using the US Army phrase "collateral damage" to rationalize Schwarzenegger's dead family, thus prompting Arnold to redecorate the guy's grungy head-quarters with a baseball bat.

In publicizing the movie, Schwarzenegger has claimed that *Collateral Damage* showcases his vulnerable side. True, he does have to fight mano-a-mano with a girl. (As usual, a signifier of revolutionary cadres is a heavy sprinkling of grim-faced warrior-women in their combat-fatigued ranks.) But, whether sprinting through the rainforest or digitally diving down a waterfall, Our Arnold is tough enough to wipe the smirk from beneath El Lobo's mask. The revolutionaries' quotes are largely from the Al Qaeda fakebook: "Americans hide behind family values … they have forgotten the reality of war, not like us." This reality is apparent when the sadistic guerrillas prove their native cruelty by exotically forcing one of their own to swallow a live coral snake.

Intermittently attempting to articulate a coherent argument, *Collateral Damage* shifts from pulse-pounding mode to something more migraine-conducive. It takes a sudden segue to fisticuffs and ear-chomping for the movie to escape from a tautological debate on moral equivalence between good vengeance and bad. ("You Americans are so naïve. You never ask, why does a peasant need a gun? You think you are the only ones to fight for your independence?" The non-sequitur riposte: "Independence to do what—kill women and children?") Similarly, in the aftermath of Arnold's single-handed decimation of the guerrilla camp, El Lobo asks the Fireman (as he is usually known) to explain the difference between them, prompting Arnold to ponderously elucidate, "I'm just going to kill you."

This is the sort of burly action flick where one coincidence pummels another, narrative necessity is a drunken roundhouse, and whatever passes for logic is a factor of the last plot device left standing. It's a small world after all, particularly in comparison to Arnold. When the star instructively yells, "You cannot fight terror with terror," at the resident CIA sleazebag (Elias Koteas), he's creating his own foreign policy; when he extends his protection to El Lobo's consort (Francesca Neri), he's acting as a nation unto himself.

Collateral damage is something that Americans have inflicted far more than they have suffered, but in this case, the phrase is synonymous with windfall profits. Just as George Bush's questionable presidency was consecrated by the War on Terror, so Schwarzenegger's flagging career should be revived. Perhaps the Fireman would again decide to run for governor of California. All together now: "Heads up. Let's … do … it!"

Fifteen months later, Schwarzenegger did successfully cast himself as protagonist and beneficiary of another extraordinary crisis, namely the drive to recall California governor Gray Davis.

The beat went on. Hollywood rolled out a well-hyped succession of combat films and the public lined up to see them. More were said to be in production. Not all would come to fruition; that they were announced was sufficient to define the moment. Titled "The Art of War," the following piece was the cover story for the *Village Voice*'s June 19, 2002 issue.

NEW YORK, JUNE 19, 2002

A landscape of smoky rubble littered with American corpses: Mogadishu, the Ia Drang valley, downtown Baltimore. For seven weeks out of the past twenty-two, the nation's No. 1 or 2 box-office attraction has been a spectacular war film. Add to these hits—*Black Hawk Down, We Were Soldiers*, and *The Sum of All Fears*—such crypto-combat, high-body-count chart-toppers as *Collateral Damage* and *Attack of the Clones*, and 2002 has been springtime for carnage, at least at the movies.

As *Black Hawk Down* instructed, "Leave no man behind." Last weekend's *Windtalkers* may have been butt-kicked by *Scooby-Doo*, but more spectacles of organized mayhem are on the way: *To End All Wars* continues the World War II revival, *Men in Black II* envisions warfare in outer space, *K-19: The Widowmaker* and *Below* bring back the Cold War nuclear submarine drama, *Gods and Generals* resurrects the Civil War. Meanwhile, on television, CBS floated the since-canceled *AFP: American Fighter Pilot*, and the VH1 reality-based series *Military Diaries* will soon be joined by ABC's Afghanistan-set *Profiles from the Front Line*.

Not since the flurry of Vietnam movies in the late 1980s has the combat film been so viable or so visible. And not since the gung-ho Reagan-era warnography of *Rambo* and *Top Gun* had the brass been so pleased. Vice President Dick Cheney took a breather from his undisclosed location to join Secretary of Defense Donald Rumsfeld at the gala Washington premiere of *Black Hawk Down*, the first movie for which (thanks to Rumsfeld's personal intervention) US troops were dispatched to a foreign country to aid in its production. *We Were Soldiers* and

The Sum of All Fears were similarly treated as official art. Mel Gibson's Vietnam War vehicle *We Were Soldiers* was previewed for George W. Bush, Rumsfeld, Condoleezza Rice, Karl Rove, and sundry military VIPs at a well-publicized White House screening. (An aide summarized the president's evaluation of the movie as "violent" but "good.") *The Sum of All Fears* had its world premiere in Washington, DC, as Paramount took care to alert the media that the producers had enjoyed considerable, even unprecedented, CIA access and Pentagon support.[1]

All of last spring's movies, if not the TV shows, predate September 11. Their inspiration came not from the attacks on New York and Washington or Team Bush's war on terror but the strong showing of *Saving Private Ryan* (which grossed $216 million and topped the box office for a month during the Lewinsky summer of '98, when Bill Clinton too was striving to show he was not just a lover but a fighter). Credit the entertainment industry, or at least producer Jerry Bruckheimer and writer Tom Clancy, with uncanny prescience. Bruckheimer's *Pearl Harbor* grossed $200 million in the spring and summer of 2001, but what truly seemed prophetic the day after September 11 was the movie's blend of blockbuster mega-disaster and historical war epic.

Bruckheimer's art film *Black Hawk Down* was rushed into theaters in late December (and subsequently furnished on video to US military bases) to capitalize on the nation's new bellicosity. Throughout the winter, this visceral spectacle of US soldiers pinned down under Somali fire effectively functioned as an example of virtual combat. *Black Hawk Down* inspired patriotic sentiment, precipitated European ridicule, and invited anti-war protest, even as it stood in for the American debacle in Afghanistan that never quite happened (and to which reporters had even less access than Operation Desert Storm).

---

1   Written and directed by Randall Wallace, *We Were Soldiers* is primarily concerned with the bloody November 1965 Battle of Ia Dang Valley, the Vietnam War's first major confrontation between US and North Vietnamese troops. Like its model *Saving Private Ryan*, *We Were Soldiers* is an extremely graphic depiction of infantry combat and, like *Black Hawk Down*, which it resembles in many ways, *We Were Soldiers* was completed before September 11, 2001. Paramount scheduled the movie to open the following summer; however, it was tested for audiences in October 2001, with one such screening attended by presidential advisor Karl Rove, and then advanced on the release schedule to open during the early stages of the war in Afghanistan—again like *Black Hawk Down*, which it succeeded as America's top-grossing movie.

The scenario structures the event. Bruckheimer co-produced *Top Gun*, the 1986 movie that military historian Lawrence H. Suid credits with rehabilitating Hollywood's image of the US armed forces. Clancy was the nearest thing the military establishment has to a Homeric bard. The writer had been recognized by the afternoon of September 11 as a near "precog" and pundit supreme for his 1994 novel *Debt of Honor*'s climactic description of terrorists wiping out the entire US government by crashing their hijacked airplane into the Capitol during a joint session of Congress. *The Sum of All Fears*, adapted from an earlier Clancy book, opened amid international jitters that the perennial Kashmir dispute might precipitate a nuclear exchange between India and Pakistan—resurrecting a cinematic mode more or less dormant since the early 1960s by bringing the Bomb home.[2]

A week before *The Sum of All Fears* opened to become the nation's top-grossing movie, a *New York Times Magazine* cover story warned of the inevitable nuclear terrorism that was bound to befall American cities. "Not if but when" is how Bill Keller's remarkably fatalistic "Nuclear Nightmares" began, going on to term the deployment of a high-radiation dirty bomb as "almost childishly simple." *The Sum of All Fears* obligingly visualized the possibility of such a radiological dispersion device detonated by foreign terrorists at Baltimore's Camden Yards, where virtually the entire US government is attending the Super Bowl. It's the ultimate advertisement for Homeland Security. The president's men are hustled out faster than you can say "anthrax." A frenzied attempt at poignant montage presents the American people as goofball cheerleaders, their faces painted in support of their team, idiotically oblivious to their imminent incineration.

In the early 1960s, imagining nuclear war was called thinking about the unthinkable. What's startling in *The Sum of All Fears* is that the nuke actually happens—rolling shock waves flinging cars into the air and swatting planes to the ground, a big black mushroom cloud rising over what

---

2   *The Sum of All Fears* was the closest movie yet to official art. A front-page *New York Times* article reported that, in terms of government support, the movie exceeded any previously made; for a modest fee of less than $1 million, the Pentagon provided Paramount with "the celluloid equivalent of a small nation's armed forces" as well as consultations with CIA officials and analysts and "numerous military experts" to give "technical assistance" (Katharine Q. Seelye, "When Hollywood's Big Guns Come Right from the Source," *New York Times*, 6/9/02).

once was Baltimore as the movie's surviving protagonists race around the white-light radioactive inferno. As *The Sum of All Fears* captured its second weekend, US Customs officials called a news conference to demonstrate their bomb detection capability. Meanwhile, the Chris Rock vehicle *Bad Company* offered a similarly radioactive terrorist scenario played for laughs and on cable TV, Turner Classic Movies topically offered historical perspective with a triple bill of *Dr. Strangelove, Fail-Safe*, and *The China Syndrome*.

The Pentagon's Office of Strategic Influence may have officially backed off its announced intention to plant disinformation in the foreign press, but it would seem that Washington takes its cues from Hollywood—as well as vice versa. Attorney General John Ashcroft timed for the Monday morning that followed *The Sum of All Fears'* second triumphant weekend his proud announcement that the currently beleaguered FBI and CIA had successfully collaborated on the arrest of one Abdullah al-Muhajir, born Jose Padilla in Brooklyn. Already detained for a month since deplaning in Chicago, Padilla was being held as a military prisoner and suspected of abetting an Al Qaeda plot to produce the very scenario *The Sum of All Fears* so vividly illustrated—the drama of a nuclear device detonated in an East Coast American city.[3]

Indeed, the attorney general received another timely cue the following month with the opening of Steven Spielberg's *Minority Report*. Having been announced on the eve of the millennium, as the Y2K panic was reaching its peak, Spielberg's science-fiction *policier* went into production in the spring of 2001 and wrapped that July. Premiering in June 2002, the director's first post-9/11 release was a tale of precognitive police work that, as many reviewers pointed out, uncannily anticipated Ashcroft's notions of preventative detention. "The guilty are arrested before the law is broken," TV spots warned, strategically placed during national and local news programs during the week of Padilla's arrest.

---

3   That Ashcroft was in Moscow when he announced Padilla's capture echoed the last-minute US–Russian cooperation that, at least in *The Sum of All Fears*, saves both nations from Mutually Assured Destruction. Of course, in 2002, the MAD doctrine was nothing more than Cold War nostalgia, hardly applicable to Israel and its neighbors, the US and Iraq, or India and Pakistan.

NEW YORK, JULY 2, 2002

Steven Spielberg's *Minority Report* posits a futuristic police force that arrests criminals before they have a chance to commit their crimes. The unexpectedly topical premise, taken from a 1956 story by sci-fi master Philip K. Dick, posits a future in which mutant "precogs" dream of murders before they occur, thus allowing the police to arrest killers in advance of their crimes. Spielberg himself has expressed cautious support for the extra-legality of the current Bush war on terror: "I am willing to give up some of my personal freedoms in order to stop 9-11 from ever happening again. But the question is where do you draw the line?"[4]

Adding to the early twenty-first-century feel, *Minority Report* opens with a zappy, gore-filled "pre-visualization." Chief inspector John Anderton (Tom Cruise) conducts the flow of images, hilariously accompanied by Schubert's "Unfinished Symphony," rewinding and recombining the evidence as though fashioning a movie on some telepathic editing console. The three pre-cogs floating unconscious in their high-security amniotic pool are not the only ones troubled by nightmares. The solitary Anderton is a secret dope fiend, haunted by the disappearance of his young son six years before. It is because of the boy's abduction that the cop has become the poster child for the Washington, DC, pre-crime unit founded by the lordly, Ashcroft-like Lamar Burgess (Max von Sydow). But is preemptive punishment a good thing? Inevitably, Anderton discovers that the pre-cogs have determined that he is destined to commit murder, killing someone he doesn't yet know.

His trademark paranoia aside, Dick's original story was mainly an exercise in the proliferation of bifurcating possibilities, closer in some respects to imagining a Borges conundrum than an Orwell police state.

---

4   Matt Drudge, who leaked Spielberg's interview online, maintained that while the director was preparing to publically support the administration in coordination for the release of *Minority Report*, his Dreamworks colleagues

> pulled out their eyes in horror as the Bush administration moved the nation's law enforcement priority from enforcement of terror crimes to "prevention" ... "Is this really happening? This is our movie!!!" a top— politically active—Dreamworks executive yelled while watching a John Ashcroft press conference last week on C-SPAN, according to sources. "Mr. Ashcroft is scary as s*%t!"
>
> (*Drudge Report*, 6/13/2002: www.drudgereport.com.)

Spielberg's movie, however, is less concerned with forking paths of pre-destination than in the process of exorcizing the past. The concept of the minority report that gives Dick's story its twist is here something of a red herring—although the screenplay does introduce such other Dickian notions as compensatory drug use and pervasive advertising.

Anticipating the proliferation of online merchandizing, Spielberg imagines an all-too-credible world in which (as with TV ratings) consumers are defined by what they watch. Eyes, in *Minority Report*, are literally windows on the soul, and the soul is that which yearns for brand-name fulfillment. Every electronic billboard is a consumer surveillance mechanism programmed to recognize a potential customer and deliver a customized personal message. This is most wickedly visualized as Anderton drags a shaking and quaking, madly prognosticating precog Agatha (Samantha Morton) through a shopping mall with the cops in hot pursuit.[5]

Minority Report is a movie of haunting images and mindless thrills. Whatever its intent, it visualizes (as well as demonstrates) a future where the unconscious has been thoroughly colonized. All human desires are grist for capitalist gratification, just as any criminal thoughts are grounds for state punishment. Although the filmmaker may have wanted to trade legal freedoms for security from terror, his recurring images of thought police drifting down from the sky or crashing through the ceiling into someone's life have a terrorizing resonance beyond the tortuous permutations of the plot. Similarly, the mechanical spiders that serve as police bloodhounds are spectacularly invasive—a key concept for the movies.[6]

---

5   John Sutherland found this maddening: "There can rarely have been a film narrative more saturated in product placement." Wryly noting the monopolistic brands of Spielberg's 2054 (all cars are Lexus, all sodas are Pepsi, the only newspaper is *USA Today*), Sutherland further observes that "in the world of *Minority Report*, there is only one nation. There is no terrorism, no ideology." Even though the movie is set in Washington, DC, "there isn't apparently, a President any more. History has indeed ended" ("Can you see the precog turning?," *Times Literary Supplement*, 7/12/2002).

6   For Andrew Sarris, *Minority Report* was itself something of an image arcade: the movie "sinks to the level of pornographically violent video games such as *Grand Theft Auto*, with some ghoulish surgery involving switched eyeballs guaranteed to titillate the tots. Indeed, the film's vaunted Pre-Crime technology ends up looking like little more than a peculiarly shaped pin-ball machine" (*New York Observer*, 7/2/2002).

There's also a rueful edge to the tawdry image emporium—part sleazy disco, part psychedelic Radio Shack—where citizens seek solace and Anderton tries to "download" Agatha's visions. And most fascinating is the bitter knowledge of its final mystery: If you can only create the right movie, you can get away with murder.[7]

Anticipating the commercial totality inherent in social networking, *Minority Report* can be seen as a prescient expression of the new social-real. At the time, it was clear that we had entered the Age of Bush. In late July, *New York Times* political commentator Maureen Dowd began a column, datelined "Los Angeles," with the hilarious news that "Hollywood agents now advise budding screenwriters how to pitch scripts by using a political analogy."

"You're in the Oval Office," they bark. "You're briefing President Bush. He's got no attention span. He doesn't care about details. Sell *him* the movie." If you can tell the story vividly and simply enough to appeal to the curiosity-challenged chief executive who likes his memos on one page, the agents figure, you might be able to win over busy, bottom-line-oriented studio executives.[8]

On the other hand, Geoffrey O'Brien noted the thematic resonance. Unlike previous adaptations from Philip K. Dick like *Blade Runner* or *Total Recall*, *Minority Report* seemed to acknowledge that the dystopia Dick saw was already here: "The technology is just too powerful for the characters to assert an existence apart from it. The very notion of background and foreground is obliterated by a visual field in which the people are little more than swirls of information oscillating among other analogous swirls" ("Prospero on the Run," *New York Review of Books*, 8/15/2002).

7   As Spielberg was quoted in the June 2002 issue of *Wired*: "Someday the entire motion picture may take place inside the mind, and it will be the most internal experience anyone can have: being told a story with your eyes closed, but you see and smell and interact with the story."

8   In the aftermath of 9/11, Dowd reported, many of Hollywood's Democrats had concluded that "W. might well be cast as president," reasoning that a leader who saw the world in bumper-sticker slogans might be more effective than one, like his predecessor, whose thinking ran to full paragraphs. "If Clinton was a talky Stephen [*sic*] Soderbergh feature, W. was a fast-cut Jerry Bruckheimer trailer" (Dowd, "Hooray for Hillarywood!," *New York Times*, 7/31/2002).

The WTC cast its non-existent shadow over the year's holiday releases. Martin Scorsese's much-anticipated *Gangs of New York* was for most a terrible disappointment although, like other movies that opened at the close of 2002, it could not be seen apart from the events of 9/11. Scorsese's concluding image was a stunning matte shot of smoky Lower Manhattan as viewed from a Brooklyn graveyard, followed by the inevitable time-lapse dissolve to the skyline as of September 10, 2001.

Scorsese's fellow New Yorker Spike Lee specifically set his in-your-face paean to ethnic vaudeville and urban lowlife, *25th Hour*, in post-9/11 Manhattan. Although the Event has no bearing on the narrative, Lee's movie opens with aerial shots of the city that include the memorializing twin columns of light beamed up from the Trade Center site and ends with Bruce Springsteen's 9/11 anthem, "The Rising"; another scene is shot in a high rise apartment above Ground Zero, which is distractingly visible through the window.[9]

25th Hour opened in New York on the same day as *The Two Towers*, which might have offered Lee an alternate title. Not only notable for featuring the first convincing human-digital cyborg performance (Andy Serkis, radically modified, as the pitiful Gollum), *The Two Towers* was a key component in what would prove Hollywood's top-grossing year of the '00s. Four out of the five worldwide top-grossing movies released in 2002 were sequels: *Lord of the Rings: The Two Towers*; *Harry Potter and the Chamber of Secrets*; *Star Wars Episode II: Attack of the Clones*; and *Men in Black II*. The fifth was *Spider-Man*, which would go on to spin off sequels in 2004 and 2007. All were essentially animated movies created from photographic material.

---

9   "Watching the beams fade into the dawn onscreen stirred up some half-buried sorrows, which I found a little jarring," A. O. Scott wrote in the *New York Times*. "The New York of the movies has always been an exaggerated, even fantastical version of the real place, and this division has seemed especially acute in the past year. Even in newer movies, the cinematic city has frequently offered a backward or sidelong escape from the post-9/11 real thing." The reviewer found "an ambience of stunned grief and a slightly giddy, slightly guilty feeling of survival [floating] through the film, which chronicles a midlevel drug dealer's last day of freedom before the start of a seven-year prison sentence."

CHAPTER NINE

2003: INVADING IRAQ

The winter of 2003 was the run-up to the Iraq War—its beginning was protested, to no avail, by hundreds of thousands of New Yorkers marching in the streets.

On March 14, George W. Bush made a televised speech to the nation maintaining that "intelligence gathered by this and other governments leaves no doubt that the Iraq regime continues to possess and conceal some of the most lethal weapons ever devised." War came on March 21, two days before Oscar Night. Continuing a trend that began during the Clinton presidency, movie stars had come to serve the Democrats as talk radio personalities served the Republicans. Political dissidence was a matter of celebrity.

Titled "When Doves Cry," the following article was the *Village Voice* cover story for the issue of March 25.

NEW YORK, MARCH 25, 2003

A cast of Bill Clinton's cronies, a vaunted 1 billion viewers in 150 countries: there were some who imagined that Oscar Night '03 might be the most widely seen peace demonstration ever beamed into the universe.

As the Desert Storm sequel drew nigh, the right-wing media shifted their enemies of choice from those *The Simpsons* calls "cheese-eating surrender monkeys" to bigmouth movie stars. Could Shock and Awe really be upstaged by Stupefaction and Narcissism? The *New York Post* suggested that the Academy Awards be canceled. Meanwhile, the Internet crackled with reports that activists like Susan Sarandon and Martin Sheen were on a blacklist and that acceptance speeches would be monitored for political content. Insiders warned a UK daily that failure to award Michael Moore's *Bowling for Columbine* the Oscar for Best Documentary Feature would be proof that Hollywood had reverted to "the witch-hunting 1950s."

What was appropriate—and what should people wear? The group Artists United to Win Without War was handing out green peace buttons; other members of the Academy sported a more abstract silver squiggle apparently meant to represent a dove. Monitoring the stars' entrance on the foreshortened red carpet from her E! Channel aerie, fashion arbiter Joan Rivers wondered what they meant. "Peace," her daughter explained. "Every idiot in the world wants peace," Joan snorted, suggesting that the morning after, the pins will wind up for sale on eBay. But what the buttons and squiggles really meant was that, for those of us who cared, the stars were making a statement—or not.

The Hollywood left had devolved to this. But then, the movies encourage semiotic readings. The green semaphore seemed more radical, if less chic, than the silver squiggle. It was less surprising to spot a green button affixed to the lapel of Michael Moore's tuxedo than Harvey Weinstein's. Salma Hayek, Daniel Day-Lewis, and Adrien Brody all wore the squiggle but not their fellow nominees Julianne Moore and Meryl Streep (although it had been reported they would). Presenter Richard Gere was besquiggled, surprise loser Martin Scorsese not. Susan Sarandon sauntered confidently out with her pin and held up two fingers in a goddessy peace sign. A shell-shocked-looking Barbra Streisand was unsquiggled, although she did make a statement in praise of protest music. There were some who devised other accessories—Matthew McConaughey's lapel had sprouted a peculiar mélange of red, white, and blue flowers—but only Jon Voight seemed to be wearing an American flag pin.

Where were movieland's macho men? Who would defend Bush's war? Mel Gibson, Charlton Heston, Clint Eastwood, Kevin Costner, Bruce Willis, and Arnold Schwarzenegger all seemed conspicuous by their absence. Had they driven their Humvees into lockdown? Were they stockpiling Poland Spring and boycotting the hippie love-in? Was it the hall? The Kodak Theater's outsize, quasi-pagan Oscar statues and the Babylonian deco splendor had the look of an Iraqi presidential palace. Had the terrorists won? There was an elephant in the room, but it wasn't Republican.

"What is a movie star?" Oscar host Steve Martin riffed. "They can be thin or skinny. They can be Democrats or ... skinny." Throughout his presidency, Bill Clinton was identified with a "cultural elite" as personified by his Hollywood cronies Steven Spielberg and Barbra Streisand; when he ran for re-election, *Variety* calculated political contributions from the fabulous 90210 zip code went Democrat by more than two to one.

Clinton and Hollywood were one. The president befriended, co-opted, and ultimately hid behind movieland activists. They responded by imagining his better self. One prime Clintonian legacy was the virtuous virtual presidency of Martin Sheen (perhaps to be embodied by the actual Howard Dean, the Vermont governor who, as an anti-war candidate, was briefly the Democratic frontrunner). The Clinton saga—as well as the histories of the Hollywood Anti-Nazi League and the Hollywood Democratic Committee, not to mention the 1968 McCarthy and 1972 McGovern campaigns—suggest that stars excel as fundraisers and campaign surrogates. Under the current Bush regime, Hollywood actors have filled a vacuum. They are themselves stand-ins without a star. The silence of elected officials combined with the exegeses of entertainment news insured that Martin Sheen and Jessica Lange, George Clooney and Janeane Garofalo would be drafted as media spokespeople to speak in opposition to Bush's war.

The Oscar producers were scarcely unaware of Hollywood's current role as America's most visible opposition. Nor did they negate it. The organizers minimized wartime hoopla; the evening's genial host never once waved the flag. Still, his deflationary razzing of the stars in attendance served to dampen their self-importance. Did they really have the right to an opinion? The anti-war remarks seemed subtle and tentative—albeit still more outspoken than those of equivocating Senate Democrats. Mexican, Irish, and Spanish presenters and recipients were far less ambiguous in their comments on the war than their American counterparts. (Of the fifty-nine Oscar winners assembled, only four—Sarandon, Day-Lewis, Anjelica Huston, and Ben Kingsley—wore the silver squiggle, and only two are American.)

The tension was palpable when arch provocateur Michael Moore advanced to the stage. But the enthusiastic standing ovation faded to silence and turned to boos when the filmmaker broke the frame by invoking the "fictitious" 2000 election and questioning Bush's "war for fictitious reasons." Moore succeeded in using the Oscars to reach the billion-person viewing audience. But despite his well-prepared statement, the filmmaker was not to be the evening's hero. The Oscars are, before anything else, the industry's main way to feel good about itself.

Would this embarrassment be the evening's moment to remember? There was no John Wayne on hand to shoot down the obstreperous Moore. As if on cue, Jack Valenti wandered out, too stunned or clueless to defend the honor of the Bush administration. Hollywood saved itself when, in a performance worthy of a second Oscar, Adrien Brody stopped the show. The surprise Best Actor winner had the youthful energy to expend ten precious seconds and who knows how much bodily fluid kissing Halle Berry and the presence of mind to express his gratitude to the Academy, thank his mother (photographer Sylvia Plachy), and—silencing the band—cite the war, enact anguish, and invoke Allah. He even wound up by naming a childhood friend who was an actual American combatant in Kuwait.

It was only then that Academy president Frank Pierson could, speaking like the fictitious president, extend an offer of peace to the Iraqi people, who were even then being bombed, a mere flick of the remote away.

In the early hours of April 2, CNN broke the story that US Army Rangers and Navy Seals had stormed Saddam Hospital in Nasiriya and rescued a prisoner of war, Private Jessica Lynch, a nineteen-year-old army maintenance worker captured in an Iraqi ambush on March 23. That morning, newscasts and newspapers put forth a picture of Pvt. Lynch on a stretcher, sheltered by a folded American flag, and it was reported that she had sustained at least one gunshot wound in her battle with Iraqi soldiers. April 3, the *Washington Post* ran a front-page story headlined "She Was Fighting to the Death" that, citing unnamed government officials, suggested that Lynch was a veritable teenaged Rambo who "fought fiercely" and sustained multiple gunshot and stab wounds. "Hollywood could not have dreamed up a more singular tale," per the April 14 issue of *Time*. Almost immediately, NBC announced plans for a made-for-TV movie to be called *Saving Private Lynch*.[1]

The Saving Private Lynch scenario dominated US war coverage even after Baghdad fell on April 9—symbolized by the rigorously staged and tightly framed toppling of Saddam Hussein's statue in the city's main square, an event that was made for TV and routinely compared to the fall of the Berlin Wall. ("Lights! Camera! Combat! Iraq Passes Its Screen Test," per weekly *Variety*'s April 14 front page: "Viewed as showbiz, the Iraq war was a winner, as expertly executed as it was scripted.") On May 1, in a photo op seemingly inspired by the 1986 movie *Top Gun*, George W. Bush piloted a Navy S-3B Viking onto the deck of the aircraft carrier *USS Abraham Lincoln* and, standing in a flight jacket before a banner reading MISSION ACCOMPLISHED, declared victory: "Major combat operations in Iraq have ended." Soon afterward, US toy companies were manufacturing twelve-inch action figures of the president in a flight suit, some labeled "Top Gun."[2]

As the Events of 9/11 deranged the 2001 Toronto Film Festival, so the war in Iraq was a tangible presence at the next international film festival I attended.

---

1   By April 15, the *Washington Post* was questioning its initial account; on May 4, the *Toronto Star* published a story, based on interviews with the hospital staff, suggesting that Lynch had neither been involved in combat, nor wounded by Iraqi soldiers and that, as the hospital was unguarded, there had been no resistance to the rescue mission. The definitive revision of the Lynch story appeared on May 18 with a BBC documentary. Describing the rescue, Dr. Anmar Uday compared it to a Hollywood film: "They cried 'go, go, go,' with guns and blanks and the sound of explosions. They made a show—an action movie like Sylvester Stallone or Jackie Chan." The operation was documented by military cameramen. Telecast on November 9 as *Saving Jessica Lynch*, the NBC telefilm took into account revisionist accounts of the incident.

2   Six months further into the war, no one could be found to take credit for the now embarrassing "Mission Accomplished" banner. On October 28, the president publicly disavowed the sign and suggested that the sailors of the *USS Abraham Lincoln* were responsible; a few days later, the ship's lieutenant commander attributed the idea to the White House advance team ("Bush Steps Away From Victory Banner," *New York Times*, 10/29/2003; Elisabeth Bumiller, "A Proclamation of Victory That No Author Will Claim," *New York Times*, 11/3/2003).

CANNES, MAY 30, 2003

The appropriate Hollywood ending for the 2003 Cannes Film Festival would have been a Palme d'Or garland for Clint Eastwood's *Mystic River*. Directed by a seventy-three-year-old legend, rhapsodically received by French and American auteurists alike, this character-driven crime thriller offered an opportunity to end a lackluster festival with a burst of manufactured glamour.

Even more interesting, a winning *Mystic River*—which, like many of Eastwood's movies, can be read as a meditation on lone-wolf, vigilante justice—would have provided a suitably ambiguous conclusion for the much discussed Franco-American tensions that, as explicated in the pages of *Variety* and the leftish French daily *Libération*, provided this festival with its particular narrative. Instead, the jury (evidently as unhappy with the quality of the competition films as the press) opted for Gus Van Sant's *Elephant*—a poetic evocation of a Columbine-like American high school shooting that was attacked by *Variety*'s Todd McCarthy as "pointless at best and irresponsible at worst," but that proved markedly more popular with French critics than Americans.

Elephant, though stronger on formal values and surface tension than social context or psychological analysis, was scarcely the least movie that the jury, headed by French director Patrice Chéreau and including Americans Steven Soderbergh and Meg Ryan, might have decorated. Strictly in terms of passion, originality, and sustained cinematic chutzpah, however, Lars von Trier's allegory *Dogville* towered over the competition. Still, speaking of unpopular foreign entanglements, the most topical and perhaps the most universally admired movie in Cannes' official section was Errol Morris's *The Fog of War*—a documentary portrait, shown out of competition, of former US Secretary of Defense Robert McNamara. Culled from over twenty hours of interviews, annotated with archival footage and declassified White House tapes, scored to Philip Glass's now axiomatic angst-drone, the movie allows the still-formidable octogenarian to reveal what he was taught by the Cuban missile crisis ("we came that close—that close!—to war") and to detail his lesser-known experiences as contributor to the World War II firebombing of Japan and later, pioneer of the automobile seat belt.

Once upon a time, McNamara personified the military industrial complex. A stellar technocrat and a brilliant efficiency expert, this so-called walking IBM machine went from running the giant Ford Motor Company (the first non-family member to do so) to administering the even more colossal US Defense Department (where he was similarly credited with putting the Pentagon under civilian control).

The young McNamara was the most iconic of Kennedy's New Frontiersmen. His bulldog look—slicked-back hair, rimless glasses— and arrogant pugnacity made him a star. Four decades before Donald Rumsfeld, McNamara invented his successor's steely smile and jaunty certitude, which is only one reason why *The Fog of War* is almost ridiculously relevant. Vietnam is the war that remains to be resolved. Senator John Kerry, the leading Democratic challenger to George W. Bush, established his integrity as a decorated and wounded Vietnam vet who became an outspoken—and consequently vilified—opponent of the war. Bush, on the other hand, used his family privilege to secure alternate service in the National Guard and then dodged even that when it proved inconvenient.

Distressingly, Morris generally allows McNamara to put his own spin on the Vietnam War. Following a line advanced by Oliver Stone among others, McNamara suggests that Kennedy was waiting until after the 1964 election in order to disengage from South Vietnam and blames Lyndon Johnson for the debacle. But Johnson's White House tapes— which is to say, the phone calls that he bugged for posterity and which were released in 1997—tell a different story. In one of the first, made six months after Johnson became president, McNamara invokes the verdict of history in warning his new boss that the US can't allow itself to be "pushed out of Vietnam." That summer, the exaggerated and bungled Gulf of Tonkin "incident," which *The Fog of War* acknowledges without pressing McNamara on his long years of dissembling about it, served to stampede the Congress into supporting Johnson's policy.[3]

While McNamara several times broaches the subject of war crimes and appears prepared to re-examine his own mistakes, he's remarkably unwilling to accept any personal responsibility. If McNamara does not

---

3   "No one does 'existential dread' as well as Philip Glass," Errol Morris was quoted as saying in smug defense of *The Fog of War*. "And this is a movie filled with existential dread." But whose? Morris's feelings are nowhere apparent and McNamara shows not the slightest degree of fear and trembling. Rather than dread, *The Fog of War* is suffused with moral equivocation. Or perhaps the "existential dread" that Morris evokes is akin to that experienced by Hannah Arendt in the face of Eichmann's "banality."

come across as a grandstanding prevaricator like Henry Kissinger, one may still well wonder how so brilliant a man can claim to have been ignorant of certain historical dynamics (the antipathy between Vietnam and China, for example) readily available to any moderately aware high school student in 1966. On the other hand, one may also be amazed to hear the octogenarian powerhouse suddenly launch into a criticism of US unilateralism. Curiously, that aside seemed to resonate more positively with American than foreign critics.

A skeptical review in *Le Monde* accused Morris of demonstrating too much sympathy for the devil. More than providing the satanic former secretary with an all-to-human face however, *The Fog of War* offers additional evidence that the road to hell—or at least, the way to Dogville—is paved with good intentions.

Opening as it did in many American cities on the same December weekend as *The Return of the King*, pundits might have been pardoned for subtitling Morris's movie, "Robert McNamara and the Ring of Power"—particularly as the wrinkled and bony former Secretary of Defense appeared as a sort of animated, Gollumized husk of his younger self. Although clearly and profoundly corrupted by power, McNamara was the only senior American official to ever admit to an error under the coercion of his own conscience alone. In their year-end meetings, the various US critics' conclaves saw more than a few votes for Best Actor cast in favor of an elderly neophyte. McNamara's bad teeth and liver-spots notwithstanding, the beauty of *The Fog of War* is entirely skin deep. McNamara concedes that mistakes were made but when asked why he didn't speak out against the war, he can only take refuge in his anguish: "I am not going to say any more than I have." As the Frodologists of the '60s might have put it, the former secretary carried the Ring of Power to the rim of Mount Doom, but refused to throw it in.

In another sort of Vietnam flashback, on August 27, five months into the Iraq War, the Pentagon held the first of several informational screenings of *The Battle of Algiers*. As the Pentagon flier put it: "Children shoot soldiers at point-blank range. Women plant bombs in cafés. Soon the entire Arab population builds to a mad fervor. Sound familiar?" The last half of *The Battle of Algiers* illustrates the flier's hook: "How to win a battle against terrorism and lose the war of ideas."

French reaction is personified by the newly arrived Col. Mathieu who accepts the mission of demolishing the revolutionary FLN. "There are 80,000 Arabs in the casbah," he tells his men. "Are they all against us? We know they are not. In reality, it is only a small minority that dominates with terror and violence. This minority is our adversary and we must isolate and destroy it." How familiar that must have sounded!

Mathieu's campaign is successful but—as he, more than anyone else in the movie, realizes—history belongs to the FLN. At one point he turns on a press conference full of hostile French journalists and forces them to clarify their own privileged positions. "I would now like to ask you a question: Should France remain in Algeria? If you answer 'yes,' then you must accept all the necessary consequences." A montage of Algerians subject to torture follows. This, one imagines, was the key moment of the Pentagon's *Battle of Algiers*. To succeed, the American occupation must consign such abuses to the Ba'athist past—indeed, the rationale for the invasion of Iraq long ago shifted from Saddam Hussein's weapons of mass destruction to his dungeons of horror. But didn't the invasion itself demonstrate that, in the war against terrorism, all means are available?

NEW YORK, JULY 2, 2003

"The future has not been written …" the young narrator solemnly muses at the beginning of *Terminator 3: Rise of the Machines*. That's true enough—although in the pre-sold universe of summer entertainment, the box-office brawn of this Arnold Schwarzenegger vehicle is as close to a given as the laws of gravity.

If it's Terminator time, there must be a Republican president running for re-election. Appearing unheralded on the eve of the 1984 election, the original Arnold Schwarzenegger robot opera, directed by then unknown James Cameron and featuring the most compelling Frankenstein monster in fifty years, provided a dystopian alternative to the Reaganite "new morning." Released as Bush I girded his loins in the summer of the New World Order 1991, Cameron's vastly inflated, post–Desert Storm *T2: Judgment Day* resurrected the president's fitness adviser as a kinder, gentler killer cyborg. (*T2* was for a time the most expensive movie ever made; Cameron modestly described it as "the first action movie advocating world peace.")

There are no term limits on sequels, and now, as the Bush II juggernaut gets ready to roll, der Arnold—once hailed by *Time* as "the most potent symbol" of Hollywood's "worldwide dominance"—returns to save the world, or at least the designated world-savior, the now grown John Connor (Nick Stahl). Soreheads will note that this JC becomes humanity's leader either by mistake or through a strategic deception—but so what? Cameron, meanwhile, has bequeathed the franchise to director Jonathan Mostow, author of the submarine thriller *U-571* and evidently a man with far less baggage. Where *Judgment Day* exhibited the profligate sprawl of a military operation, the leaner, less grandiose *Rise of the Machines* has the feel of a single Hummer careening through an earthquake in downtown Burbank.

Dispatched once more on a mission from the future, the latest model of the Arnold android materializes in the middle of the Mojave Desert. Born naked and flexing into this world, he makes his now traditional foray to an unsuspecting human watering hole; in short order he denudes a snippy male stripper of his fetishistic glad rags to re-create his own ultra-butch image. Somewhat less paternal here than he was in *T2*, Schwarzenegger is in fine, which is to say humorously ponderous, form. His refurbished Terminator remains an unsocialized machine—if not without a certain professional pride. Referred to disparagingly as a "robot," he's quick to correct: "I'm a cybernetic organism."

The first two *Terminator* movies projected a sort of muscle feminism in the person of Nautilized Linda Hamilton's warrior woman. But this time around, despite Claire Danes's intermittent facility with a variety of guns, there's an undercurrent of chick bashing. Arnold's antagonist, the ultra-sophisticated T-X (Kristanna Loken), is a robo-babe with a tailored leather jumpsuit and a bionic arm. Her default setting on permanent hissy fit, this svelte femmebot has an irresistible habit of cocking her head and glaring with impersonal curiosity at the victim she's about to vaporize. What's more, she can fry Arnold's circuits.

Back in the mid '80s, *Terminator* inspired an impressive degree of academic discourse—thanks to its tough-girl heroine, the convoluted, bizarrely oedipal time-travelling premise that had John Connor being fathered by his future best friend, and Arnold's then new-minted status as Hollywood's reigning action superstar, the blockbuster personified.

As befits a third outing, *Rise of the Machines* offers little that is novel. All temporal mind-bending and kinky genealogy are subsumed in the comforting notion that our world is about to come under the malign control of a single, giant, self-aware computer program. Indeed, the program probably wrote the movie, which could be most efficiently described as a quasi-videogame featuring a pair of unkillable antagonists.

The opening joust's mega-bumper-car ride makes for nearly as impressive a carnival of destruction as the great freeway battle in *The Matrix Reloaded*. The fighting, however, is much more hands-on. Responding to Mostow's directorial joystick, the endlessly regenerating Terminator and Terminatrix alternately lift and slam, shove and hurl, toss and pound, crush and heave each other, in a clanky *ballet mécanique* that could easily be re-imagined as terminal foreplay.

Terminator 3 was still in movie theaters when a special election to recall California's governor was announced on July 27. Schwarzenegger declared his candidacy on *The Tonight Show* on August 7—a different sort of "cybernetic organism": part performer, part politician. In a sense, the president followed suit. The following piece, headlined "Lights, Camera, Exploitation," was the cover story for the August 28 edition of the *Village Voice*.

NEW YORK, AUGUST 28, 2003

In the end, 9/11 turned out to be a made-for-TV movie, or rather, the basis for one—a shameless propaganda vehicle for our superstar president George W. Bush.

The upcoming Showtime feature *DC 9/11: Time of Crisis* is a signal advance in the instant, ongoing fictionalization of American history, complete with the president fulminating most presidentially against "tinhorn terrorists," decisively employing the word problematic in a complete sentence, selling a rationale for preemptive war, and presciently laying out American foreign policy for the next eighteen months. "We start with bin Laden," Bush (played by Timothy Bottoms) tells his cabinet. "That's what the American people expect ... So let's build a coalition for that job. Later, we can shape different coalitions for different tasks."

Scheduled for cablecast on September 7, *DC 9/11* inaugurates Bush's re-election campaign fifty weeks before the 9/11 Memorial Republican National Convention opens in Madison Square Garden. *DC 9/11* also marks a new stage in the American cult of personality: the actual president as fictional protagonist.[4]

That Bottoms is reconfiguring his role in the Comedy Central series *That's My Bush!* (a gross-out sitcom canceled a month before 9/11) provides a uniquely American twist. In the aftermath of the first Iraq war, Bush the elder was brought down in part by Dana Carvey's devastating campaign of ridicule on *Saturday Night Live*. Drafting the clownish Bottoms effectively preempts that strategy. Indeed, casting a former Bush travesty in the role of the serious Bush only reinforces the telefilm's agenda, namely that the events of September 11 served to render divine Bush's dubious mandate.

A movie that attempted to reconstruct Bush's actual activities on 9/11 would be fascinating, if not entirely heroic. A detailed attempt to account for the president's movements and actions on what he later termed that "interesting day" may be found at the Center for Cooperative Research website (cooperativeresearch.org): Bush had just arrived at a Florida elementary school for a pre-planned 9 a.m. photo op when he was informed that a plane had crashed into the WTC fifteen minutes before. Bush would later make the impossible claim that he saw the event televised live. (In early December, the president told an Orlando audience he'd been watching TV that morning and saw "an airplane hit the tower of a—of a—you know … and I said, 'Well, there's one terrible pilot.'")

As Secret Service men evidently were watching TV in another classroom, however, news of the second crash reached him almost immediately. Bush's startled response, documented on video for all eternity and seen by millions, is restaged in the movie: As Chief of Staff Andrew Card appears beside Bush and whispers in his ear, the president responds with visible shock and panic (the real Bush was more expressive than

---

4   There are, of course, precedents. "One of the original aspects of Soviet cinema is its daring in depicting contemporary historical personages, even living figures," André Bazin dryly observed in his 1950 essay, "The Myth of Stalin in the Soviet Cinema." It was one of the unique characteristics of Stalin-era Soviet movies that their infallible leader was regularly portrayed, by professional impersonators, as an all-wise demiurge in suitably grandiose historical dramas. So it is with *DC 9/11*, where documentary footage of the collapsing WTC is punctuated by the pronouncements of Bottoms's Bush.

Bottoms). Missing from *DC 9/11* is the president's next move—picking up a children's book called *The Pet Goat*.

By then, back in the real DC, Secret Service men had already burst into Dick Cheney's office and bodily carried the vice president to a secure location in the White House basement. Meanwhile, responding to Press Secretary Ari Fleischer's hastily scrawled instructions ("DON'T SAY ANYTHING YET"), Bush actually remained in the classroom for almost ten minutes, taking his time thanking the kids and the teachers ("Hoo! These are great readers ...") shortly before boarding Air Force One, where he was informed that his plane was the next terrorist target.

DC 9/11 subtly re-jiggered these events so that Cheney was hustled into the White House basement only after Bush is aloft—the inference being that the entire leadership was equally dazed and confused, and that relocating Bush was part of the solution rather than one of the problems.

According to *The Washington Post*, Cheney, seconded by Condoleezza Rice, instructed Bush not to return to Washington. Nevertheless, the movie does attempt to deal with the circumstances that had the president largely incommunicado for the rest of the day. According to the *Post* account, there was little debate on Air Force One—the plane banked sharply and flew south to Barksdale Air Force Base in Louisiana, where Bush's first official statement was made at 12:36 p.m. He appeared hesitant and nervous—as does Bottoms in the movie. Within the hour, Air Force One had taken off for another base, and not until that evening, after eight hours flying from Florida to Louisiana to Nebraska to Washington, did the president address the nation.

The threat to the president's plane was soon recognized as bogus, although it took weeks for the White House to acknowledge it. By September 13, however, presidential image-maker Karl Rove had released his script: "I'm not going to let some tinhorn terrorist keep the president of the United States away from the nation's capital," Bush had supposedly complained, a line further improved in *DC 9/11* as "If some tinhorn terrorist wants me, tell him to come and get me! I'll be at home, waiting for the bastard!" Simultaneously, the real Rice was detailing Bush's instant grasp of the situation, explaining that he was the first in his administration to understand the meaning of the events.

This is the story of *DC 9/11*. Screenwriter and co-executive producer Lionel Chetwynd had access to top officials and staffers, including Bush, Fleischer, Card, Rove, and Rumsfeld—all of whom are played by look-alike actors in the movie (as are Cheney and Rice, John Ashcroft, Karen Hughes, Colin Powell, George Tenet, and Paul Wolfowitz). The script was subsequently vetted by right-wing pundits Fred Barnes, Charles Krauthammer, and Morton Kondracke. Chetwynd, whose vita includes such politically charged movies and telefilms as *The Hanoi Hilton*, *The Heroes of Desert Storm*, *The Siege at Ruby Ridge*, *Kissinger and Nixon*, and *Varian's War*, is a prominent Hollywood conservative—a veteran of the 1980 Reagan campaign who, after Bill Clinton's election twelve years later, was recruited by right-wing pop culture ideologue David Horowitz to set up the Wednesday Morning Club ("a platform in the entertainment community where a Henry Hyde can come and get a warm welcome and respectful hearing," as Chetwynd later told *The Nation*).

Chetwynd bonded with Dubya in March 2001 when, at Rove's suggestion, *Varian's War* was screened at the White House; Chetwynd was subsequently involved in various post-9/11 Hollywood–Washington conclaves and currently serves Bush as part of the President's Committee on the Arts and the Humanities. Shot largely in Toronto, *DC 9/11* was eligible for Canadian film subsidies, but it is, in nearly every other sense, an official production.[5]

*   *   *

---

5 The Clinton administration was characterized by a cycle of movies featuring Hollywood presidents; a culmination of those fantasies, *The West Wing* TV series is a virtual presidency set in an ongoing alternate universe. But only once before *DC 9/11* has a reigning president been portrayed in the context of the entertainment machine. An FDR stand-in appeared briefly in the notorious wartime propaganda epic *Mission to Moscow* (1943), his back turned discreetly to the camera as he instructs the actor playing Ambassador Joseph Davies to go to Stalin's Soviet Union and "get the hard-boiled facts behind the most dangerous situation in history." Roosevelt reaped no domestic political capital from *Mission to Moscow* (on the contrary). The real precedent for *DC 9/11* is the similarly titled *PT 109* (1963), which reconstructed the wartime heroics of then president John F. Kennedy. While no Hollywood producer ever suggested bringing Dwight Eisenhower's military exploits to the screen, Warner Bros. purchased rights to Robert Donovan's bestselling *PT 109* soon after JFK's inauguration. Kennedy's well-publicized escapade as a PT-boat skipper was already an integral part of his image; it was the basis for Kennedy's first congressional campaign in 1946 and figured prominently in the 1960 election. *PT 109* was designed to be the greatest campaign poster ever created—in widescreen and living color.

Would JFK have had the audacity to promote a docudramatization of the Cuban Missile Crisis as part of his bid for reelection? As political as *PT 109*, *DC 9/11* models Bush on Kennedy's appearances in the 1974 telefilm *The Missiles of October*, the 1983 miniseries featuring telepresident-to-be Martin Sheen as Kennedy, and particularly, on the 2000 feature *Thirteen Days*—selected for the first official Bush White House screening, with Senator Ted Kennedy and Caroline Kennedy in attendance. But however hagiographic, these were period pieces memorializing a dead leader.

The turgid *DC 9/11* would doubtless have been more entertaining with Harrison Ford or Arnold Schwarzenegger or even Ronald Reagan in the role of the president. *DC 9/11* is instead the spectacle of Reagan in reverse: rather than being a professional actor who entered politics, Bush is a politician who has been reconfigured, packaged, and sold as a media star—dialog included. Indeed, that metamorphosis is the movie's true subject.

The basic Dubya narrative is the transformation of a roistering Prince Hal into a heroic Henry V. In *DC 9/11*, the young Bush—spoiled frat boy and drunken prankster—is subsumed in the image of the initially powerless president. The movie is thus the story of Bush assuming command, first of his staffers (who attest to his new aura with numerous admiring reaction shots) and then the situation. He is the one who declares that "we are at war," who firmly places Cheney (Lawrence Pressman) in his secure location—not once but twice. (To further make the point, Chetwynd has Scott Alan Smith's Fleischer muse that the press refuses to get it: "The Cheney-runs-the-show myth is always going to be with some of them.") Rudy Giuliani, who eclipsed Bush in the days following the attack, is conspicuously absent—or, rather, glimpsed only as a figure on television.

Rumsfeld (impersonated with frightening veracity by Broadway vet John Cunningham) emerges as the Soviet-style positive hero, embodying the logic of history. In the very first scene, he is seen hosting a congressional breakfast, invoking the 1993 attack on the WTC, and warning the dim-witted legislators that that was only the beginning. Rumsfeld is the first to utter the name "Saddam Hussein" and, over the pooh-poohs of Colin Powell (David Fonteno), goes on to detail Iraq's awesome stockpile of WMDs. But there can be only one maximum leader. Increasingly tough and folksy, prone to strategically consulting his Bible, it is Bush who directs Rummy and Ashcroft to think in "unconventional ways."

This new Bush is continually educating his staff, instructing Rice in the significance of "modernity, pluralism, and freedom." (As played by Penny Johnson Jerald, the president's ex-wife on the Fox series *24*, Condi is a sort of super-intelligent poodle—dogging her master's steps, gazing into his eyes with rapt adoration.)

Ultimately, *DC 9/11* is less a docudramatic account of historical events than a legitimizing allegory. In glamorizing a living president, it is an opportunistic piece of political mythmaking—a scenario that effectively bridges the highly irregular maneuvering that brought a popular-vote loser to power in 2000 and the exaggerated, even fabricated, claims with which his regime orchestrated the US invasion of Iraq.

Bush's approval rating was hovering around 50 percent on the morning of September 11. Indeed, Saddam Hussein and Osama bin Laden have done so much for Bush's presidency one might reasonably suspect they're being held in a witness protection program. If the Iraq war is integral to America's transformation from republic to empire, then *DC 9/11* is part of the process, described by Mark Crispin Miller as Bush's "incarnation as America's Augustus."

Several incidents in the Iraq war—the semi-fictional Saving Private Lynch saga, the made-for-TV toppling of Hussein's statue, the outrageous *Top Gun* photo op with which Bush announced victory—are ready to be excerpted in Republican Party 2004 campaign propaganda. *DC 9/11* is that propaganda. The "Battle Hymn of the Republic" swells as Bush flies into Ground Zero, where he astonishes even Rove (Allan Royal) by spontaneously vaulting a police barricade to hop on the rubble and grab the microphone. A nearby fireman, compelled to tell the president that he didn't vote for him, swears allegiance, mandating Bush to "find the son of a bitch who did this." Once Bush realizes that "today, the president has to be the country," Rove considers the image problem solved. Bush, he explains, has become commander in chief and taken back "control of his destiny." The climax is Bush's televised, prime-time September 20 speech—a montage of highly charged 9/11 footage that ends with the real-life, now fully authenticated Bush accepting the adulation of Congress as he fingers the talismanic shield worn by a fallen New York police officer.

As long as there are parents and children in this world, people will yearn for the illusion of a wise, selfless, divinely inspired leader. As expressed in *DC 9/11*, this desire is far less complex than the bizarre wish-fulfillment provided by *The West Wing*—unless a political miracle occurs and that fantasy materializes with the election of Howard Dean. Both of these presidential soap operas offer utopian visions of political leadership. But unlike *The West Wing*, *DC 9/11* gumps a fictionalized hero into real catastrophe to create the myth of a defining moment, and stake its claim on historical truth.

On October 7, in the first history-changing cinematic event since 9/11, movie star Arnold Schwarzenegger was elected California governor with 48 percent of the vote, more than his two closest rivals combined.

CHAPTER TEN

2004: BUSH'S VICTORY

In ten months, George W. Bush would also face the voters. Before that, the single most significant American movie of the post-9/11 decade—not to mention a movie that, in its choice of subject matter, was designed to rival the Events of 9/11 and even put them in perspective—had its much anticipated premiere.

NEW YORK, FEBRUARY 18, 2004

Welcome, friends, to Medieval Times: jihads, crusades, fundamentalist fanatics of all persuasions, and this week, thundering into your neighborhood mall alongside *Welcome to Mooseport* and *Confessions of a Teenage Drama Queen*, is Mel Gibson's $25 million celluloid sacrifice, *The Passion of the Christ*.[1]

Less reverential than razzle-dazzlin', more an episode in the history of show business than a religious epiphany, Gibson's blood-soaked

---

1 Because *The Passion of the Christ* had its New York press screening only two days before the movie opened, the above review was composed under mild duress, written to space for *The Village Voice* in less than two hours on the afternoon that the paper was put to bed. Admission to the preview, held at the Broadway Screening Room, was strictly regulated with the door guarded by a beefy security man. Was the distributor afraid that one of us might attack the screen?

126-minute account of Jesus Christ's last hours on earth has been flogged for months with everything from souvenir nine-inch nails and contested papal endorsements to death threats against *New York Times* op-ed columnist Frank Rich and bizarre anti-Semitic radio rants by the filmmaker's eighty-five-year-old father. (Where's the White House screening?) They do know what they do—the question is, will it do them any good?

The Passion of the Christ opens on a dark and stormy night in what might be a foggy Scottish glen with the Jewish police arriving to arrest Jesus (James Caviezel). His two-fisted, brave-hearted disciples fight back; in an action montage replete with slo-mo and thud-thud, Peter slices off one cop's ear. Jesus picks it up and reattaches it—a prosthetic miracle that sets the stage for the muscular action and cosmetic wonders to come. Before anything else, *The Passion* establishes itself in the realm of recent fantasy epics: The Aramaic sounds like bad Elvish, a brief interlude in epicene Herod's degenerate court suggests a minor detour to the *Matrix* world, the music is straight out of *Gladiator*, and much of the movie is haunted by the androgynous, cowled Satan (Rosalinda Celentano) seemingly risen from George Lucas's cutting room floor.

Greatly extrapolated from the four Gospels, *The Passion of the Christ* has Jesus dragged before the Jewish high priest Caiaphas (Mattia Sbragia) to be denounced for blasphemy—then punched, smacked, and spat upon, not for the last time, by the scurvy mob. Although Caiaphas fails to convince the stern and skeptical Pontius Pilate (Hristo Naumov Shopov) that blasphemous Jesus deserves to die, the noble Roman does agree to fifteen minutes of chastisement by his palace orcs. Jesus is beaten, first with rods and then studded whips, until his back resembles a side of flayed beef. Satan and his mini-me are trolling the crowd as Pilate washes his hands and the unsatiated onlookers cry out for crucifixion. The old blood libel is there, albeit prudently untranslated from the Aramaic. Is this movie anti-Semitic? Let me put it this way: iconographically, Jesus and his disciples are already Christians; Judas is the only one tasteless enough to call Jesus "rabbi."

With the chastisement serving as visceral climax and without much in the way of dramatic relief, *The Passion* reaches the point of diminishing returns well before Jesus has to carry his cross through the filthy rabble of Jerusalem and up Golgotha hill. A tilted camera and mega close-ups add to the tumult, but the movie's last forty-five minutes are less grueling than one might expect. Filigreed with caramelized blood, Caviezel's

skin-crack makeup has by then ceased to be convincing, numerous agonized reaction shots from Mary (Romanian actress Maia Morgenstern)
and Mary Magdalene (Monica Bellucci) notwithstanding. Given that a
chiropractor is listed in the credits, one can well believe that the actor
suffered—was his ordeal worse than De Niro's in *Raging Bull*?[2]

At last, the pain pageant ends—the heavens open, the earth quakes,
and Satan's wig flies off. In the final moments, Jesus emerges from his
grave, tanned, rested, and ready—accompanied by appropriately kick-ass
martial music. Payback time.

**From a sociological point of view, *The Passion* is the key event in
American movies between 9/11 and the election of Barack Obama—
not only for its subject matter, and its attitude toward that subject
matter, including a brutal new "realness"—but for the means by which
it was promoted and exhibited.**

**With more pre-sales than any movie in history, *The Passion of
the Christ* opened for Lent and became the highest grossing independent (and for the US, foreign-language) film ever made. Gibson
courted negative publicity—he cast himself as a victim by provoking
the presumably Jewish media to "crucify" his outsider film—even as
he mobilized a mass audience. To some degree his constituency was
the same that George W. Bush's key political advisor Karl Rove would
address some months later in the 2004 election. As was soon noted,
The Passion held as much appeal for evangelical Protestants as traditional Catholics—and perhaps even more, given that evangelicals had
little that was comparable to Catholicism's thousand years of religious
pageantry.[3]**

---

2   Was the director's? Gibson made it known that his was the hand holding
the first nail driven into Caviezel's palm.

3   In an essay on *The Passion* published in the Spring 2004 issue of *Logos*,
Rhonda Hammer and Douglas Kellner make an extended series of comparisons
between Bush and Gibson: "Bush has famously declared that Jesus was his
favorite philosopher and part of Gibson's highly effective publicity for the film
was stressing his deep Christian beliefs ...

Both Gibson and Bush Junior are born-again Christians who overcame
struggles with drugs and alcohol to embrace a highly fundamentalist
Christianity (albeit of different denominations). Both are Manichean to
the core, see themselves on the side of Good and see their enemies and

Along with the War in Iraq and Schwarzenegger's ascension to the governor's mansion in Sacramento, *The Passion* demonstrated the power of a media-driven scenario. In a quasi-underground response, the first documentaries to contest the Bush administration's world-view and tactics began to appear.

NEW YORK, MAY 12, 2004

Every conflict is a contest of competing narratives—which is why the international Arab news channel Al Jazeera is an American *bête noire*. As the voice of Arab nationalism, Al Jazeera spins a story line that is not necessarily ours. Can an independent fly on the wall elude the web?

A no-frills documentary that reports on Al Jazeera's Iraq war reportage, Jehane Noujaim's *Control Room* offers a unique perspective on the military adventure officially known as Operation Iraqi Freedom. This absorbing, significant, and shamelessly entertaining movie not only goes through the looking glass but, no less significantly, turns the mirror back on us.

Control Room, which begins in March 2003 with the United States poised to invade Iraq, is set entirely in the realm of information—namely the Gulf state of Qatar, where Al Jazeera is based, along with the American military information station Centcom. The filmmakers never leave Qatar. This science fiction realm of white sand beaches, humongous satellite dishes, and frenzied media mavens is the front line of an image war that turns actual once George W. Bush appears as a televised holo-gram to issue his ultimatum to Saddam Hussein—and then the bombs start falling.

Noujaim, a young Egyptian-American graduate of the Pennebaker-Hegedus school of *cinéma vérité*, co-directed the 2001 doc *Startup.com*. Here, having organized her entry to Al Jazeera by strategically hanging out in the station's commissary, she continues her exploration of corpo-rate culture at the cutting edge. Noujaim doesn't ask the Al Jazeeristas too many tough questions. But while they describe their operation as

adversaries as Evil. Both are morally righteous and accept redemptive violence in the struggle for the Good ... And both deploy their respec-tive political and cultural power to advance the ends of their conservative version of Christianity, arguably with highly destructive effects.

"a wake-up call" for the Arabs, their values are surprisingly Western. Al Jazeera has been threatened and/or banned by a number of authoritarian Arab regimes, including Saddam Hussein's.

Control Room is a McLuhan-esque immersion populated by a varied cast of articulate types—all resembling the filmmaker in that they are naturalistically rife with contradiction: "Between us," the suave and cynical senior producer Samir Khader says, "if I'm offered a job with Fox, I will take it [and] exchange the Arab nightmare for the American dream." He plans to send his kids to America to be educated and hopes that they remain. The portly Sudanese journalist Hassan Ibrahim, a former classmate of bin Laden's, onetime Deadhead, and ex-BBC man, is another defender of American democracy. Understanding the US does not, however, preclude identification with the Iraqis. Assuming a mandate to focus on the war's "human cost," the Al Jazeera staff seems puzzled by the Western media's reluctance to do the same.

Truth has long since been the first casualty of the image war. Lieutenant Josh Rushing, an earnest and slightly bewildered young American information officer (with a Hollywood background) provides the US point of view; at a climactic moment in the movie, he realizes that Al Jazeera is the Arab equivalent of Fox News. Indeed, the title *Control Room* takes on a somewhat different meaning as the filmmakers observe the management of the American press. The army's (purposeful?) failure to provide the press with decks of "most wanted" playing cards inspires a desperate petulance. The unfolding Jessica Lynch story eclipses what is going on in Baghdad. The American press greets with high-five enthusiasm the spectacle of US troops circling the statue of Saddam Hussein—indifferent to the transparently staged nature of the event.

Meanwhile, Al Jazeera—already in America's doghouse as Al Qaeda's communiqué venue of choice—has crossed the line with tasteless telecasts of Iraqi civilian casualties, including severely wounded children, images of dead American soldiers, and statements by disoriented American POWs. Implying the usurpation of US prerogatives, Donald Rumsfeld accuses Al Jazeera of faking evidence ("willing to lie to the world to make their case") while "pounding the people in the region day after day." Soon after, US forces shell the Palestine Hotel (with fatal results for three war correspondents), fire on the headquarters of Abu Dhabi TV, and bomb Al Jazeera's Baghdad office, killing a cameraman.

As *Control Room* shows, this intimidation worked. The US was now free to create its own TV show, culminating in Bush's *Top Gun* "mission accomplished" visitation. "The whole war is like an American movie," the headscarf- and jeans-wearing Syrian producer Deema Khatib notes. "You know how it will end, but you want to see how it happens." You might think that a smart American occupying force would be listening to Al Jazeera (as well as watching it), but then as this infuriating and essential movie shows, victory creates its own storyline.[4]

The spring of 2004 saw the first attempts to demystify the war hysteria embodied in and fed by the bellicose blockbusters of early 2002. Thus, the must-see movie at the 2004 Cannes Film Festival was Michael Moore's *Fahrenheit 9/11*, which brought hordes of TV camera crews to interview critics exiting the hastily scheduled extra screenings, while Moore himself managed to join a French union protest and proclaim his solidarity with the local proletariat. After Moore won the competition it was announced, per one excited French headline, that the festival had produced "*la Palme d'Or qui défie Bush*." And the more that the jury, headed by Quentin Tarantino, defiantly insisted that only aesthetic considerations had ruled its decision to garland *Fahrenheit 9/11*, the more shrewdly political its choices seemed. "It validates cinema," jury member Tilda Swinton declared of Moore's documentary, and in a sense, the Palme validated Cannes as an Event. One's conversations with international colleagues—not to mention the questions Americans were continually asked by attending news crews— were more apt to concern the upcoming election than any celluloid discovery.

NEW YORK, JUNE 16, 2004

A master of PR, Michael Moore may well be exploiting the Walt Disney Company's refusal to distribute the movie—but that doesn't make

---

4 Not until the so-called Arab Spring, seven years later, was it possible to find the Al Jazeera narrative, mainly on YouTube. As reported in early 2011, Al Jazeera's English-language channel had attracted new interest for its twenty-four-hour coverage of the protests in Egypt. Given the near complete refusal of any US cable or satellite company to carry the channel, YouTube began promoting a live stream (Brian Stelter, "Al Jazeera Finds New Paths In U.S.," *New York Times*, 2/1/11).

Disney's refusal any less craven or political. *Fahrenheit 9/11* has few new revelations, but it does make a compelling narrative and, as such, could even be an intervention.

Last winter, Moore fired a shot across the bow of our hijacked ship of state when he characterized George W. Bush as a Vietnam-era "deserter." With his much ballyhooed, frankly partisan *Fahrenheit 9/11*, Moore launches a torpedo squarely at the ongoing campaign to finally get the president elected. *Fahrenheit 9/11* is effective in undermining the administration's rationale for invading Iraq and unrelenting in its caustic critique of official mistruths. Although overlong and hampered by a sometimes rambling argument obviously updated to encompass the recent Senate hearings and abuse revelations, the movie is the least grandstanding and most purposeful of Moore's career.

Moore shamelessly exploited 9/11 in *Bowling for Columbine*, but *Fahrenheit*'s first half-hour—which, tightly edited and scored for maximum impact, segues from the stolen election of 2000 and Bush's 2001 summer vacation through the events of 9/11 and the cowboy invasion of Afghanistan to dwell on the oil politics uniting the Bushies with the Saudis—is succinct and hilarious in making its points, as well as being infuriating and tragic. The film, which runs approximately two hours, achieves this height only once more: a painful, gruesomely explicit montage of Battlefield Iraq appropriately salts the wounds with tough-guy inanities from our shameless Secretary of Defense.

In Cannes, where locals express incredulity at learning that, hardly a marginalized scribbler of samizdat, Moore is actually one of America's bestselling authors, *Fahrenheit 9/11* was wildly over-praised as film-making. (Moore was repeatedly hailed as a new Eisenstein—although, if anything, his wise-guy vertical montage is ultimately derived from Kenneth Anger's underground biker doc *Scorpio Rising*.) Moore's métier is not the scene but the shot—in context. Self-promotion aside, his most formidable talent has turned out to be editing found footage. In *Fahrenheit 9/11*, Moore wisely keeps his onscreen stunts to a minimum. Still, he finds it difficult to resist his least attractive urge, namely the mocking of those ordinary Americans whom he purports to champion.

Such contempt is not his alone. Moore includes the president's suggestion that ordinary Americans fight terrorism by visiting Disney World—if not Michael Eisner's delighted in-house e-mail that hailed Bush as Disney's "newest cheerleader." (Refusing to allow subsidiary

Miramax to release Moore's movie was the least Eisner could do for Bush.) But a well-wrought account of the administration's use of absurd terror alerts, an elaboration on ideas advanced in *Bowling for Columbine*, dissipates once Moore drops Bush to make fun of an assortment of terrorized Americans, hapless peaceniks, and befuddled state troopers. The flipside to this derision is Moore's sentimentality—most apparent in his willingness to milk the grief of a Flint gold-star mother. And yet, if it registers 1,000 voters or swings 500 votes in Michigan …

Fahrenheit 9/11 is current enough to include the 9/11 Commission hearings and footage of (relatively mild) prisoner abuse. Although overlong and hampered by a rambling argument, the movie does make a compelling narrative. (It concludes with a chilling quote from neocon darling George Orwell: "The war is not meant to be won—it is meant to be continuous.") It also succeeds as entertainment. Enough of a showman to recognize the old razzle-dazzle, Moore easily unmasks the administration's officials as dogged, if inept, disciples of the patriotic bromide, military pageant, "big lie" combo pioneered by Nazi propaganda theorist Joseph Goebbels. Moore has his democratic aspects, as well as his demagogic ones. It's in his satire of official rhetoric that he comes closest to functioning as a media tribune.

If Moore is formidable, it's not because he is a great filmmaker (far from it), but because he infuses his sense of ridicule with the fury of moral indignation. *Fahrenheit 9/11* is strongest when that wrath is vented on Bush and his cohorts. Dana Carvey did more than anyone in America, save Ross Perot, to drive Bush *père* from the White House. There are sequences in *Fahrenheit 9/11* so devastatingly on target as to inspire the thought that Moore might similarly help evict the son.[5]

Unlike Michael Moore's, Hollywood's several liberal interventions into the 2004 presidential race tended to avoid 9/11 and downplay the war in Iraq. The disaster film *The Day After Tomorrow* blamed catastrophic climate changes, which some in fact read as a metaphor

---

5   A week before the election, the British magazine *Total Film* named Bush "Movie Villain of the Year" for his performance in *Fahrenheit 9/11*. A poll of some 10,000 movie fans had the US president out-scarifying Spiderman's nemesis Doctor Octopus and the new *Texas Chainsaw Massacre*'s Leatherface, as well as Gollum and Daryl Hannah's *Kill Bill* assassin Elle Driver—but that was the UK.

for 9/11, on an American administration run by a bellicose anti-ecological vice president; Jonathan Demme's remade *Manchurian Candidate* advanced a sense of oil-fueled corporate conspiracy.

As usual, Republicans far surpassed Democrats with their capacity to construct scenarios in life, rather than on theater screens. To reiterate only the most successful of these, volunteer Vietnam veteran John Kerry was effectively recast as a coward or worse, while the combat-averse Bush and Cheney were portrayed as resolute wartime leaders.[6]

Although Steven Spielberg consulted on one of Kerry's campaign films, he made no election year statement per se. In a sense, the extraordinary pageant of Ronald Reagan's funeral on June 11—subsuming all political conflict in a simplified, sentimental, personality-driven narrative—was the year's preeminent example of Spielbergization.

The Terminal, which opened two weeks later and was the first Spielberg feature to have been entirely conceptualized during wartime, inaugurated the director's post-9/11 trilogy of terror to which *Minority Report* might be considered a prologue. Based on the true story of an Iranian national stranded for years in a Paris airport, *The Terminal* directly—if squeamishly—addressed another example of the new social-real in the new hell of air travel and America's corresponding fear of the foreign or Muslim-looking. The outlander, in this case, was Tom Hanks. Winner of consecutive Oscars for playing the mentally challenged Forrest Gump and the AIDS-afflicted hero of

---

6   Both candidates were represented as fit, trim, athletic outdoorsmen although the image of Kerry in windsurfing gear was also subject to ridicule (Pia Catton, "Now It's a Battle of Manly Images for Kerry, Bush," *New York Sun*, 7/20/2004). More serious were the aspersions cast on Kerry as soldier.

After several weeks during which the Bush campaign and its surrogates unrelentingly besmirched Kerry's wartime record, the Democratic candidate was reportedly mining *Fahrenheit 9/11* for one-liners. Kerry cited close ties between Saudi Arabia and the Bush administration both at the Democratic Convention and afterwards and, addressing a gathering of black and Latino journalists in early August, evoked a notorious scene from *Fahrenheit 9/11*, depicting Bush's confused response and seven-minute delay in reacting to the events of September 11. "Previously, Mr. Kerry has steered clear of Moore for fear of alienating swing voters," *The Guardian's* Washington correspondent noted. Now he was linked to Moore. "The former Republican New York mayor Rudolph Giuliani criticized the tactics, saying John Kerry had to be frustrated 'if he is armchair quarterbacking, based on cues from Michael Moore'" (Suzanne Goldenberg, "White House race gets nasty," *The Guardian*, 8/7/2004).

Philadelphia, Hanks need hardly have stretched his persona to portray one of Spielberg's benign, if not lovable, "others"—particularly as his previous role for the director was as the martyred leader and embodiment of American decency in *Saving Private Ryan*.[7]

NEW YORK, JUNE 23, 2004

A comedy about a stateless Eastern European tourist stranded indefinitely in the limbo of Kennedy International Airport, *The Terminal* sounds—at least on paper—like it might be director Steven Spielberg's exercise in Beckett lite. Fear not, it isn't even *Minority Report* lite. "After *Catch Me If You Can*," the press notes quote the filmmaker, "I wanted to do another movie that could make you laugh and cry and feel good about the world."

To that end, Tom Hanks's Viktor Navorski first appears as a real goatfucker—stooped, grizzled, and no doubt smelly, clutching a rusty Planters Peanuts tin and babbling in an invented Slavic language as he attempts to clear US customs. When it develops that a coup in Viktor's (imaginary) Krakozhia homeland has effectively invalidated his visa, he shaves his stubble and graduates to increasingly accomplished, cutely accented English. It's a role that might once have bellowed Robin Williams, and indeed, Hanks's stranger in a strange land bears a more than passing resemblance to the repellently cloying Russian immigrant Williams played in the Reagan-era heart-warmer *Moscow on the Hudson*.

Part genius and part idiot, at once the hero and victim of globalism, Viktor inhabits the airport the way Robinson Crusoe (or Hanks's character in *Cast Away*) did his desert island—although, unlike Crusoe, he is quite diffident when the terminal's exasperated security boss, Frank Dixon (Stanley Tucci), gives him several opportunities to sail through the

---

7   During the summer of 2004, the entertainment press reported Spielberg at work on a serious thriller—dealing with the 1972 massacre of Israeli athletes at the Munich Olympics and the clandestine Mossad campaign against the responsible Palestinian terrorists. Then, reportedly because the director feared this project itself might become a target for Islamic terrorists, the movie was postponed. In its place, Spielberg would remake the science-fiction chestnut *War of the Worlds*, which went into production immediately after Bush's election.

doors into New York. In the movie's most evocative scene, the terminal serves as a huge Skinner box in which Viktor is monitored as he learns which buttons to press to get refunded quarters. Hanks exhibits a certain physical grace, particularly in his *pas de deux* with a surveillance camera. Less solitary than Crusoe, Viktor finds multiple Man Fridays. He bonds with a multi-ethnic band of buddies—the most memorably offensive of whom is Kumar Pallana's paranoid little janitor. Pushing the scenario toward workplace sitcom, these elves facilitate Viktor's platonic romance with a gorgeous, sweetly neurotic stewardess (Catherine Zeta-Jones) while upholding the traditional notion of America as melting pot, Viktor's difficulties with the customs cops notwithstanding. "The country's detaining so many people there's no goddamn room anywhere," Dixon says—writing a check that *The Terminal* would never cash. Despite its inane premise (the full idiocy of which isn't disclosed until late in the movie) and numerous incidental illogicalities, the film was inspired by a real situation, namely that of Merhan Karimi Nasseri, the Iranian-born traveler who—having lost his documents—has been living on a red plastic bench at Charles de Gaulle Airport since 1988 (and although for some years free, refuses to leave). The case has prompted two previous movies, a 1993 French comedy and a 2001 British-made hall-of-mirrors doc, in which Nasseri plays himself. DreamWorks also paid Nasseri for the rights to his story—which has been denuded of its rich absurdity.

Antic without being funny, *The Terminal*'s attempts at humor are largely predicated on calculating how many pratfalls can be derived from a wet floor. The enormous set is an engineering marvel—and it's not just an IQ test for Viktor. While one can only imagine what Jacques Tati would have done with this arena, Spielberg uses it mainly for product placement. (There's no one better at inserting a TV image or a corporate logo.) Relentlessly behaviorist, the filmmaker seldom fails to pat the puppy and, applying John Williams's melodic treacle, woo the viewer with cheap sentiment.

The Terminal's press book quotes Spielberg's boilerplate assertion that he "had an immediate affinity for Viktor's story." It would be fascinating to just know what the filmmaker meant—is he feeling trapped, stateless, alien? Does he deem the new xenophobia and the profiling of foreigners justified? In any case, it's clear that *The Terminal* reflects the post-9/11 airport angst that all passengers have experienced. To that end, making Viktor a Middle Eastern, a South Asian, or even a Bosnian tourist would have given this trite exercise an edge—and a measure of human pathos.[8]

As the election neared, another Hollywood liberal of Spielberg's generation launched a strike against the Bush presidency.

NEW YORK, AUGUST 4, 2004

The Manchurian Candidate, directed by John Frankenheimer in 1962, with Frank Sinatra in the lead role, is a chunk of American history and, on paper, Jonathan Demme's new version seems the most superfluous remake of a pop classic since Gus Van Sant's shot-for-shot *Psycho*. On the screen however, it's something else.[9]

Slick yet somber, Demme's *Candidate* lacks the wicked, giddy insolence of its predecessor. Despite a few jokes, the tale of a programmed "sleeper" assassin, a high-level political conspiracy, and an election-year coup is not primarily played for gleeful dark comedy—there's a grim, even brutal, quality to the craziness. Recalling Alan Pakula's post-Watergate, crypto-Manchurian remake *The Parallax View* almost as much as Frankenheimer's original, the ambience is moody rather than cartoonish. The 1962 movie was an uncanny vision of the Kennedy era; it remains to be seen how closely Demme's much-hyped version, strategically timed to open the day after John Kerry's nomination, will reflect the nation's state of mind.

Those familiar with the 1962 *Candidate*—which had the distinction of opening on the tensest day of the Cuban Missile Crisis and, despite the seemingly indestructible urban myth, was a box-office hit—will be

---

8   *The Terminal*'s most devastating and hilarious critique would arrive two years later in the person of Sacha Baron Cohen's post-Soviet visitor, Borat.

9   Sinatra's daughter Tina had long been interested in a *Manchurian Candidate* remake, but the project was only given the go-ahead in September 2001. The new version was co-produced by Democratic activist Scott Rudin for Paramount Pictures, whose head of production, Sherry Lansing, was a contributor to the Kerry campaign—as was Sumner Redstone, CEO of Paramount's corporate parent, Viacom. Several writers were involved but, according to Rudin, once he and Daniel Pyne (who previously adapted *The Sum of All Fears*) shifted the emphasis to corporate chicanery, "You could feel the script start to be alive."

less surprised than amused by Demme's update. The bogus military hero Raymond Shaw (Laurence Harvey in the original, Liev Schreiber here) and his commanding officer Ben Marco (Denzel Washington in the Sinatra part) have their brains washed by the enemy not during the Korean War but Operation Desert Storm; it isn't Shaw's stepfather who is a vice-presidential candidate but Shaw himself, and his monstrously Machiavellian mother (Meryl Streep) is not a behind-the-scenes player but a senator from New York. (The resemblance some observers have found between Streep's fast-talking steel magnolia and Hillary Clinton has far more to do with fear of Clinton than Streep's witty performance.)

There is no McCarthy-like demagogue in the remake—or rather, demagoguery has been dispersed and built into the workings of the national entertainment state. Similarly, the Communist villains are replaced by Manchurian Global—part Halliburton, part Carlyle, part Parallax Corporation. Coup d'état has been reformulated as "regime change," and there's a red-meat evocation of "the first privately owned and operated vice president of the United States." Paranoia is more orchestrated, with a steady background of terrorist and counter-terrorist chatter and a sense of constant surveillance, as patriotic pageantry is even more hysterical and Pavlovian (and, in the deployment of heroic New York City firefighters and Mount Rushmore, makes a reasonably accurate prediction of Republican campaign ads).

Demme, who works a clever permutation on the original ending, is more than capable of doing the thriller thing—even with material that will strike a good percentage of his audience as familiar. As an intelligent genre flick, the movie plays to his strengths. His direction of actors has never been better. Streep's character is a wholly autonomous creation, while both Washington and Schreiber give more emotionally nuanced and richly neurotic performances than Sinatra or Harvey (although Schreiber is unable to top the latter's sheer unpleasantness). And Kimberly Elise actually makes sense of Janet Leigh's surreally inconsequential part. Indeed, following a dozen years of docs, light comedy, and p.c. weepies, *Candidate* represents Demme's best dramatic filmmaking since *The Silence of the Lambs*.

Perhaps coincidentally, *Silence of the Lambs* was itself part of an earlier Gulf War culture. Released in the midst of Desert Storm, it was a bonafide phenom—passionately embraced by critics and audiences alike. (As pointed out at the time by a skeptical Jonathan Rosenbaum, the mass fascination with the monstrous Hannibal Lecter was an evident displacement for a nation then waging the most sanitized war in human history: Rosenbaum reminded Lecter's critical fans that "we're currently killing without compunction at a far greater rate than all the real serial killers in our midst combined.") In a way, the new *Candidate* represents the return of the *Lambs*' repressed—madness is real and it exists in the middle-American heart of darkness. In that movie too, a female senator found her child on the demon's altar.

Although the original *Candidate* was an anthology of Cold War anxieties, it fulfilled its prophetic mission with the election-altering shootings of Martin Luther King and Robert Kennedy in 1968, and George Wallace four years later. These days, however, government through the strategic elimination of political leaders is no longer an issue, at least in the US. Nor is the construction of history's secret agent. Thus, the most retrograde aspect of the new *Candidate* is the use of the old-fashioned José Delgado-type brain implants—even if Washington's discovery of one does afford Bruno Ganz's resident behaviorial scientist a hilarious line: "These are only theoretical."

As blatant and odious as the current cabal may be, it is hardly the nation's first bought-and-paid-for political leadership. As demonstrated by Homeland Security's blandly issued threat of a cancelled election (timed, many noted, to upstage the naming of vice-presidential candidate John Edwards) and the terror alerts that are certain to figure in the upcoming campaign, it's not the assassins who are being programmed with sinister microchips—it's the body politic.

The second *Manchurian Candidate* belongs to Bush II nearly as much as the original did to JFK. The movie was in production during the run-up to and early months of the Iraq war, with dialog rewritten in the light of unfolding events. And, from the opening theme, Wyclef Jean's cover of the anti-Bush anthem "Fortunate Son," through the references to "no-bid contracts," computerized voting and constant terror alerts, to the elaboration of a corporate conspiracy to install a "sleeper" as president, the remake is an unambiguous attack on the current American administration.

A week before the second *Candidate* had its premiere, *New York Times* columnist Paul Krugman imagined a scenario for "The Arabian Candidate" in which Islamic fanatics installed a puppet US

president who presented himself as the leader in a war against terrorism; opening in the US less than twenty-four hours after the Democratic National Convention nominated Senator John Kerry, the new *Manchurian Candidate* struck Krugman's colleague, Frank Rich, as being so blatantly partisan that it "could pass for the de facto fifth day of the convention itself."[10]

It was, however, the party of Reagan that staged the summer's most effectively cinematic spectacle. The following report ran as part of the cover story for the August 25 issue of the *Village Voice*.

NEW YORK, AUGUST 25, 2004

Strategically staged in the realm of the perpetual orange alert, the Republican National Convention was supposed to be the 9/11 convention—with the fallen Twin Towers as its invisible backdrop and a backbeat of subliminal terror threats as the theme song. There would be a select group of gallant 9/11 widows in the Madison Square Garden gallery, gaggles of Republican delegates in outsized fire-chief hats posing for souvenir snapshots alongside New York City's Bravest, Arnold Schwarzenegger would appear in full *Collateral Damage* mode, former

---

10 Of course, rightwing websites were already attacking Kerry as a Manchurian candidate—a bogus war hero under the control of billionaire George Soros—just as Bush's one-time Republican rival, Senator John McCain, had been smeared in 2000 as another such "candidate," brainwashed in a North Vietnam POW camp. All of the candidates had their Manchurian aspect—not least the third-party perennial, Ralph Nader, who, as several commentators pointed out, seemed determined to ensure Bush's victory and thus a pro-corporate agenda he ostensibly opposes, in a second consecutive election. While the movie was in release, a mysterious squarish bulge visible beneath President Bush's suit jacket during his first debate with John Kerry led to much media speculation that he was wired with some sort of radio receiver.

Demme's movie, too, was attacked (in *The New Republic*) as a "Naderite yelp against Democratic backsliding," as well as characterized, more approvingly, as "the most extravagantly Chomskyite movie Hollywood has ever made" (*In These Times*). Significantly, its release coincided with the remarkable success, at least in New York's alt-film world, of the Canadian horror-doc *The Corporation*, which applies the Diagnostic and Statistical Manual of Mental Disorders to demonstrate that corporations are by nature psychopathic—self-absorbed, irresponsible, manipulative, and unable to empathize or feel remorse.

Mayor Rudy Giuliani and New York governor George Pataki—each in his Yankee baseball jacket—would be running rival tours of Ground Zero, and then finally George W. Bush would accept his divine mandate while intoning the sacred mantra "September 11" with robotic regularity.

It may all still happen, but even as we slept, the 2004 RepCon inexorably morphed into a scripted remake of something else. Are we facing a replay of the fabled Democratic convention of 1968? Is it going to be Chicago redux? The events of 9/11 may have obliterated the '70s, '80s, and '90s, but never the '60s. They're back ... The nation will be fighting that war until the last boomer is in the ground. As the city kvetched in anticipation of the invading out-of-towners, the *New York Post* revealed that a posse of "extremists with ties to the 1970s radical Weather Underground," recently released from prison, were headed our way, quoting a "top-level source" that they were "trained in kidnapping techniques, bomb making and building improvised munitions."[11]

Had the *Post* gotten word that the crowds of anti-Bush demonstrators were to be infiltrated by special-op provocateurs? Might order really break down? What kickass campaign images those might provide! Back in the day, Abbie Hoffman called the 1968 Chicago police riot "an advertisement for Revolution," and sure enough, Republican political commercials—some of them even designed by the future Fox News honcho Roger Ailes—took the Yippie entrepreneur at his word. The Democratic candidate, a ridiculously ebullient Hubert Humphrey, was juxtaposed with footage of Chicago street fighting, accompanied by "There'll Be a Hot Time in the Old Town Tonight."

Wild in the streets and Vietnam on the brain: just like old times. Even as the RepCon cranked up and the biggest festival of guerrilla theater in a quarter-century mobilized to meet it, the Swift Boat Veterans for Truth prepared to release a new wave of commercials. These featured then-Vietnam Veterans Against the War representative John Kerry's April 1971 testimony before the Senate Committee on Foreign Relations. In the finest moment of his political life, Kerry spoke powerfully of the cost of the war and its atrocities on the men who fought it: "How do you ask a man to be the last man to die for a mistake?" That was less than a month

---

11   The Weather Underground would figure in the 2008 campaign as well, with Republicans making much of candidate Barack Obama's minor association with his Chicago neighbor, former Weatherman and current college professor, William Ayers.

after Lieutenant William Calley was found guilty of murdering twenty-two Vietnamese civilians at My Lai and a few weeks after then president Nixon ordered him released from the Fort Benning stockade. Meanwhile, a thousand anti-war vets camped out on the Washington Mall ...

But three weeks of Swifty smears, paid for by Bush's Texas supporters and telepathically masterminded by Karl Rove, have successfully muddied the Mekong. According to a recent *Los Angeles Times* poll, Kerry lost two points and Bush gained three during the August doldrums. Thus, Bush is poised for his RepCon coronation with a slight lead while, having had his combat performance successfully demeaned, Kerry is about to be recast as a long-haired hippie protester—his own Willie Horton.

We may wind up with some version of Chicago, but for all the creativity of the assembled demonstrators, it will only be on television. The other convention that the RNC resembles is RepCon '72, the last wartime conclave organized by a ruling party—a rigorously planned and flawlessly orchestrated pseudo-event. No detail of the media scenario was considered too inconsequential. A special elevator behind the speaker's rostrum insured that no one would appear taller to the broadcast audience than the president. Above the podium were three twelve-by-twenty-five-foot screens that replayed the RepCon's defining moments: Nixon's arrival in Miami, a pro-Republican rock concert, the president embraced by Sammy Davis Jr. Whenever important images were shown—like the campaign film *Portrait of a President*—the hall lights were shut off, compelling the networks to transmit the Republican programming rather than their own "live" reporting.

"We actually prepared, down to the minute, a script for the whole convention," campaign worker David Gergen recalled. By one account, a team of BBC reporters was mistakenly handed an actual copy, complete with applause cues, scheduled "spontaneous" floor demonstrations, and specified prime-time features. In fact, there were many, many more anti-war demonstrators at Miami Beach in 1972 than there had been in Chicago four years before, but because they hardly ever made TV (and because the demonstrators' encampment was strategically flooded with Quaaludes), they effectively did not exist.

If the '04 RepCon goes according to plan, the nation will be treated to a post-Olympic four-night series of three-hour telethons set off by wraparound coverage of the most egregious street demos. These action highlights will effectively replace the Republican color commentary that helped undermine the inept production that was the Boston DemCon. Indeed, several of those "commentators" will be onstage: Rudy G (a 1972 McGovern supporter), Arnold (who back then, and even later, dreamed of becoming a mighty "dictator"), and poor John McCain, smeared by the Rove(r) Boy Swifties of 2000 as the original Manchurian Candidate.

Speaking of *The Manchurian Candidate*, the Democrats may know how to make a movie in Hollywood, but the Republicans have long since perfected the art of making a movie in "life." So when was it decided that the entity known as "George W. Bush" would parachute into Madison Square Garden on Thursday night to deliver his acceptance speech, spending less time in New York than he did last Thanksgiving at the Baghdad airport? With sacred ground now hostile territory, Bush can be a *High Noon* hero for just clippin' his gerunds and showin' up.[12]

Is master terrorist Osama at large? Is Afghanistan ungovernable and Iraq a free-fire zone? Do the North Koreans still have their nukes and are the Iranians busy building theirs? Does that anthrax guy roam free? And what about the dirty bomb? Who cares—one way or another, New York City has been pacified! Republicans rule! Smoke and mirrors, or tear-gas canisters and TV cameras? Either way, the mission is accomplished.[13]

---

12   The Republican Convention struck *New York Times* pundit Maureen Dowd as a Western with Bush and Cheney as "the 'Magnificent Seven,' steely-eyed, gun-slinging samurai riding in to save the frightened town.

The vice-president played up the Western motif by giving ABC an interview at his Wyoming ranch.

"The cowboy riding tall in the saddle and holding the reins for a little girl on her pony could have been Shane," wrote Alessandra Stanley in her TV Watch column in *The Times*.

Meanwhile, the president's father was on the radio, comparing Kerry to Jane Fonda ("Westerns and Easterns," *New York Times*, 9/12/2004).

13   As Chris Smith would later point out, Karl Rove "didn't need to show ground zero when the networks would do it for him, allowing the GOP to use the city as a whole, from the Statue of Liberty to a midtown firehouse, as the soundstage for the Bush industrial film ...

Heck, even the protests played to Bush's advantage. When United for Peace and Justice hit the streets, 400,000 people strong, it was a dignified, uplifting display of democracy in action. So a few unlucky bicyclists spent a night locked up in an oily former bus garage. Nobody in Ohio

On September 8, the CBS news show *60 Minutes Wednesday* presented four documents critical of President Bush's 1972–73 National Guard service. Almost immediately, the story shifted from the question of Bush's special treatment in and absences from the National Guard to the provenance of the material. The documents were attacked as forgeries and CBS was compelled to admit a failure to authenticate them prior to broadcast. The disgraced network fired a number of *60 Minutes'* top producers and Dan Rather, the star CBS news reporter who broke the story, resigned as anchorman in 2005. It has never been established who forged the documents or supplied them to Rather.

Late in the campaign, the anti-*Fahrenheit 9/11*, a curiously and effectively retrograde example of artisanal animation ...

NEW YORK, OCTOBER 14, 2004

A would-be equal-opportunity offender, *Team America: World Police* sets out to skewer both hemispheres of the American brain—and mainly yours, dear liberal. This shish-kebab is cooked on one side. No matter how you parse it, the *South Park* guys' election-season intervention is a flag-waving, fag-baiting farce that—all puppet all the time—celebrates, even as it debunks, good old-fashioned American know-how.

As animated filmmaking, *Team America*—directed by Trey Parker from a script co-written with partner Matt Stone and Pam Brady—is far more audacious than any Pixar opus. It's a Bruckheimer-style action spectacle with puppets fighting, dancing, and having sex in a variety of positions while being manipulated by absurdly visible strings. From the opening shot of a French marionette show in a marionette world to the final gag of a live cockroach blasting into outer space, *Team America* is at once grandiose and tacky, elaborate and deflationary.

---

saw that. The larger image communicated to the nation was that George Bush and the Republicans were tough enough and confident enough to walk right into their enemies' backyard and endure some dissent.
(Chris Smith, "The Republicans Picked Our Pockets,"
New York, December 14, 2004.)

The geopolitics are brazenly insulting. Battling bin Laden's minions on the banks of the Seine, the inanely gung-ho *Team America* commandos inflict maximal collateral damage—toppling the Eiffel Tower, pulverizing the Arc de Triomphe, and blowing up the Louvre. Then, like good Americans, they retreat to their Mount Rushmore fortress to await further instructions from an eminently fallible supercomputer code-named I.N.T.E.L.L.I.G.E.N.C.E. So much for satirizing the war on terror—*Team America* has its own fear factor.

Often funny but seldom uproarious, *Team America* purveys a post-9/11 irony that's founded on a combination of schoolyard insult, belligerent patriotism, and the absence of irony. The villains are Kim Jong Il, an irate little puppet who furnishes Arab terrorists with WMDs; Michael Moore, who appears outside Mount Rushmore with a hotdog in each hand and a bomb strapped to his belly; and a gaggle of prominent Hollywood stars led by Alec Baldwin, head of the Film Actors Guild. So far as the latter's acronym goes: how much of Parker and Stone's anxiety is based on the fact that their songs are the movie's wittiest aspect—are they closet show-tune queens?

In the service of human interest, *Team America* recruits a replacement commando from the Broadway hit *Lease*. (He's first seen singing "Everyone Has AIDS.") His job is acting, something that intrinsically amuses animators Parker and Stone. Their marionettes vomit, bleed, and explode into organ parts. Indeed, these puppets show more guts than the filmmakers, who direct their fire at very soft targets: French and Egyptian civilians, a Communist dictator, and a bunch of Hollywood showboats. Despite some pre-release Drudge-stoked hysteria regarding an "unconscionable" attack on the administration, no American politicians appear in the movie. (The movie has since garnered the Fox News seal of approval.) Nor do any media moguls. The filmmakers never satirize anyone who could hurt their career—not even Michael-Moore enabler, Harvey Weinstein.

True, *Team America* is not family friendly. Parker and Stone are so proud of their rap about the relationship among dicks, pussies, and assholes—"pussies are only an inch and a half from assholes … Only dicks can fuck pussies and assholes"—that it's delivered twice. If war is hell, then Team Americans are dicks, Hollywood liberals are pussies (as well as F.A.G.s and presumably "girlie men"), and terrorists are assholes. For bellicose Bush supporters, being praised as stupid dicks in a dirty-mouthed animation may be as welcome as an endorsement from Vincent Gallo. But that's only if they're looking for irony. Soulfully sung, *Team America*'s comic faux-country ballad "Freedom Isn't Free" would have moved the RNC to tears. And although the *Team America* fight song may never be broadcast on the public airwaves, that's not to say that it won't get lots of play among the troops in Baghdad. "America, Fuck Yeah" is so on target that it's less a joke than a ready-made anthem.

Team America is obviously too profane and bawdy—that is, too "Hollywood"—for Bush's fundamentalist base or a neocon prig like Michael Medved (except perhaps late at night when he's all alone). But, fuck yeah, it's the perfect date flick for a drunken frat boy trying to impress right-wing skank Ann Coulter.[14]

On November 2, George W. Bush narrowly defeated John Kerry, 286 electoral votes to 251, while winning 50.7 percent of the popular vote. The publication, soon after, of Gary Indiana's corrosive pamphlet, *Schwarzenegger Syndrome: Politics and Celebrity in the Age of Contempt*, gave me the opportunity to analyze America's most successful star-pol since Ronald Reagan, in *Film Comment*'s November/December issue.

It's Arnold's movie, we're only just watching it. As in *The Last Action Hero* (1993), the fiasco of Arnold Schwarzenegger's comic-humanizing phase, the Arnold character keeps crossing back and forth from the movie to the movie-within-the-movie. No base goes untouched or, should we say, no breast goes unfondled.

---

14   In 2008, the conservative *National Review* ranked *Team America* twenty-fourth in a list of the twenty-five "Best Conservative Movies" of the past quarter-century: "It's amazingly vulgar and depicts Americans as wildly overzealous in fighting terror. Yet the film's utter disgust with air-headed, left-wing celebrity activism remains unmatched in popular culture."

Other Bush-era movies on the list include *The Lives of Others* (no. 1), *The Incredibles* (no. 2), *300* (no. 5), *The Pursuit of Happyness* (no. 7), *Juno* (no. 8), the *Lord of the Rings* trilogy (no. 11), *The Dark Knight* (no. 12), *Master and Commander* (no. 16), *The Lion, the Witch and the Wardrobe* (no. 17), *We Were Soldiers* (no. 19), *United 93* (no. 23), and *Gran Torino* (no. 25). That *The Passion of the Christ* is conspicuously absent—it is not even found among the twenty-five runners-up—attests to its status as something more than a movie. (John J. Miller, "The Best Conservative Movies," nrd.nationalreview.com).

Two summers ago, the expensive expanse of well-lit torso known as "Arnold Schwarzenegger"—a product, Gary Indiana notes in his deadly serious and laugh out-loud hilarious rant *Schwarzenegger Syndrome*, that was "as familiar as any canned tuna or packaged cake the average voter might pick up at Ralph's"—declared itself a candidate for governor of California. To vote for the Arnold was, per Indiana, an act of brand loyalty; at the same time, it was wonderfully flattering, "as if the Queen of England had suddenly abdicated to stand for election in the House of Commons."

As the media's Klieg lights lit up California and the carnivalesque life-movie that no one, least of all Arnold, needed to dub *Total Recall 2*, got underway, the superstar candidate campaigned mainly on the TV talk shows of his fellow celebs. "By his artful use of these venues," Indiana writes, "Schwarzenegger cultivated the impression that he was conde-scending to run for governor, an impression that carried an implication of sacrifice, which in turn could only be accounted for by a powerful wish to serve the public."

There is a sense in which all of our stars are public servants, ful-filling the socially cohesive function of entertaining the nation. But self-aware Arnold had already made public service part of his personae. As an Austrian-born émigré, he was the greatest of the extraterrestrial/immigrant/supernatural Strangers in Paradise who wandered through the movies of the 1980s, validating America's suburbs and shopping malls. Indeed, by the time Ronald Reagan left office, the Arnold was a strategic asset. His films grossed $1 billion worldwide during the '80s; on the eve of the Gulf War, *Time* declared him "the most potent symbol of worldwide dominance of the US entertainment industry."

In 1990, Arnold (one of the few American action stars who cannot be construed as anti-authoritarian) had appointed himself the nation's *Kindergarten Cop*. In an ancillary promotional move, George H. W. Bush anointed the actor the Chairman of the President's Council on Physical Fitness and Sports. Schwarzenegger began his career as a Bush family retainer and pump-you-up Republican. He campaigned for Bush Sr. against Pat Buchanan during the 1992 New Hampshire primary—and even before. For, as though to summon the white men who represent the GOP's most important minority, the Terminator has always appeared when a Republican president ran for reelection.

Materializing unheralded late in the 1984 campaign, the original

Terminator provided an amusingly dystopian action alternative to the relentlessly positivist Reaganite "new morning." Released in the post-Desert Storm, New World Order summer of 1991 as Bush I girded his loins, the vastly inflated *T2: Judgment Day* cast the nation's fitness chairman as a kinder, gentler killer-cyborg. And as the Bush II juggernaut prepared to roll in the summer of 2003, Arnold returned in *Terminator 3: Rise of the Machines.*

T3 proved an excellent trailer for *Total Recall 2.* As Indiana explains, Schwarzenegger understood that California's special election afforded the only possible moment during which he could become governor— "calculation is, after all, his foremost skill." That and a flair for the mean-spirited *bon mot,* as demonstrated by the robotic blitz of applied movie-dialog sound-bites with which the candidate communicated. Like the kid in *The Last Action Hero,* anyone could join in the fun. Give Gray Davis the old *hasta la vista, baby* and terminate California's problems. "This language of coercion, plucked from fictions that glorified force as the preferred method of problem-solving, formed an intoxicating, vaporous mirage in the sketchy shape of a political 'platform,'" writes Indiana in what I take to be his definition of the Schwarzenegger Syndrome. "The Schwarzenegger bandwagon was a flying carpet, floating elusively between the hemorrhoid-crimson Mars of *Total Recall* and the carnage-strewn freeways of *Terminator 2,* films in which the candidate rescued humanity from slavery and annihilation."

California had been raped by Enron, Ross Perot, and sundry other energy providers but, as a savior, Arnold's first and most cherished project has always been himself. He began as a body-builder—an activity that, Indiana notes, is "devoted entirely to self-display," as well as the most conspicuous form of self-improvement. Becoming a movie star was only another stage in Schwarzenegger's will to power. In a sense, Jack Smith prophesied Arnoldian stardom in his 1962 analysis of Maria Montez, when he suggested that rather than imagine themselves exotic beings in an Arabian Nights universe, stars would degrade the audience through the evidence of their crass concern with the material world: "Fantasies now feature weight lifters who think now how lucky and clever they were to get into the movies and the fabulous pay ... think something like that on camera—it's contagious and you share those thoughts ..."

Contagious, yes: lucky clever Schwarzenegger was the blockbuster made human. But his career went soft during the touchie-feelie Clinton years. "While it was okay for the Arnold of the eighties to kill 275 people onscreen, it is not for the Arnold of the nineties," the star told reporters on the set of *The Last Action Hero*. In the following year's *Junior*, a comedy wherein the Arnold was made pregnant, he played his own feminine side. Married into the Kennedy clan, Schwarzenegger had floated the idea of a Senate campaign as early as 1991. The prospect seemed ludicrous. In 1993, his onetime rival Sylvester Stallone made *Demolition Man*, a suspiciously Schwarzeneggerian vehicle set in a future "liberal" dystopia whose monuments include the Schwarzenegger Presidential Library.

After a clownish turn in the gayest of *Batman* movies, Arnold's aspirations reached the acme of absurdity in his 1999 millennium-pegged bomb *End of Days*. Casting himself as the despairing ex-cop Jericho Cane, Schwarzenegger went one-on-one with Satan. (Having taken possession of Gabriel Byrne, the devil demonstrates his evil by walking up to a strange woman in a low-cut gown, grabbing her breasts and making her like it.) *End of Days* is mainly set on the Sodom and Gomorrah mean streets of midtown Manhattan. But its version of urban apocalypse was a few seasons premature.

Just as George W. Bush's questionable presidency was consecrated by the War on Terror, so Schwarzenegger's flagging career was revived by his embodiment of irate American vigilante derring-do in the 9/11-delayed *Collateral Damage*. The late 2001 success of *Black Hawk Down* demonstrated the New Bellicosity's box-office appeal. January's National Football League playoffs were saturated with *Collateral Damage* spots and *Terminator 3* was rushed into production. And so Arnold was reborn from the ashes of Ground Zero, a virtual hero of the post-9/11 world.

Back to the future: In a manner unseen since the Ronald Reagan of 1984, Schwarzenegger created his own movie within the hyper-designed triumphalist pseudo-event of the 2004 Republican National Convention. But, not until he became president (actually, not until he took John Hinckley's bullet and lived) did Reagan rise to anything like Arnold's iconic stature. Improving on the truth where necessary, Schwarzenegger used his primetime speech to pledge allegiance to America and recall his fearful boyhood in Austria's Russian zone: "I saw tanks in the street …" When, in a skillful inoculation, he dubbed the Democratic National Convention "True Lies" and called the Democrats "economic girlie men," the delegates, "soaked in the star's luster" per the *New York Post*, jumped to their feet, screaming with delight.

Arnold, as Indiana puts it in his hilarious account of this Nuremberg moment, had "resurrected the specter of Communism and the moral aporias of the Cold War by burnishing his own history with wild hyperbole no nativist politician could have convincingly pulled off. It was propaganda in the service of narcissism, one of the many skills that George W. Bush himself had barely developed beyond the most rudimentary and obvious level." Bush, however well he had learned to project the Texican, was only a Hollywood neophyte.

Last year, the *New York Times* noted with a surprise that was itself somewhat surprising that California's "Action-Figure Governor" had proved a "surprise hit" in Hollywood. But there's nothing Hollywood loves more than success (unless it's propaganda in the service of narcissism). What's truly remarkable is how long it has taken rightwing Republicans to admit how much they love, love, love, love the Team America action-figures that Hollywood's liberal commie Jewish feminist pansies have sold the American public.

The day after his election, Arnold himself pointed out that, "it's all about leadership." (No need to add the emphatic, "stupid.") As the world's reigning action star, Schwarzenegger specialized in enacting the masculine. His vehicles were distinguished by can-do attitude and insouciantly surplus carnage—on a per capita basis, he racked up the highest body count in movie history. And, unlike his macho predecessors, Arnold was an equal opportunity killing machine. Eliminating the woman is the premise of *The Terminator* and it provided Schwarzenegger's best movie *Total Recall* with its money shot—plugging Sharon Stone pointblank through the forehead with the words "consider this a divorce." Even in *Collateral Damage*, the Arnold goes mano-a-mano with Italian fashionplate Francesca Neri.

While a tone of muscle-feminism was set by Linda Hamilton's warriorwoman in the first two *Terminator* movies, *T3* was explicitly founded on chick bashing. Arnold's antagonist is a robo-babe with a tailored leather jumpsuit who, at one point, has her head shoved in a toilet bowl. "How many times do you get away with this," Schwarzenegger excitedly told *Entertainment Weekly*, "take a woman, grab her upside down, and bury her face in a toilet bowl? I wanted to have something floating there." This image surfaced so to speak during a campaign debate a few months later when the Arnold attempted to intimidate adversary Arianna Huffington by telling her he had a role for her in *Terminator 4*.

Heh, heh. As demonstrated by *Total Recall 2*, bullying women is intrinsic to Schwarzenegger's appeal. As governor, the Overdeterminator cannot help but denounce the California Nurses Association as a special interest group and brag that they hate him because, "I'm always kicking their butt." No question but that the Arnold would have his career role campaigning against Hillary Clinton.

When the Arnold takes his super-guzzling, militarized Humvee on the road or holds court in his Bedouin-style smoking tent, when he compares the legislature to a kindergarten, when he calls state senators "girlie men" and threatens to terminate them, when he boasts of dominating the state's nurses, he is inviting us to relive his greatest hits. As Indiana makes clear in his Tom Paineful pamphlet, the Schwarzenegger Syndrome liberates the Last Action Hero at last. It allows for embracing, in so-called real life, the Neanderthal homilies and bully-boy will-to-power that the Arnold's movies have always concealed behind the fig leaf of self-reflexive irony.

CHAPTER ELEVEN

2005: LOOKING FOR THE MUSLIM WORLD

As Bush began his second term, a first draft of US history—at least in Iraq—continued to be written by a series of independent documentaries and embodied by a new cycle of Hollywood political thrillers.

NEW YORK, MARCH 2, 2005

Documentaries, like spinach, are supposed to be good for you and healthy for the body politic. The most striking thing about *Gunner Palace*, Michael Tucker and Petra Epperlein's fascinating, if not entirely satisfying, digital video portrait of US forces in Iraq, is that it addresses a hunger for leafy greens—which is to say, images of the war—that you may not have known you had.

Those who lived through the Vietnam period—and perhaps even more those who didn't—are familiar with that war's lysergic jungle iconography, rock chopper soundtrack, and druggy "Born to Kill" ethos. *Gunner Palace*, which John Kerry screened for his fellow senators last month, begins to provide a comparable simulation. Its points of reference are not Motown and Westerns but rap and reality TV. Indeed, this often chaotic camcorder documentary—produced during Tucker's two two-month stretches embedded with the 2-3 Field Artillery—most often suggests a combination of *The Real World* and *Cops*, set to a plaintive gangsta beat.

The "Gunners" are barracked in one of Uday Hussein's pleasure palaces. "We dropped a bomb on it and now we party in it," one of Tucker's roommates explains. The ambience suggests a post-nuclear Las Vegas—a bunch of small-town kids with automatic weapons camped out in an abandoned luxury hotel, splashing around in the pool, putting golf balls amid the rubble of a goonish *Arabian Nights* fantasy. But these children of Oprah and the internet are nothing if not self-conscious. Most are happy to perform for Tucker's camcorder, clowning in burnoose or expressing inanities they might have heard on TV. The most articulate are the group's rappers: "When those guns start blazing and our friends get hit, that's when our hearts start racing and our stomachs get woozy," Specialist Richmond Shaw concludes his number. "Cuz for y'all this is just a show but we live in this movie."

The brass is nonexistent but the kids are documented having fun with their Iraqi interpreters—middle-aged guys to whom they give nicknames like Mike Tyson and Superstar. (Throughout the movie, these men are killed off-camera or exposed as spies.) Unable to get jiggy with the local women, the soldiers seem to enjoy themselves most when playing with Iraqi kids. One goes to an orphanage and presents a three-year-old with a SpongeBob SquarePants doll: "He's one of my heroes." (Does that constitute child abuse or only cultural imperialism?)

Gunner Palace is set almost entirely in Baghdad, mainly in late 2003, when Saddam, still at large, was being blamed for the insurgency, with additional material filmed in early 2004. GWB had declared major combat to be over ten months before, but the movie resounds with the rifle fire of "minor combat." Meanwhile, more distant than guerrilla mortars, upbeat official bulletins whistle overhead: Secretary Rumsfeld conveys his best wishes to the Iraqi people. "Life has improved, Comrades. Life has become more joyous," as J. V. Stalin told the All-Union Convention of Stakhanovite Workers in 1935.

Adrenaline pumps whenever the Gunners go on downtown patrol. If Vietnam reminded Michael Herr of Fort Apache, this feels more like Fort Apache, the Bronx—complete with glue-sniffing twelve-year-old street kids. The soldiers sense hidden hostility all around them—hardly a paranoid response in a world where any stray plastic bag might conceal a roadside bomb. The movie might be subtitled "Incomprehensible Doings on the Iraqi Street." Nerves are raw. Sometimes the guys enjoy "scaring the natives," by rolling through town with feedback blasting from their

Hummers. A psy-op to the barrio carries intimations of *Black Hawk Down*, although, with a nod to *Apocalypse Now*, the men play a bit of "Ride of the Valkyries" to set the mood.

No weapons are found in most of the raids we see. Often, however, the Gunners take prisoners anyway—and there's more resonance than the filmmakers may have originally intended when the soldiers threaten unruly (usually English-speaking) captives with being "sent to Cuba." Tucker, who comes from a military family, is an empathetic observer of these ordinary enlisted men and one woman. We never see any casualties, although he takes pains to telegraph his suffering when some of the soldiers he's embedded with die.

Mainly, however, Tucker seems to partake in the mood of disassociated bewilderment. Floating on the surface of confusion, *Gunner Palace* has a raw home-video quality that's often quite beautiful. Much of the movie is hardly more than an immersion in sights and sounds. Vivid as it is, *Gunner Palace* is dominated by what isn't shown. It's the human face of Abu Ghraib.

The most complicated Iraq movie appeared that year at Cannes— straightforward, yet highly duplicitous, conceived (just across the border) in Canada but set in the heart of the USA. David Cronenberg's *A History of Violence* "isn't so much a comment on America," Andrew Sarris would write after the movie opened in the States, "as it is a comment on American movies and the violent ecstasies they have provided to audiences around the world. There is a spiritual price to be paid ..." Exactly: Sarris articulated precisely the anxiety felt in Hollywood in the days and weeks following the Events of 9/11. As a variant on the Western, our most beloved and instructional genre, as well as one only barely alive since the end of the Vietnam War, Cronenberg's movie has something to say about the Western's persistence both in our culture and our reptile brain.

CANNES, MAY 18, 2005

The veterans showed their strength this year at Cannes. Still, the toughest movie I saw in competition, David Cronenberg's droll and ruthless meta-thriller *A History of Violence*, came away empty-handed—just as

Cronenberg's *Spider* was ignored by the 2002 jury. What does it take? Beginning with *Dead Ringers* (1988), or even *The Fly* (1986), Cronenberg has been, film for film, the most audacious and challenging narrative director in the English-speaking world. But then, Hou Hsiao-hsien—arguably the greatest narrative filmmaker working anywhere over the last fifteen years—left Cannes without a prize as well.

A work for hire, as well as Cronenberg's biggest budget ever, freely adapted by Josh Olson from John Wagner and Vince Locke's graphic novel, *A History of Violence* manages to have its cake and eat it—impersonating an action flick in its staccato mayhem while questioning these violent attractions every step of the way. The movie is deeply involving. Still, with its Hitchcockian "wrong man" theme and continual implication of the viewer, it's as coolly distanced as its title would suggest. In the very first minute a scarily hard-bitten killer walks on camera and perfects the flat perspective by straightening a chair. Cronenberg's tone is too disconcertingly dry to be ironic and too scary to register as absurd. "It's not tongue-in-cheek," he remarked at his press conference. "It's funny." In a way, it's a successful version of Michael Haneke's audience-bashing *Funny Games*, and the over-appreciative press screening audience drove one Viennese programmer to shout, "Stop laughing you fucking piece of shit critics and take this film serious!" In other words, it's a movie that could drive you crazy.[1]

Cued by Howard Shore's unobtrusive Western score, *A History of*

---

1   Watching the North American premiere of *A History of Violence* a few months later with a hometown crowd from the upper balcony of the cavernously vertical Roy Thomson Hall was the closest the 2005 Toronto International Film Festival came to providing a hockey game atmosphere. "Wow, you're a rowdy audience," festival topper Piers Handling exclaimed—although most of the anticipatory screams were for Viggo Mortensen. Still, the minister of culture was on hand to laud Toronto as "one of the top two [film festivals] in the world, second only to Cannes" and introduce the director *The Toronto Star* had that morning hailed as "a true Canadian artist." "We might be second to Cannes," Cronenberg noted, "but we know this is the only screening that counts." Indeed, where the Cannes jury snubbed *A History of Violence* as too pop, the Canadian audience responded viscerally—laughing at Cronenberg's adroitly timed jokes and spontaneously applauding his artfully choreographed outbursts of righteous mayhem, before subsiding into shocked silence. Despite its focus on the use value of violence, in life as well as the movies, Cronenberg's film attracted relatively little political analysis—beyond the vaguely expressed idea that it somehow felt right for now.

Violence illustrates, as its title suggests, the return of the repressed—or, if you prefer, the vicissitudes of an over-determined superhero destiny. A pair of cartoonishly chiseled normals (Viggo Mortensen and Maria Bello) live with their CGI-perfect children in a Disneyland-idyllic small town that might have been designed for the game players of Cronenberg's *eXistenZ*. In one romantic scene, Mortensen and Bello pretend to be teenagers; in their next tryst, they no longer know who they are. In between, the couple and their kids have been irrationally terrorized by a series of criminals, most impressively Ed Harris's mutilated gangster.

Tense and atmospheric, with a real sense of animal menace, *A History of Violence* is a hyper-real version of an early '50s B-movie nightmare— albeit one where the narrative delicately blurs dream and reality, the performances slyly merge acting with role-playing, the location feels like a set, and blood always oozes from lovingly contrived prosthetic injuries. Each lie builds on another. Innocuous interaction is rife with hints to turbulent inner lives and violent fantasies. Innocent scenes are booby-trapped to explode on a second viewing. One child is shot; another wakes up screaming to be told by her father that "there's no such thing as monsters."

It's the monsters that keep *A History of Violence* from projecting a world as hermetic as the madman's mind in *Spider*. The violence is amazingly staged and increasingly cathartic. But whether directed at high school bullies or cold-blooded killers, it never fails to rebound uncomfortably on the spectator. By the time William Hurt appears as a godfather from the City of Brotherly Love, *A History of Violence* has succeeded in incriminating virtually all of its characters in its particular "history," not to mention the audience (and maybe the species too). Only in the light of that recognition can Superman return to Smallville and seek his place at the table.[2]

Steven Spielberg's *War of the Worlds* had its world premiere in Tokyo on June 13, 2005, opening in the US two weeks later: the morning after President Bush addressed the nation from the Army base at Fort Bragg, North Carolina, defending the US war in Iraq lest "we yield the future of the Middle East to men like bin Laden." *War of the Worlds* was released amid a surge of urban terror and fratricidal violence—in

---

2   Among its other distinctions, *A History of Violence* was the last major Hollywood movie to be released on VHS as well as DVD.

Iraq, where the number of civilian casualties in the two years since Bush's "Mission Accomplished" announcement now approached 25,000. No more lovable aliens. No less than the president, Spielberg invoked the trauma that was said to have precipitated America's current war. There were, however, alternative analyses of the disaster.

NEW YORK, DECEMBER 7, 2005

The most widely discussed docu-agitprop since *Fahrenheit 9/11*, Adam Curtis's *The Power of Nightmares* takes a similarly confrontational stance toward Bush-world disorder. But the counter-narrative offered by this three-part, three-hour BBC account of the so-called War on Terror is more complex and seductive.

Curtis's thesis assumes the failure of liberalism. Each episode begins with the assertion that, where once they promised us social utopia, politicians now vie to be the most persuasively frightening. Then, like a gavel rapping for attention, Curtis presents the rogues' gallery: Bush, bin Laden, and Blair. The movie's first and most provocative hour argues that the Islamic fundamentalist Sayyid Qutb, a founder of the Muslim Brotherhood, and neocon guru Leo Strauss were evil twins—both reacting against the perceived selfish individualism of America's post–World War II affluence. But where Qutb may have been a true believer, Strauss was more cynical in teaching that religion and nationalism are necessary illusions for social cohesion.

Beginning in the mid '70s, so Curtis argues, the neocons and their allies set out to defeat Henry Kissinger's ruthless pragmatism. Among other evidence, he provides fabulous footage of Donald Rumsfeld lying about the Soviet danger. Then too, America was threatened by undetectable weapons systems—all the more present because unverifiable—and an international "terror network," albeit one coordinated by Moscow. (According to Curtis's CIA interviewees, much of the evidence for this was actually black propaganda invented to scare our NATO allies and taken as truth by the Committee on the Present Danger.) Meanwhile, despite Qutb's 1966 execution, his ideas spread—influencing the Iranian revolution, the assassination of Anwar Sadat, and through his disciple Ayman al-Zawahiri, the jihadist terror of Osama bin Laden.

Curtis discusses the convergence of neocon and jihadist interest in

Soviet-occupied Afghanistan. But his narrative comes unraveled both in his under-emphasis on Desert Storm's unintended consequences and over-emphasis on the conservative "political terrorism" directed against President Bill Clinton. Just marking time until back in power and relentlessly exploiting 9/11, Rumsfeld, Cheney, and Wolfowitz set about conjuring a spook house of sleeper cells, dirty bombs, and Iraqi WMDs.

In his final episode, Curtis makes his most controversial assertion. Buttressed by the French political scientist Gilles Kepel, he argues that Al Qaeda was essentially invented by the neocons as a means to prosecute bin Laden—and the reason that it disappeared was because it never really existed. This is not an easy sell in the shadow of no Twin Towers and one wonders how Curtis's line would play in the UK in the aftermath of last July's bombings. In fact, he has recently provided a perfunctory disclaimer: "Although we in the West face a serious terrorist threat, the apocalyptic vision of Al Qaeda portrayed by politicians and the media over the past four years is both a distortion and an exaggeration."

That's a more reasonable take, but *The Power of Nightmares* is essentially polemical. As partisan filmmaking it is often brilliant and sometimes hilarious—a superior version of *Syriana* (which also prudently subtracts Israel and the Palestinians from the Middle East equation). Cinematic argument is founded on juxtaposition, but where Michael Moore's montage is essentially comic, Curtis is more visionary in his connections. He enlivens his frequently fantastic archival footage not just with sarcastic pop songs, but repeated clips from the 1940 *Thief of Bagdad*, the surreal mid-50s industrial spectacular *Design for Dreaming*, and Leo Strauss's favorite TV shows (*Gunsmoke* and *Perry Mason*).

At heart, Curtis's worldview feels closer to that of Don DeLillo than to Noam Chomsky. The desire for narrative coherence is crucial to the understanding of any social formation—and fear of a phantom enemy is a necessary ingredient for social control. Curtis is certainly on target in addressing the role of necessary fiction in clouding our minds. But go forewarned that *The Power of Nightmares* also demonstrates what it proposes to demystify.[3]

---

3   The great conservative documentary of the year, as well as the second highest-grossing documentary ever (after *Fahrenheit 9/11*) turned out to be the French-made *March of the Penguins*, praised by Christian and conservative commentators as a defense of monogamy, a parable of religious faith, and an argument for intelligent design. Speaking of Hollywood's underserved

The day *War of the Worlds* opened, Spielberg began shooting *Munich*— the culmination of his 9/11 trilogy. In many respects a reiteration of the earlier movie, it also opened with a history-changing cinematic event (and might have modestly proposed itself as another).

NEW YORK, DECEMBER 14, 2005

The war on terror is a grim business, and so is *Munich*, Steven Spielberg's sincerely self-important account of the assassination campaign waged by Israeli secret agents against the Palestinian group that perpetrated the murder of eleven Israeli athletes at the 1972 Olympics.

The film is sluggish and repetitive, yet it exerts a certain clinical fascination. *Munich* isn't so much a dramatization of the Israeli-Palestinian conflict or a rumination on the morality of counterterrorism as a filmmaker's *cri de cœur*. More than politics, it's predicated on Spielberg's faith in the redemptive nature of Hollywood entertainment, as well as his ongoing attempt to be all things to all people—not just a *macher* but a *mensch*.

Thus, although made from an Israeli perspective, Munich doggedly seeks to humanize the Palestinian other. Nor are Mossad and Black September the only odd couple. Initially written by Eric Roth (awarded an Oscar for the quintessentially depoliticized *Forrest Gump*), the script was revised by Tony Kushner (who won a Pulitzer for writing the highly politicized *Angels in America*). American neo-cons and Palestinian nationalists are likely to find common ground in their objections. All are united in victimhood as Spielberg attempts to feel his way into a situation that confounds rational analysis.

Munich heralds itself as tragedy with a bombastic faux Jewish lament as a group of inebriated American athletes give a gang of Palestinian terrorists a leg up over the wall and into the Olympic village. There they storm the Israeli compound, shooting some athletes and holding the rest hostage. The games continue, even as the whole world watches the debacle on TV. Spielberg compresses the gist of the Oscar-winning doc

---

culturally conservative audience, talkshow host Michael Medved declared that *March of the Penguins* was "the first movie they've enjoyed since *The Passion of the Christ*. This is *The Passion of the Penguins*" (Jonathan Miller, "March of the Conservatives: Penguin Film as Political Fodder," *New York Times*, 9/13/2005).

One Day in September into a superbly edited McLuhanite frenzy; as with *Saving Private Ryan*, nothing else in the movie can match its opening. The terrifying introduction is the most powerful scene in the movie in part because it conjures up the hitherto only imagined hijacking of four American airliners on September 11. And like *Saving Private Ryan*'s D-Day, it whets a frightened audience's desire for revenge. In the first of many unlikely but metaphorically charged scenes, Golda Meir personally organizes a Mossad hit squad, to be led by her favorite bodyguard, codenamed Avner (Eric Bana). The team is given eleven targets; their mission takes them from Rome to Paris to Cyprus to Beirut to Athens to London. The source for this narrative, coyly denied by Spielberg until the moment of the movie's release, was George Jonas's 1984 *Vengeance*—an oft-disputed and essentially unverifiable account of the operation, told to the author by the pseudonymous Avner.

As in *Vengeance* and its 1986 HBO adaptation, *Sword of Gideon*, Spielberg's Mossad commandos are both super-competent and morally confused. Perhaps even more perplexed, as they are essentially functioning in the world of 2005. Eric Bana's Avner is a troubled blank, rendered even more so by his unit's gallery of mildly colorful types: the neurotic bomb maker (Mathieu Kassovitz), nervous diplomat (played as Abba Eban by Ciarán Hinds), bellicose muscle Jew (Daniel Craig), stolid forger (Hanns Zischler), and their manipulative handler (Geoffrey Rush), all primed to answer one question with another.

Avner's men are given eleven targets. However, they inadvertently kill other people, add more names to the list, and refuse to terminate the operation. (The Lillehammer fiasco in which an innocent Moroccan waiter was shot dead is not included; in *Vengeance*, it was blamed on another Mossad unit.) While point-blank shooting is the rule on both sides, Palestinians are humanized as nice neighbors or caring parents. Collateral damage, on the other hand, is usually reduced to some stray arms and legs.

The action ranges from Rome to Paris to Cyprus to Beirut to Athens to London, yet nobody seems to know what Avner's men are up to— except the omniscient French outfit that sells them their information. In *Vengeance*, this family-run spy service is known as Le Group. In *Munich*, they're more like Lutece, serving up pretentiously "traditional" cuisine even as they plan Avner's menu. (Turns out he's quite the chef himself.) These gourmet anarchists function as the inadvertent comic relief in what is essentially a half-baked action film, studded with philosophical raisins: "How do you think we got control of the land—by being nice?"

As the quest for vengeance continues, *Munich* becomes an increasingly dark and rainy nightmare, intermittently illuminated by flashes of anguish. "We're supposed to be righteous—that's a beautiful thing," the bomb maker wails even before his colleagues take it upon themselves to murder a freelance Mata Hari (Marie-Josée Croze). Avner winds up permanently haunted. "You are what we prayed for," his mother reassures him in the movie's ultimate expression of Jewish patriotism, while suggesting that in his brute application of justice he is a successor to the Golem of Prague. But even she doesn't want to know just what he did.

Burdened by moral ambivalence, *Munich* is a tough slog through a morass of unconvincing human interactions. At one point, Le Group tricks the Mossad men into sharing an Athens safe house with an unwitting group of PLO operatives: "You don't know what it is not to have a home," one tells Avner, as Al Green croons his 1972 hit "Let's Stay Together" obtrusively in the background. This pop anthem addresses us all. *Munich*'s least convincing, most utopian scene is pure Spielberg in its search for common ground ... in America—an Oslo summit that dare not speak its name.[4]

Late in the movie, there's a moment of coarse, if undeniable, authenticity: Attacking his material with far less finesse than demonstrated in the opening sequence, Spielberg completes the circuit by flashing back one last time to bloody '72. The remaining Israeli hostages are driven to the airport and then, in a paroxysm of panicked violence, massacred

---

4   Although strongly criticized by American neoconservatives, *Munich* has relatively little to do with Israel per se—except insofar as it expresses an ambivalence felt by many American Jews regarding the Jewish state. Much of the blame for this "moral equivalence" was assigned to screenwriter Tony Kushner, an outspoken critic of Israeli policy and, in a sense, heir to the left-wing screenwriters of the 1940s. Replying to his own critics, Spielberg made the suggestive gaffe of defending himself against "the sin of moral equivocation." On one hand, and in what Spielberg might characterize as an example of "ultra-realism," the terrorists of that other Black September are typically evoked in terms that blatantly anticipate Al Qaeda. On the other, in a more fantastic mode, *Munich* doggedly seeks to humanize these Palestinian others. Neither the lovable outlanders of *The Terminal*, nor the terrifying aliens of *War of the Worlds*, the movie's semi-differentiated Palestinians represent a new dialectic, united with their Israeli enemy in common victimhood.

by their captors. As the German police bungled their rescue operation, so Spielberg mangles this sequence by intercutting it with Avner's agonized conjugal relations and scoring the montage with a strident reprise of the film's opening lament. Is this the filmmaker's big bang theory? His tantrum? In a textbook case of abuse, Spielberg surrenders to his own despair and lashes out … at the audience.

Munich was praised as the most downbeat, and thus least Hollywood, movie Spielberg ever made. However harrowing in parts, *Schindler's List* and *Saving Private Ryan* both contrived (as the filmmaker would say of *The Terminal*) to make you laugh, cry, and feel good about the world. No such consolation exists here: on the eve of the Oscars, Spielberg spun *Munich* as "a prayer for peace." But rather, it seems the filmmaker's unhappy justification for the war against terrorism.

Largely uncommented on, in the substantial op-ed midrash that attached itself to the film's text, was *Munich*'s implicit suggestion that there was an Israeli connection to Bush's war and that the connection is intrinsic. *Syriana*, 2005's other serious movie about terror and the Middle East, solved this problem by leaving Israel out of the equation altogether. *Munich*, however, makes it clear that we defend Israel because we could be next—and, as the final shot of the lower Manhattan skyline makes abundantly clear, we were! In a unique spin on Old Testament foreshadowing, the War on Terror that the movie shows to have been initiated by the Israelis, is now ours to complete. In Spielberg's dramatization, the Mossad mission prophesies Bush's— but without promising any resolution. "Every man we kill is replaced by worse," the unhappy Avner warns. "There is no peace at the end of this."

Like *The Terminal* and no less than *War of the Worlds*, *Munich* sought to express support for an American foreign policy doctrine. The difference, in *Munich*'s case, was that this policy, namely the war in Iraq, was one that the movie (or Spielberg) could not, in good conscience, support. Small wonder that the movie was so depressed. How does one dramatize opposition to the war? Had even one prominent Democratic politician provided a clue? More to the point, how could one make the rational intervention Spielberg dreamed of making without sacrificing the emotional manipulation that is the filmmaker's stock-in-trade? Let's stay together, indeed.

Despite *Munich*'s faults, however, Spielberg and his writers Tony Kushner and Eric Roth deserve credit for attempting to address The Thing. So too Albert Brooks, whose valiant attempt to analyze the nature of post-9/11 Hollywood, proved an even greater failure. Dropped by Sony Pictures around the fourth anniversary of 9/11, *Looking for Comedy in the Muslim World* was subsequently acquired by Warner Bros. Independent Pictures.

NEW YORK, JANUARY 18, 2006

Too provocatively titled for its first distributor, Albert Brooks's *Looking for Comedy in the Muslim World* is nothing if not high-concept. This is the most self-reflexive of Hollywood's post-9/11 movies—wondering, as it does, just what exactly the patriotic entertainment industry can do to help make things right.[5]

Looking for Comedy is a crypto-sequel to Brooks's *Real Life*, a meta-act in which Brooks plays himself—as a failure. He's introduced attempting to audition for the real Penny Marshall, casting a remake of *Harvey*. When she hears who's next, her displeasure is evident. "I don't want to go a Jewish way," she tells her staff. War-on-terror paranoia or simply social realism? This is the first time the J-word has appeared in a Brooks movie—let alone been used to characterize his persona. But the subject at hand ensures it won't be the last.

---

5   The *Los Angeles Times* published excerpts from a letter sent Brooks by Sony Chairman Michael Lynton maintaining that "recent incidents have dramatically changed the landscape that we live in and that this, among other things, warrants changing the title of the film." (The incident to which Lynton referred was a report, evidently false although printed in *Newsweek*, that, in the course of an interrogation at Guantánamo, a Koran had been flushed down the toilet. Despite a subsequent retraction, the alleged desecration inflamed widespread Muslim anger.)

For Brooks, the title was crucial. "Even if you didn't see the movie, you'd see two words you'd never seen put together before—comedy and Muslim," he told reporter Patrick Goldstein. "Comedy is friendly—it's the least offensive word in our language," adding that Sony's demand that the title be changed made him "so upset I was throwing up at 3 a.m." (Patrick Goldstein, "Funny Choices," *Los Angeles Times*, 9/27/2005).

As far back as *Stand Up and Cheer* (1934), Hollywood proposed a "Department of Entertainment." Now, possibly confused with Mel Brooks, if not Steven Spielberg, Albert is summoned to Washington, DC, to meet with former senator Fred Thompson (playing himself) and take a role in the government's plan to "instrumentalize laughter." Specifically, he is to travel to South Asia to determine the Muslim sense of humor. The suggestion is that the idea came from George W. Bush: "The president has a pretty darn good sense of humor." (And he does appreciate happy news.)

Thompson hypnotizes Albert by dangling a Medal of Freedom before his eyes, even as he confounds him with the need to write a 500-page report. The mildly Kafkaesque situation, with Albert obsessing over the report (as he will in his inimitable fashion, for the remainder of the movie), is heightened when he is shown flying coach to India in the company of two cheerfully incompetent State Department aides, obviously modeled on K.'s helpers in *The Castle*. Set up in a shabby office in a building full of outsourced call banks, Brooks stages his own casting call, looking for an assistant—who isn't a Mel Gibson fan and doesn't realize that he's a Jew.

Looking for Comedy in the Muslim World is predicated on the absence of Muslim comedians—although somehow the *New York Times* manages to report on the phenomenon every six months. Baffled by the local TV and defeated in his attempts at on-the-street interviews, Albert decides to organize a comedy concert—handing out flyers on the streets of Old Delhi (a most flavorsome location). In the movie's lengthy set piece, Albert appears in a school auditorium, absurdly dressed in native garb to greet his supremely unresponsive audience with a resolution to discover "what makes you guys chuckle." The act, partly derived from Brooks's old routines, is doomed to bomb—all the more spectacularly once Albert moves into conceptual territory with fake ventriloquism and faux improv.

The humor in *Looking for Comedy in the Muslim World* is so dry that those expecting boffo yuks might well be looking for water in the desert. Moreover, the movie is complicated by two paradoxes—one annoyingly obvious, the other fascinatingly implicit. The first is the use of India, which, although home to 150 million Muslims, has six times as many Hindus; the second is that Brooks's comic sensibility travels so badly. Woody Allen may bestride the world like a colossus, but—the brilliance of *Real Life, Modern Romance*, and *Lost in America* notwithstanding—not even the French have shown any interest in Albert Brooks. I'd hazard that this has something to do with the untranslatable subtlety of his one-liners (dependent as they are on situation and delivery) and the uningratiating nature of his persona (complete with refusal to acknowledge blatant neuroses).

Brooks is the great uninflected narcissist of the movies. Never quite recovering from Albert's lovingly staged and fabulously failed stand-up routine, *Looking for Comedy* goes cloak-and-dagger, complete with disturbing intimations of the martyred *Wall Street Journal* reporter Daniel Pearl. Almost despite itself, this is a deeply pessimistic movie—not least in blandly suggesting that, the universality of stupid pet tricks aside, the mindless application of cannabis sativa may be the only surefire chuckle bait. Stoned, even the most terrifying Muslims love Brooks's lame routines, and that's all he really wants. "I killed, everything worked!" he exults.

In the end, *Looking for Comedy in the Muslim World* is a satire of American solipsism. (The perfect accompanying short subject would be a précis of Bush aide Karen Hughes's Middle Eastern goodwill mission.) Brooks plays a character so self-absorbed he visits the Taj Mahal and manages not to notice it. As the film ends, who can fail to appreciate the care with which he steps on his own apocalyptic punchline? That's the joke.

CHAPTER TWELVE

2006: SEPTEMBER 11, THE ANNIVERSARY

No commercial post-9/11 movie was more avidly anticipated than the Wachowski brothers' first post-*Matrix* statement, *V for Vendetta*; and none proved more disappointing. Reflecting turmoil within the newspaper, the following review ran as the March 8 *Village Voice* cover story.

NEW YORK, MARCH 8, 2006

V for Vendetta—produced by the Wachowski brothers and directed by James McTeigue—is nothing if not topical, as well as supremely tasteless, in its fantasies.

The action is set in a totalitarian London dominated by fake news and ruled through xenophobic panic. Historically, however, the movie takes a longer view. A pre-credit sequence walks through the seventeenth-century Gunpowder Plot, in which Guy Fawkes and a cabal of Catholic fanatics hid thirty-six barrels of explosives beneath Parliament to blow the British government to kingdom come. England's not-quite 9/11 (a pretext for a crackdown on Catholics and foreigners), this thwarted conspiracy—celebrated every year as Guy Fawkes Day—has an even more hysterical significance. Had it been successful, the explosion might have vaporized half of London and thus, in its state-of-the-art carnage, offered a foretaste of Hiroshima.

V for Vendetta was scheduled to have its world premiere in London on November 5, 2005, the very day of the Plot's 400th anniversary. The opening was delayed out of deference to last summer's London subway bombings, as well it might have been. What's remarkable about the Wachowski scenario, as opposed to Moore's original, is the degree to which it stands Fawkes on his head—recuperating this proto-suicide bomber as a figure of revolt. (Moore, incidentally, has disassociated himself from the film.)[1]

A movie of multitudinous comic book tropes, with the mysterious V (Hugo Weaving) haunting London in an insouciantly smiling Guy Fawkes mask, *V for Vendetta* is predicated on secret identities, floridly alliterative dialogue, and gnomic bromides: "There are no coincidences, only the illusion of coincidence," V grandly explains. In other words, it's all about the plot. (McTeigue's pedestrian mise-en-scène is elaborate without being particularly detailed.) Like the movie in which he dwells, V is partial to nineteenth-century fictions like *The Count of Monte Cristo*, even as his social function is grotesquely hyper-contemporary.

His name and origin unknown, V is both blank slate and screen for projection, even as he orchestrates, literally, a twenty-first-century gunpowder plot. His full-face disguise recalls the ski masks of the Italian Red Brigades; his slashing trademark is a recognizable permutation on the anarchist "A." This empty signifier argues for terror as a semiotician might—an attack on symbols—and he paraphrases Emma Goldman on the revolutionary importance of dancing. (His subterranean museum of solitude boasts a Wurlitzer jukebox although, as a romantic, he's partial to Julie London's "Cry Me a River.") With his mocking fixed grin, V as a political superhero plays Joker to his own Batman.[2]

Moore's stories appeared throughout the '80s, conflating Thatcherite Britain and Orwell's dystopia, imagining a post–World War III regime founded on racial purity, sexual conformity, and Nazi-style concentration camps. The Wachowskis tweak this premise to tweak the US. It's

---

1   When *V for Vendetta* had its premiere at the Berlin Film Festival in February 2006, director McTeigue stressed that the movie had not been cut or reedited, while producer Joel Silver maintained that "It's a great time for this movie. It's a controversial film and it's a controversial time. It's going to make people think" (Mark Kermode, "You call it a disaster. Hollywood calls it a vehicle," *London Observer*, March 12, 2006).

2   It's as if the terrorist menace of *V for Vendetta* called the 2008 mega hit *The Dark Knight* into existence.

2020, the year of perfect vision, and to no one's disappointment, America has collapsed in chaos. Awash in secret detention camps and biological weapons (including avian flu), the UK is a Muslim-phobic fascist state (Koran consigned to the Ministry of Objectionable Material) ruled by a fascist Chancellor who came to power in a biological Reichstag Fire and appears—both to colleagues and the TV-fuddled masses—as an outsize video image. (Winston Smith in the 1984 *1984*, John Hurt plays a sort of Big Brother here.) Meanwhile, V's lone disciple, Evey (Natalie Portman), daughter of two disappeared social activists, works in a version of Orwell's Ministry of Truth. Given V's essential abstraction, she's the movie's most human presence. A former Broadway "Anne Frank," Portman adds Saint Joan to her baggage—once captured and processed by the police, she looks like a diminutive, doe-eyed Falconetti.

V and Evey meet cute when he saves her from police gang rape. Other forms of social control include a snarling Bill O'Reilly type known as the Voice of London. His opposite number (Stephen Fry) is a subversive chat show host who ridicules the Chancellor and pays the price for his music hall stunt. Clearly, the Wachowskis have not entirely abandoned the idea of *The Matrix*. When V blows up London's central criminal court, the Old Bailey, the fake news goes into major damage control, bragging that it was an intentional demolition job. Fog City is so shrouded in conspiracy that, in tracking down the mystery terrorist, the government's hangdog investigator (Stephen Rea) has no alternative but to investigate himself.

If *The Matrix* betrayed the Wachowskis' acquaintance with Jean Baudrillard, *V for Vendetta* suggests they've been perusing political philosopher Antonio Negri—both the old ultra-left Negri of *Domination and Sabotage* and the new Michael Hardt–collaborating Negri of *Empire and Multitude*. (The latter book even name dropped *The Matrix* as an example of how Empire feeds on the creative "social productivity" of the ruled.) V's dictum that "people shouldn't be afraid of their government, the government should be afraid of its people"—is a Cracker Jack box restatement of Negri and Hardt's notion of democracy for all. And the theorists would surely approve of V as the antithesis of a Leninist revolutionary elite.

This hero not only has no name but also no actual personality. (Why hire Weaving? The role could have been played by a computer program.) At a key moment in *V for Vendetta*, the Negri-Hardt multitude—mysteriously networked and absurdly masked like their faceless non-leader—takes to the streets and waits expectantly. Their patience is rewarded by a superbly irresponsible finale that conflates the "1812 Overture," the Rolling Stones, Malcolm X, and Gloria Steinem. Absorbing even in its incoherence, *V for Vendetta* manages to make an old popular mythology new. Impossible not to break into a grin: It's the thought that counts.[3]

Six years after *V for Vendetta* had its London premiere, the movie had lodged itself in international popular culture as a symbol of revolt. In late September 2011, the hacker-activist group Anonymous, which had used the movie's Guy Fawkes mask in previous demonstrations, introduced them into the leaderless "Occupy Wall Street" movement camped out in Lower Manhattan's Zuccotti Park. When the protests went global in mid-October, the mask was seen in other American and many European cities, including London where Wikileaks founder Julian Assange wore one to address the crowd at Occupy London Stock Exchange.[4]

Not all attempts to subvert the Bush regime had the same staying power.

---

3   *V for Vendetta*'s greatest apostle was *Vanity Fair* columnist James Wolcott who saw the film at an early, celebrity-enriched screening and used his blog to proclaim it "the most subversive cinematic deed of the Bush-Blair era." Wolcott found *V for Vendetta* genuinely populist—"unlike the other movies dubbed 'controversial' (*Fahrenheit 9-11, The Passion, Munich, Syriana*), it doesn't play to a particular constituency"—and blatantly confrontational. The movie "doesn't just depict a *1984* dystopia—it advocates radical remedy, and illustrates what it advocates with rhapsodic, operatic, orgasmic flourish … [It's an] angry, summoning Tom Paine moral dispatch that puts our pundits, politicians, and cable news hosts to shame" ("The Red and the Black," James Wolcott's Blog, 2/27/2006: www.vanityfair.com/online/wolcott/2006/02/the-red-and-the.html).

After the movie opened, Wolcott blogged again to mock the tepid reviews it received from New York critics. *V for Vendetta* proved only a moderate success, grossing $70.5 million in the US and finishing no. 36 for the year, one spot ahead of Oliver Stone's *World Trade Center*.

4   Indeed, Amazon.com's best-selling mask for Halloween 2011 would be the grinning visage of Guy Fawkes (JoAnn Wypijewski, "The Body Acoustic," *Nation*, 11/14/2011).

NEW YORK, APRIL 12, 2006

Wanna knock the prez? Let's make a show ... preferably on television. Paul Weitz's new satire *American Dreamz* imagines the Bush regime as an episode in the history of American entertainment and the nation's number one TV show *American Idol* as the quintessence of US democracy. So what else is new?

The vision of America as a vast, ratings-driven amateur hour is not without promise, but Weitz's movie, named for the most popular TV program in its parallel universe, is disappointingly soft in its individual characterizations. Indeed, as befits a director whose slice of the American pie has been predicated on a self-proclaimed "franchise" of gross-out comedies, the movie is mainly about tolerance. (He knows, firsthand, that the American people have it.)

American Dreamz is a movie with two world-historic players and a raft of wannabes. Host of the eponymous TV show, Hugh Grant plays the role of the smarmy swine with convincing self-loathing. "I envy myself deeply," he tells his gorgeous girlfriend as she leaves him. Scouting new contestants, Grant actually finds one as callous as he—an Ohio cheerleader (singer-actress Mandy Moore) who is as eager to exploit her Iraq war-injured boyfriend as she is to mimic Christina Aguilera.

Moore's ultimate rival is a *Chorus Line*-loving Iraqi mujahid (avid newcomer Sam Golzari) sent to America by his disgusted comrades as a sleeper agent who will never be activated. Installed at the Beverly Hills home of his unsuspecting, bizarrely nouveau relatives, Golzari winds up on Grant's show. America is the land of opportunity—his queeny cousin submitted an audition tape, and when the show's representatives turn up, they take Golzari for the applicant. (Like Steven Spielberg in *Munich*'s second-worst scene, Weitz is pleased to exaggerate the appeal of American pop music for the Arab world.)

Meanwhile, America's president (Dennis Quaid) has just been returned to office. In a paroxysm of rebelliousness, he elects to stay in bed and read a newspaper rather than meet the press. Harking back to the sitcom protag of Comedy Central's *That's My Bush!* the Weitz conception of our maximum leader as a timid moron is hardly unsympathetic. "My mom wanted to show my dad any idiot could do it," Quaid explains to his sweetly medicated wife (Marcia Gay Harden), pushing the movie's talent show premise into the political realm.

As one might expect, too much information precipitates a presidential breakdown; Quaid is shown surrounded by books, with Benjamin Barber's prophetic *Jihad vs. McWorld* prominently positioned for the camera. Whether or not the president takes Barber's argument seriously, Weitz does: Barber's pre-9/11 formulation, "When Jihad and McWorld collide on television, there is little doubt about who wins," turns out to be the movie's article of faith and *deus ex machina*. The president's controlling chief of staff (Willem Dafoe), a combination of Karl Rove and Dick Cheney, who in one of their funnier exchanges assures Quaid that "I'm there for you," wants to restore the president's plunging poll numbers by positioning him as a guest judge on Grant's show. At this point, the mujahideen—who, like everyone else in this universe, are addicted to American TV—catch Golzari's act and, realizing that he has a chance to go all the way, designate him their suicide contestant.

The eerie spectacle of a jihadist prancing through "The Impossible Dream" notwithstanding, *American Dreamz* should really have been funnier. At least it's not boring. Paddling vigorously through some mid-movie doldrums, Weitz unexpectedly brings everything together for a suitably madcap finale involving multiple betrayals and malfunctions, a remote-controlled president, star-struck terrorists, and an on-air marriage proposal. It's not exactly *The Manchurian Candidate*, but the whole world is watching. Golzari's rendition of "My Way" is nearly equaled by a heartfelt plea to "deal with reality" (including the admission that Middle East problems will never be solved). As if to prove the point, Weitz detonates a suicide bomb as a punch line.

To make its point, however, *American Dreamz* could not possibly be insulting enough. (Compared to the genuinely illiberal *Team America*, this is a love pat—despite Trey Parker's cameo as a doomed contestant, the long-haired "Rocky Man.") Quaid's president is neither the petulant charmer we know and loathe nor the vain and cunning Bush of David Hare's heroic docudrama *Stuff Happens*—although perhaps Weitz did see Hare's play when it was staged in Los Angeles last summer. At any rate, *American Dreamz* poses the same essential question: "To what degree is this country culpable for its actions?" the dancing mujahid wonders. "Are Americans responsible for America?"

Ultimately, *American Dreamz* is less social satire than social realism— the contestants are virtually indistinguishable from those on the real *American Idol*; the pols are as comfortably stupid as we might wish them to be. Bottom line and end of the day: *American Dreamz* is still flattering. The movie may have been made with the barest modicum of style and taste, but it is never as crass as its presumed audience.[5]

The month after *American Dreamz* opened brought the final episode of *The West Wing*—the popular TV drama that began its run on NBC in September 1999 and, over the course of its seven seasons, offered in the person of Josiah Bartlett (Martin Sheen) a liberal and rhetorical alternative to the Bush presidency.[6]

The utopian world that was *The West Wing* featured numerous crises of all sorts, many involving terrorism, but not 9/11. The show was essentially forward-looking. Its final season featured a race to succeed Bartlett pitting a Republican candidate highly evocative of Senator John McCain (Alan Alda) against a youthful Democratic representative (played by Caribbean actor Jimmy Smits). The Democrat won.[7]

And now, as the fifth anniversary of 9/11 approached, so did its "naturalistic" movie representations, discussed in a May 10 *Village Voice* cover story.

---

5   As reported by critic Caryn James, *American Dreamz's* opening weekend grosses were "deadly"—less than $4 million. In analyzing the movie's failure, James actually deemed it deficient in cultural narcissism: "The concept of the Cheney figure as the puppet master and the president as a dunce is an antique of political humor. The terrorists are funnier because they are saturated in American popular culture. In this film they don't hate us; they love us, or at least our entertainment" ("Critic's Notebook: Pop Beats Politics in the Race For Laughs," *New York Times*, 4/26/2006).

6   "In *The West Wing* version of the West Wing," Clive James wrote, "the frantically energetic inhabitants speak modern American English in its highest state of colloquial eloquence. In the Bush administration's West Wing, a hold area for somnambulists, any speech by the President sets a standard so low that Donald Rumsfeld is elevated to the oratorical status of Edmund Burke" ("In the grip of the eagle," *TLS*, 4/4/2003).

7   Fox's *24*, the great TV beneficiary of 9/11, having begun its run less than two months after the Trade Center fell, continued its War on Terror through the 2010 season.

NEW YORK, MAY 10, 2006

The movies love mayhem, and inevitably, the televised events of 9/11 were experienced by millions as a sort of real-life disaster film. Is a movie about 9/11 then a disaster movie about a disaster movie?

Oliver Stone's upcoming *World Trade Center* is in some sense a remake of the 1974 *Towering Inferno*; Paul Greengrass's *United 93* could be construed as a revisionist sequel to the '70s *Airport* series. One may be mega- and the other meta-, but both take their disasters extremely seriously. *World Trade Center* will likely be promoted as the most significant event in American history since *JFK*; *United 93* is already the first movie since *The Passion of the Christ* to position itself as something other than entertainment.

Long ago, Susan Sontag wrote that only in the movies could one "participate in the fantasy of living through one's own death and more, the death of cities, the destruction of humanity itself." Yes, and what's more, enjoy it! The old-school disaster movies that glutted theaters during the run-up to the millennium eschewed all but the most perfunctory human interest in F/X spectacles of wholesale urban destruction. *Armageddon, Deep Impact*, and *Godzilla*—three of 1998's top-grossing movies behind *Titanic*—featured the destruction of New York City. Magical thinking perhaps, but on September 11, 2001, Hollywood felt implicated. Was Al Qaeda guilty of intellectual piracy? Within days, studios and studio execs were recalling, recutting, and canceling movies.

The summer of 2004 brought a new sort of disaster film—one with pretensions to responsibility. In old-school disaster films, nature was the terrorist. And while greedy, mendacious, or foolish individuals might be at fault, the system was essentially sound and sufficiently internalized to allow a natural leader to emerge from the chaos, often in uniform. *The Day After Tomorrow*, however, clumsily inserted itself into the presidential election by transparently blaming the Bush administration for the threat of global climate change.

A few months later, the puppet animation *Team America* satirized the whole notion of the new socially responsible disaster film, but last summer Steven Spielberg gave the mode its first real hit: *War of the Worlds* deliberately evoked the trauma of 9/11, complete with political allegory in which a deadbeat dad becomes a heroic solid citizen. The movie was not meant to be seen so much as experienced—or rather, since it re-imagined the recent past, re-experienced. (The summer's other great disaster show, Hurricane Katrina, reflected less well on the nation's leadership—as did the recent TV movie *Fatal Contact*, remaking *The Birds* in the light of avian flu.)

Poseidon, which occupied the 'plexes last weekend, is an old-fashioned disaster flick, and not only because it remakes the 1972 *Poseidon Adventure*. *Poseidon* is pure showbiz and all business: the audience doesn't have to wait for the catastrophe. The movie is total action, predicated on the beauty of mayhem and the suspense of survival. Hundreds of extras may "die" for our amusement, but who cares? In lit-crit terms, *Poseidon* is a comedy—ending with the construction of two marriageable young couples. Yet the shadow of 9/11 is not altogether absent. The classic Vietnam- and Watergate-inflected disaster films of the early '70s showed heroism under stress practiced by nearly everyone except top public officials; *Poseidon*'s principals include an ex-mayor of New York.

United 93 resembles an old-school disaster film in that it has been constructed as an Event everyone must see to fully participate in American life. But unlike *Airport* or *Poseidon*, *United 93* is not much fun—if anything, it is a ritual ordeal. Although time will tell how the movie will play overseas, it's possible that the enjoyment demographic is strictly Al Qaeda. Zacarias Moussaoui was reported to have "smiled broadly" when the Flight 93 tape was played during his trial twelve days before Paul Greengrass's film had its world premiere on the opening night of the 2006 Tribeca Film Festival.[8]

Why was *United 93* made, and why should people want to experience it? Is the movie a commercial enterprise, a form of knowledge, a sort of group therapy? Thanks to Greengrass's brilliant direction, *United 93* looks and sounds like a documentary—but it is a dramatic reconstruction. Despite the existent phone calls and flight recording, there can be no absolute certainty of what happened during the flight. The fatal stabbing of the plane's captain and co-pilot, as well as a first-class passenger and one flight attendant, can only be surmised—and yet are witnessed by those who see the movie.

---

8 The Tribeca Film Festival had a long-standing connection to 9/11, having been founded in early 2002 by Robert De Niro and producer Jane Rosenthal, with the announced purpose of restoring morale (and business) to the residential neighborhood closest to Ground Zero.

Since the ending is known, *United 93* substitutes anxiety for suspense. Perhaps twice as much screen time is devoted to the FAA and air force command centers as to the plane itself. Is the system working? "We're trying to get the military involved—we're not getting an answer," beleaguered air traffic controllers cry. The military, for its part, can't find the president or vice president. (The spectator may insert a mental cutaway to Bush in Florida, reading *The Pet Goat*.) Greengrass forestalls the disaster, wringing maximum tension from the viewer's foreknowledge that the passengers are doomed.[9]

Considering how frequently the actual Flight 93 was invoked by Bush in late 2001 and throughout 2002, a White House screening for *United 93* has been conspicuously absent. Still, the movie did secure an early, enthusiastic endorsement from Rush Limbaugh. The talk show star characterized *United 93* as "inspirational" while calling for the sort of leadership shown aboard the flight and describing his own experience of watching the movie: "The overwhelming emotion I had was sheer anger at the terrorists, bordering on hatred …"

Rage strengthened Limbaugh's resolve: "This movie is going to refocus, for those who see it, the exact reason we are in the war on terror." (It's worth noting that Limbaugh almost certainly saw the movie with its original end title, "America's war on terror had begun." Before release, this Pavlovian cue was removed.) Nor was that the only political conclusion that Limbaugh drew. Recognizing Bush's association with Flight 93, Limbaugh attempted to inoculate the

---

9   As *War of the Worlds* was both reviled and praised for exploiting 9/11, *United 93* was said to be said—by whom?—to have been made "too soon." But how could the movie be too soon, when the story itself was twice dramatized that season on TV? Discovery Channel's *The Flight That Fought Back* annotated reenactments with interviewed family members; a few months later the docudrama *Flight 93* attracted 6 million viewers, the most-watched program in A&E history.

Less immediate and more intimate than *United 93*, *Flight 93* was specifically designed for home viewing: At the heart of the movie are the agonizing phone conversations between the passengers and their distraught families, most of them located in beautiful suburban neighborhoods. Although not nearly as artful or coherent as *United 93*, *Flight 93* received generally respectful reviews and was praised by the conservative *National Review* as a metaphor for the War on Terror: "The bad guys wield box cutters, invoke the name of Allah, and kill people; the Americans vote, say the Lord's Prayer, and fight back." The movie was not only appreciated for its Realness but its politics.

president by predicting that only the craziest lefties would use *United 93* to scapegoat him.

Throughout the spring of 2002, as the first saber-rattling over invading Iraq began, Bush repeatedly cited the heroic sacrifice of the Flight 93 passengers. "They realized that the hijacked plane they were on was going to be used to kill. And they decided to serve something greater than themselves. In this case, they served their country. They said a prayer, they told their loved ones they loved them, and they drove a plane into the ground." Flight 93 was thus recuperated as a glorious defeat, like the Alamo or the Battle of Bataan.

But Greengrass's interpretation of events is secular. He promotes official incompetence over conspiracy, shows hijackers and passengers addressing their God, and eschews nationalist appeals. *United 93* even tends to collectivize heroism—a sore point for certain families who maintain that some passengers were more heroic than others. Even the line "Let's roll," first used by Bush as a rallying cry two months after 9/11, is barely heard—and may refer to the use of a serving cart as a battering ram.

United 93 suggests that, rather than patriotic self-sacrifice, the desperate passengers were motivated by self-preservation. They storm the cockpit preparing to take control and land the plane. Flight tapes indicate that the hijackers deliberately crashed the plane before the passengers could breach the cockpit. Bush's scenario—"they said a prayer" and "drove the plane into the ground to serve something greater than themselves"—actually more closely describes the terrorists.

As a commercial moviemaker, rather than a historian, Greengrass had his primary contract with the audience. The ordeal must provide catharsis, and the one *United 93* offers is far more primal than Bush's Flight 93 rhetoric: in the gospel according to Greengrass, the passengers not only enter the cockpit but actually appear to kill the hijackers.[10]

---

10   This thrilling finale is underscored with martial drumbeats. (As master manipulator Alfred Hitchcock demonstrated in *The Birds*, the absence of music would have been enormously disconcerting—let alone the unresolved non-ending Hitchcock gave his absurdist disaster film.) Still, audiences were not eager to experience *United 93*; for all its critical accolades and awards, the movie grossed only $31 million in the US (even less than *Children of Men*) and barely qualified as one of the year's hundred top-grossing movies.

And then there was Oliver Stone's long-awaited, much-hyped, programmatically apolitical statement.

NEW YORK, AUGUST 2, 2006

Oliver Stone's *World Trade Center* lands today—its title as emphatic and its subject as world-historical as any movie since Stone weighed in with *JFK*. The surprising thing about this commission job, directed from Andrea Berloff's script, is not its factuality but its restraint.

Master of the sledgehammer, Stone spent millions of Paramount dollars recreating the post-9/11 "pile" on a back-lot Ground Zero. Still, *World Trade Center's* most impressive effect is its delicate editing. The epoch-defining disaster is rendered in shorthand—the shadow of a plane, the thud of the impact—and largely mediated by TV. For the most part, Stone favors discreet cutaways and meaningful blackouts. He's a good soldier.

So are his protagonists. Twenty years a Port Authority cop, John McLoughlin (Nicolas Cage) rises at 3:29 a.m., squeezes past sleeping wife Donna (Maria Bello), checks their slumbering brood, and heads to work, the car radio providentially blasting "sun comin' up on New York City." As he arrives at the Port Authority Bus Terminal, younger officer Will Jimeno (Michael Peña)—soon his buddy in horror—threads through the heedless crowd of Ratso Rizzos and Travis Bickles. Their daily briefing has a military quality; when news arrives that a plane has struck the WTC, John and company head for the war zone. It's their duty: "We're going downtown."

The ghastly doomsday vision is slightly sweetened with CGI. Only one person is glimpsed leaping from ninety stories up. In the most startling image, John and Will—who have volunteered to evacuate trapped office workers—watch the collapse of the second tower from the lobby of the first one, a roiling tidal wave of ash and debris. As befits a new-style disaster film, spectacle is subsumed in subjective experience—in this case, being buried alive.[11]

---

11   A. O. Scott's review noted another instance of subjectivity: "The film's astonishingly faithful re-creation of the emotional reality of the day produces a curious kind of nostalgia … [*World Trade Center*] offers both a harrowing return to a singular, disastrous episode of the recent past and a refuge from

Pinned beneath twenty feet of rubble, the two cops might be coal miners in a caved-in shaft. (Cage's character is physically constrained; like his director, the actor is effectively subdued.) But *World Trade Center* draws heavily on Stone's wartime experience—as well as Hollywood war movie conventions. The guys cite *G.I. Jane*: "Pain is your friend." Not just the WTC but battlefield and home front have collapsed. These casualties are devoted family men who share their situation with wives waiting at home for a uniformed messenger of death. Bello is a study in controlled anguish while Maggie Gyllenhaal's pregnant Allison Jimeno is all elbows, rushing headlong in and out of her New Jersey frame house.

Stone has dutifully repeated his studio-given mantra that *World Trade Center* is "not a political movie." (As if that were possible: Even the musical cues suggest the mawkish piano doodling that's been a campaign ad staple since Reagan ran for re-election.) But once Stone uncorks a virtual crane shot up from the pile to a communications satellite and then the Whole World Watching, a context unavoidably appears. The first responder is a heroic George W. Bush, followed by a Sheboygan police officer excoriating the "bastards," and then another guy exclaiming, "This country's at war!" Somewhere in Connecticut, an ex-Marine who likes to be called Staff Sergeant (Michael Shannon) gets the heavenly call and marches to the rescue: "God made a curtain with the smoke to shield us from what we're not yet ready to see," he says as he approaches the Pile.[12]

What hath Oliver wrought? For the hard right, Stone is the most hated "Hollywood liberal" post-Jane Fonda and pre-Michael Moore. But *World Trade Center* is Stone's rehabilitation. It's not just courage that's honored, it's God's Will. It isn't only men who are saved, it's their families—and their family values. Raised from the dead, John pays Donna the ultimate tribute: "You kept me alive."

The key to converting disaster into entertainment is uplift. You may not be convinced by the suggestions of divine intervention—Stone

---

the ugly, depressing realities of its aftermath" ("Pinned Under the Weight of Shattered Towers, and 9/11 History," *New York Times*, 8/9/2006).

12 Stone characterized *World Trade Center* as a memorial, but it was also a simulation. Perhaps the most amazing thing about the movie was its set which recreated the iconic WTC wreckage (as well as a portion of the underground shopping concourse, complete with vintage 2001 handbags, clothing, and shoes on display) in and around the Marina del Rey airplane hangar where Howard Hughes built his ill-fated Spruce Goose. (David M. Halbfinger, "A Ground Zero Grows in Los Angeles," *New York Times*, 12/12/2005.)

doesn't seem to have been—but then *World Trade Center* obeys a more crucial show business commandment. By focusing on two of the twenty people pulled alive from the pile that crushed some 2,700, the movie employs the *Schindler's List* strategy: Spectators can invest their emotions in the handful of individuals miraculously chosen to survive the disaster rather than the overwhelming anonymous multitude who perished.

"It brought out the goodness," a voiceover concludes. It is inspiring that John and Will headed into the WTC; it is heartwarming that Staff Sergeant searched for them. Last seen, he's looking ahead to his next mission: "They're going to need someone out there to avenge this." Is it possible to conceive of 9/11 as anything other than the narrative put forth by George W. Bush? Stone's end title notes that Staff Sergeant subsequently served two tours in Iraq. Who will extricate our brave soldiers from the rubble of that disaster?[13]

The Toronto Film Festival marked the fifth anniversary of 9/11, an event which rocked the 2001 festival, with the North American premiere of *Death of a President*, described by festival co-director Noah Cowen as "the most dangerous and breathtakingly original film I have encountered this year" and coyly listed in the festival catalogue as *D.O.A.P.*

---

13   Even more than *United 93*, *World Trade Center* was adopted by the conservative media, praised in advance of its release by rightwing media watchdog L. Brent Bozell ("a masterpiece"), the *National Review* ("God bless Oliver Stone"), and syndicated evangelical Christian columnist Cal Thomas ("one of the greatest pro-American, pro-family, pro-faith, pro-male, flag-waving, God Bless America films you will ever see"). In addition Paramount engaged the publicity firm Creative Response Concepts, involved in numerous right-wing causes, most famously advising the group Swift Boat Veterans for Truth which successfully tarnished candidate John Kerry's war record during the 2004 campaign. (See David M. Halbfinger, "Odd Bedfellows Align to Market Film About 9/11," *New York Times*, 7/27/2006.) For all its good press, *World Trade Center* failed to get a single Oscar nomination—not even for art direction—and grossed a relatively modest $70.3 million.

TORONTO, SEPTEMBER 11, 2006

Manufactured history guarantees a manufactured controversy: Gabriel Range's *Death of a President*, which docu-dramatizes the 2007 assassination of George W. Bush, has been preceded by a long, raucous fanfare.

Excoriated on talk radio, damned as a snuff film, banned by two theater chains, the British production has also garnered celebrity disendorsements. It was criticized unseen by assassination movie veteran Kevin Costner ("We can't, like, wish …") and denounced (also unseen) by Senator Hillary Clinton: "That anyone would even attempt to profit on such a horrible scenario makes me sick."

Is *Death of a President* more exploitative than *JFK*? (That was a snuff film.) And didn't Fox turn a buck on *Independence Day*, which jovially incinerated the White House when Mrs. Clinton was actually living there? The difference is *lése majesté*: *Death of a President* presents the "real" Bush in a fictional situation. (It's the opposite of the egregious telefilm *DC 9/11: Time of Crisis*, which featured a fictional Bush.)

Dramatically inert but a minor techno-miracle, Range's movie is a faux documentary with fake talking heads and seamless digital effects. Invented characters are gumped into actual news events and vice versa. The editing and audio sleight-of-hand are nearly as impressive. Range, who previously "documented" the collapse of British transport, used actual Chicago street protests to provide the illusion of crowds breaking police barriers to mob the presidential limo. But that's not the money shot. The assassination occurs when, leaving the Sheraton, supposedly surrounded by 12,000 flag-burning demonstrators, the president elects to work the rope line.

Death of a President's method and location recall Haskell Wexler's *Medium Cool*, which staged a fictional story against the chaotic backdrop of the 1968 Democratic convention. But Range skews more theoretical than sensationalist—and if he's celebratory, it's not in the way Rush Limbaugh imagines. Bush is presented as a martyr. (Appropriately, the movie is distributed by the company that released *The Passion of the Christ*.) Range may be overcompensating, but he has the slain president praised throughout by adoring staffers and mealy-mouthed acolytes; even at the hospital, a functionary tells the press the chief surgeon has "never seen such a strong heart in a man of the president's age." The obvious reference is Ronald Reagan. If the attempt on Reagan's life offers Range a dramatic template, the mass amnesia occasioned by Reagan's funeral is far more crucial—and not just because it provides Dick Cheney's eulogy. Bush is but a special effect. *Death of a President* is really a movie about 9/11—an essay on a national tragedy used to create an even greater tragedy. (That's the scenario that really should have made Senator Clinton "sick.") It's also a movie about itself—a demonstration of reality shaped to fit a particular hypothesis. There doesn't seem to be any irony there. Range saves that for the investigation. The system is flooded with detainees while, in the matter of suspects, use value trumps truth. President Cheney suggests that his security adviser "take another look" at Syria. The infinite elasticity of "national security" enables a new Patriot Act to trample the Bill of Rights. But *Death of a President*'s warning about blowback has its own unintended consequences: What follows the assassination is so awful that anyone might be excused for leaving the theater convinced of the urgent need to keep Bush alive.

The world was awash in *cinéma vérité* forty years ago, when British maverick Peter Watkins more or less invented the faux documentary with *The War Game*. He's been refining the form ever since, but *Death of a President* has nowhere near Watkins's agitational fervor. (Or his critical intelligence: Even if you believe that Bush is the worst president in history, it matters not whether he is impeached, falls from his bicycle, or gets raptured up to heaven—the damage has been done.) *Death of a President* is ultimately just an exercise. A far more subversive political mockumentary premiered in Toronto is coming. I invite President Bush, Senator Clinton, and all politicians to get down with *Borat*.[14]

NEW YORK, NOVEMBER 1, 2006

Borat: Cultural Learnings of America for Make Benefit Glorious Nation of Kazakhstan is funnier than its malapropic title—the Toronto Film

---

14   *Death of a President* was a sensation in Toronto, where it won the International Critics (FIPRESCI) Prize and one local critic called it "an incredibly realistic political thriller," compared it to Peter Watkins's *The War Game* and Costa-Gavras's *Z*, and recommended it be seen by "every thinking person" (Peter Howell, "DOAP terrifies with realism," *Toronto Star*, 9/11/2006). It fared less well in the US.

Festival audience with whom I saw the movie wasn't laughing so much as howling—and even more difficult to parse.[15]

Eyes wide, face fixed in an avid grin, Sacha Baron Cohen's ersatz Kazakh TV reporter, the ineffably oafish Borat Sagdiyev, goes looking for America. It's a documentary of sorts. The road trip—he's afraid to fly "in case the Jews repeated their attack of 9/11"—takes him from New York to Los Angeles (where he hopes to bag va-va-voom gal Pamela Anderson) by way of Mississippi, and well beyond the boundaries of taste.

America, the "greatest country in the world" per Borat, first appears as a subway car, where the friendly Kazakh introduces himself to passengers and, as is his custom, attempts to double-kiss the men. Predictable agitation is trumped when Borat's cheap suitcase drops open to release a live chicken.

The alert viewer may glimpse director Larry Charles among the startled commuters, but by and large, Baron Cohen's lumpen performance art—replete with all manner of public display and daredevil idiocy—is skilled at concealing its tracks. In the most spectacular example, Borat's bedroom tussle with his heavyset "Kazakh" producer (Ken Davitian), caught masturbating with a picture of Pamela, escalates into a naked chase down the hotel elevator, through the lobby, and into a banquet of the local mortgage brokers' association.

Not simply a jackass, Borat (like Baron Cohen's earlier creation Ali G) specializes in one-on-ones with unwary professionals, snared by

---

15   The screening was an event in itself. A near-hysterical line ringed the downtown Ryerson University campus for the midnight world premiere of this candid-camera US journey. Desperate fans jostled TV crews—or were they plants, offering $150 a ticket?—as Borat made his grand entrance escorted by a horse. Twenty minutes into the movie, shortly after friendly Borat begins kissing strange men on the New York City subway, the projector broke down and the screening became theater: The immigrant projectionist apologized onstage as Borat materialized to praise the "minor nation" of Canada ("our countries are very similar and not only because of the projector system"), and Michael Moore erupted out of the audience to offer his services. The screening was canceled, but the next day's makeup presentation afforded a wonderful festival coincidence: I dashed from Borat's climactic attempt to stuff Pamela Anderson into his "wedding sack" to an in-progress showing of *The Pervert's Guide to Cinema*—a continuation of Borat by other means—with wild and crazy Slovenian film theorist Slavoj Žižek holding forth for two and a half hours, in richly accented English, on the unconscious desires instilled by Hollywood movies.

their willingness to humor a hapless foreigner and desire to appear on (even Kazakh) TV. Stooges range from a self-identified humor consultant ("Do you ever laugh on people with retardation?" Borat wonders) to a car salesman (asked if the automobile is outfitted with a "pussy magnet") to a pair of pols, former Georgia representative Bob Barr and perennial Republican candidate Alan Keyes. What did they know—and when did they know it? Keyes realizes something before our eyes when, after a long, faux-naïve account of a Gay Pride rally, Borat says, "Are you telling me that the man who tried to put a rubber fist into my anus was a homosexual?"

How does Baron Cohen keep a straight face? If ever there was a movie that demanded a documentary devoted to its making, it's this one. (Press notes assert the filmmakers were reported as terrorists and trailed by the FBI.) That both Barr and Keyes are right-wing moralizers suggests something about the Baron Cohen agenda. It's hardly coincidental that the antique store he trashes specializes in Confederate memorabilia. Interviewing "veteran feminists" or Atlanta homies, Borat baffles them with his chauvinist stupidity. Picked up by a van of South Carolina frat boys or chatting with the owner of the Imperial Rodeo, however, he has alarmingly little difficulty getting them to articulate the idea of reinstituting slavery or making homosexuality a capital offense.

Baron Cohen gleefully involved the government of Kazakhstan in a campaign against Borat by showing up at the White House on the day President Bush hosted Kazakh president Nursultan Nazarbayev with an invitation, also extended to other "American dignitaries Mel Gibson and O. J. Simpson," to preview his new documentary. But his target isn't really an imaginary version of Nazarbayev's nation (nor its enemies, the "evil nitwits" of Uzbekistan whom he accused, while in Washington, of putting forth "disgusting fabrications" that Kazakhstan practiced religious tolerance and gender equality); it is rather the domain of the "great warlord Premier Bush," red states in particular. "I think the cultural differences are just vast," the Mississippi matron hosting Borat for dinner at her Magnolia Mansion (on Secession Drive) confides to the camera while her guest is away from the table. Those differences become unbridgeable when Borat returns with a stool sample, and then with the arrival of his indescribably inappropriate date, recruited from the back-page ads of the local alt-weekly.[16]

---

16   Correctly recognizing *Borat* as a political film, and characterizing it as

The movie's set piece has Borat—wearing an American-flag shirt and looking like Saddam Hussein plugged into the wall—entertain a Virginia rodeo with his Kazakh version of "The Star-Spangled Banner." Borat's introductory declaration of support for America's "war of terror" gets an ovation, his fervent wish that George Bush "drink the blood of every man, woman, and child in Iraq" a slightly less enthusiastic one. The crowd starts booing, however, when they hear him sing, "Kazakhstan is the great country in the world—all other countries are run by little girls." (Borat manages to complete this anthem; a report in *The Roanoke Times* suggests that Baron Cohen and his crew had to be hustled out of the place before they were lynched.)[17]

It's almost anticlimactic when Borat wanders into a Pentecostal church and, in the presence of a Mississippi congressman and justice of the state supreme court, is baptized in the spirit. "Does Jesus like me?" he cries, his impassioned babble lost in the mass glossolalia and the strident "Kazakh" fiddle music arising on the soundtrack. To what faith does Borat subscribe? It's an interesting, never answered question. At one point, he's told to shave off his mustache so that he doesn't look Muslim—"just Eye-talian." But there's no suggestion that Borat is Muslim; his only religion seems to be anti-Semitism.

"a triumph for truly pissed-off Americans," *The Nation's* critic Stuart Klawans noted, unique among commentators, that the movie appeared during the 2006 campaign and opened on the weekend preceding the election: "Moviegoers have clearly elected to go with the swift, the mobile, the riotously vulgar; and it doesn't surprise me that they made this choice just days before the general population voted (far less decisively) for change." Klawans further observes that *Borat* is a documentary that, rather than an imaginary Kazakhstan, is about an actual place that mirrors it—a place of "race-hatred, arms-dealing, seething hostility and unrestrained horniness," not to mention "religio-jingoism."

17   "If he had been out there a minute longer, I think somebody would have shot him," local television host Robynn Jaymes told reporter Laurence Hammack. "Had we not gotten them out of there, there would have been a riot," according to the rodeo producer Bobby Rowe, to which his wife Lenore added, "It's a wonder one of these cowboys didn't go out there and rope him up" ("Rodeo in Salem gets unexpected song rendition: A man purportedly from Kazakhstan launched into diatribe instead of 'The Star-Spangled Banner,'" *Roanoke Times*, 1/9/2005). After the election of Barack Obama, such tactics would be appropriated and instrumentalized by conservative activists—most successfully when an employee of the community organizing group ACORN was duped into offering aid to an outlandishly dressed pimp.

Borat is not just blatant but proselytizing; his statements precipitate the latent anti-Semitism around him. (The most outrageous example, not in the film, is the widely circulated TV bit, first broadcast over HBO on August 1, 2004, in which Borat incites the patrons of the Country West Dancing & Lounge in Tucson, Arizona, to join him in singing a Kazakh folk song, "Throw the Jew Down the Well.") Small wonder the Anti-Defamation League has expressed concern. The organization deemed it unfortunate that Borat is identified with an actual nation—as if the joke would work if Baron Cohen were passing himself off as a TV reporter from some imaginary Upper Slobovia—but that's a displacement. Their real anxiety is that by satirizing anti-Semitism, Borat will legitimize it.[18]

It's a measure of Baron Cohen's dexterity that he plants his alter ego on both sides of the Jewish Question. "Kazakhstan"—actually shot in Romania—is a nightmare Eastern Europe where peasants bunk with livestock, torment Gypsies, and stage a traditional "Running of the Jew," chasing giant-fanged puppets through their muddy village. But as a native of this barbaric shtetl, Borat is also a non-Christian other who—by

18   Several conservative commentators suggested that Baron Cohen was himself guilty of class or ethnic prejudice. John Tierney called the filmmaker a bully and apostle of "imperial liberalism," defined as "the pressure on third world countries to mandate Western notions of individual rights even when they conflict with local customs and family traditions," and a sneering "Cambridge-educated comic affecting moral superiority" ("The Running of the Yokels," *New York Times*, 11/11/2006). David Brooks concurred, adding that "We Jews know all about Borat's Jewish snobbery—based on the assumption that Middle America's acceptance of Jews must be a mirage, and that underneath every Rotarian there must be a Cossack about to unleash a continental pogrom" ("The Heyday of Snobbery," *New York Times*, 11/16/2005). Charles Krauthammer praised Brooks's analysis but thought it required elaboration: *Borat* and particularly Baron Cohen's 2004 Tucson performance, provided "an unintentionally revealing demonstration of the unfortunate attitude many liberal [sic] Jews have toward working-class American Christians, especially evangelicals" ("Just an Anti-Semitic Laugh? Hardly," *Washington Post*, 11/24/2006). In other words, the overeducated, snobbish, liberal Baron Cohen was himself making trouble for his fellow Jews. David Edelstein's review in *New York* magazine (11/6/2006) compared Baron Cohen's provocation to the "most notorious scenes" in Claude Lanzmann's *Shoah* in which the director uncovers a reflexive anti-Semitism among Poles who lived near the Nazi death camps, suggesting that Lanzmann's "gotcha journalism" provided a precedent for Baron Cohen's "riotous libel on Eastern Europe."

virtue of his primitive nature—ridicules the hypocrisy of the dominant social order.[19]

The ADL identifies Baron Cohen as an "observant" Jew. (I'm not sure what that means, but it seems less revealing than the subject of his Cambridge dissertation, namely the role of Jews in the American civil rights movement.) In any case, this comic has a distinctively Jewish sensibility. As sociologist John Murray Cuddihy notes in *The Ordeal of Civility*, his classic account of newly enlightened Jewish thinkers assimilated into the modern world, Marx, Freud, and Claude Lévi-Strauss were all similarly obsessed with "the raw, the coarse, the vulgar, the naked" and exposing the way in which these things were sublimated by the civil "niceness" of Western culture. So too, Borat (who might add the superstitious, the stupid, the sexist, and the xenophobic to that list).

Indeed, the man who invented Borat is a masterful improviser, brilliant comedian, courageous political satirist, and genuinely experimental film artist. Borat makes you laugh but Baron Cohen forces you to think.[20]

The 2006 campaign was largely dominated by public dissatisfaction with the war in Iraq—although YouTube brought down Senator George Allen, Republican of Virginia, who twice during the course of a campaign appearance on August 11, 2006, used the presumed racial slur "macaca" to address the tracker S. R. Sidarth, an Asian-American filming the event for Allen's Democratic opponent Jim Webb. Democrats would recapture Congress, regaining the Senate

---

19   Stuart Klawans's *Nation* review opens by placing Sasha Baron Cohen in the tradition of "another English comedian sporting curly hair and a funny mustache" (and, he might have added, one frequently mistaken for a Jew), Charles Chaplin, noting that Borat, like the Little Tramp, was both scurrilous and somehow lovable ("the audience instinctively warms to him and even wants to protect him, the most obscenely offensive movie character of our time"). He concludes by speculating that to understand public excitement about *Borat* ("their sense that Borat is doing something in the world") one should look to the "directness of Cohen's attack, and the deceptive simplicity of his method. These are Chaplin qualities" ("Coming to America!," *The Nation*, 12/4/2006).

20   *Borat* was barred from distribution in Jordan, Kuwait, Bahrain, Oman, and Qatar, as well as Russia, where it had been scheduled to open on November 30, 2006, and its denial of certification by the Federal Culture and Cinematography Agency represented the first such restriction, save for pornography, since the end of Soviet censorship. ("'Borat' Is Not Approved for Distribution in Russia," *New York Times*, 11/10/2006.)

after four years in the minority and winning control of the House of Representatives for the first time since 1994. Responding to the loss of his majority, President Bush announced the resignation of Defense Secretary Donald Rumsfeld.

A month later, Mel Gibson let the second sandal drop ...

NEW YORK, DECEMBER 6, 2006

Apocalypto has a faux Greek title and an opening quote from historian Will Durant that ruminates on the decline of imperial Rome. It may seem an odd way to comment on the supposed end of an imaginary, unspeakably barbaric Mayan civilization—but WWJD? Mel Gibson means to be universal.

Not just a walk in the park with Mel and the guys (in this case a large cast of mainly Mexican Indians speaking present-day Yucatec), this lavishly punishing picture is the third panel in Gibson's "Ordeal" triptych. *The Martyrdom of the Braveheart* and *The Passion of the Christ* have nothing on *The Misadventures of the Jaguar Paw*, junior citizen of a generally jovial, practical-joke-loving sixteenth-century Central American social unit. Given the absence of any identification, and with regard to their good looks and family values (that is, keeping pet monkeys and having babies), these noble savages might be called the Sugar Tit tribe.[21]

Over the course of *Apocalypto*'s 140 subtitled minutes, Jaguar Paw (American actor Rudy Youngblood) endures two calvaries. After the Sugar Tit village is overrun, sacked, and more or less crucified by a marauding group of "civilized" Mayans, JP is dragged through the jungle, carrying his cross (as well as his brothers) to the Temple of Doom. After he's saved from ritual sacrifice by a timely miracle—his Mayan captors are so degenerate they've forgotten the astronomy they invented—there's an hour of running barefoot, bleeding, back home to the *cenote* where he

---

21   In a widely reported incident on July 28, 2006, Gibson was stopped for speeding in Malibu, California, and subsequently charged with driving under the influence of alcohol. During the course of his arrest, Gibson became abusive—telling one police officer that "Fucking Jews [were] responsible for all the wars in the world" and calling a female sergeant "sugar tits"—and attempted to urinate on the station house floor. Gibson subsequently apologized and entered an out-patient addiction recovery program.

stashed his pregnant wife and child. JP dodges spears, vaults waterfalls, and slogs through quicksand. It's a nonstop sprint—complete with irate mama jaguar nipping at his keister.

Following the gory trail marked by *Braveheart* and *The Passion of the Christ*, *Apocalypto* is a blatantly sadistic spectacle—albeit not without a certain chivalry. Women are raped and children butchered but Mel shows no taste for such savagery. (You might even call him protective: in one feeble bid for a PG-13 rating, the surviving children of Sugar Tit village are left to fend for themselves in the charge of a teenage babysitter.) Mel is a glutton for male punishment. There's not a man in this movie who isn't scourged, bashed, or punctured—unless he's disemboweled.

Unlike its predecessors, however, *Apocalypto* is unburdened by nationalist or religious piety—it's pure, amoral sensationalism. By those standards, the most engaging sequence is played in the evil heart of the Mayan sacred city. Give the devil his due: Hieronymus Bosch or Matthias Grünewald would have appreciated Mel's vision of paganism run wild. The place is a monstrous construction site cum marketplace where life is cheap (and so are the extras), and the blood pours over the stone monuments like molasses on Grandma's griddle cakes. It's political too: gesturing muck-a-mucks in feathered masks rise from their human footstools atop garish temples to address the juju-dancing mob below.[22]

No mean panderer he, Gibson has compared the "fear-mongering" Mayan leadership to "President Bush and his guys" and their ritual human sacrifice to the deployment of US troops in Iraq. He may also be recycling material from his canceled miniseries. The spectacle of a village torched and its peaceful inhabitants rounded up and marched to a remote industrial complex run by slave labor under the heel of gratuitously cruel, fetish-bedecked warriors, there to be systematically mass murdered on the altar of some irrational ideology does suggest Poland circa 1944.

22   Writing in *The Guardian*, Dr. Giles Fraser, the vicar of Putney as well as a lecturer at Oxford, took me to task for characterizing *Apocalypto* as "pure, amoral sensationalism," and so giving Mel Gibson an alibi: "Unfortunately this film is yet another chapter in [Gibson's] none too healthy obsession with Judaism. For Mayan pyramids, read Jewish temple. Gibson knows that Jewish temple worship only involved animal sacrifice. None the less, his Mayan high priest draws from some of the worst caricatures of the bloodthirsty Jews invented during the middle ages." ("A Christian snuff movie that links blood with salvation," *Guardian*, 1/10/2007.)

There's no denying this holocaust—complete with vast corpse-disposal pit—or is there?[23] Maybe the Mayans really did bounce human heads down the steps of their pyramids but, being as their civilization collapsed hundreds of years before the Spanish conquest, how would we know? "A lot of it, story-wise, I just made up," Gibson confessed to the Mexican junketeers who visited his set last year. "And then, oddly, when I checked it out with historians and archaeologists and so forth, it's not that far [off]." Or far out, for that matter. Irrational as it may be, Mel's sense of history does have a logic: JP's trip to hell ends when the Christians arrive.[24]

NEW YORK, DECEMBER 11, 2006

History repeats itself: eleven Decembers ago, Universal had the season's strongest movie—a downbeat sci-fi flick freely adapted from a well-known source by a name director. With a bare minimum of advance screenings and a total absence of hype, the studio dumped it. This year, they've done it again.

The 1995 castoff was *12 Monkeys*, Terry Gilliam's remake of Chris Marker's *La Jetée*; this year's victim is *Children of Men*, Alfonso Cuarón's dank, hallucinated, shockingly immediate version of P. D. James's novel. Never mind that Cuarón saved the Harry Potter franchise and, with *Y Tu Mamá También*, directed the highest-grossing Spanish-language movie ever released in America (or that *Children of Men* was respectfully received at the Venice Film Festival and topped the British box office the

---

23   Gibson made the Bush analogy in an onset interview during which he also maintained that the project was inspired by his efforts to preserve parts of the Guatemalan rain forest: "The parallels between the environmental imbalance and corruption of values that doomed the Maya and what's happening to our own civilization are eerie." ("Exclusive: You'd think Mel Gibson was all done with violent movies about the past told in a foreign tongue, right? Think again," *Time*, March 27, 2006.)

24   Three days before *Apocalypto* opened, Sharon Waxman reported that, given the movie's early positive buzz, Oscar voters were confused as to whether the movie should be given award consideration. ("Praise for Gibson Film, Quandary for Oscar Voters," *New York Times*, 12/5/2006). The movie received three nominations (make-up, sound editing, and sound mixing), but no awards.

week that it opened), this superbly crafted action thriller is being treated like a communicable disease.

Ever sensitive to buzz, critics have gotten the message and are steering clear. When the New York Film Critics Circle met last week, *Children of Men* got only a handful of votes, mainly for Emmanuel Lubezki's sensational cinematography. Earlier this month, *The New York Times* imagined Academy members in surgical scrubs, with a "news analysis" noting the unusual goriness of the year's Oscar contenders: *The Departed, Flags of Our Fathers, Blood Diamond, Apocalypto,* and *The Last King of Scotland.* A more resonant and gripping movie than any of these, *Children of Men* wasn't even mentioned. [25]

This despite the vivid Fleet Street terror bombing that establishes London 2027, the jolting, bloody car chase—shot in what looks like a single take—that eliminates one of the stars, and the year's most brilliantly choreographed action sequence. *Children of Men* vaults into another dimension with one more long-shot tour de force as Clive Owen's protagonist dashes from a nightmare prison camp through an urban free-fire zone, cradling a newborn baby. (Not since John Woo's *Hard Boiled* has an infant been put in such egregious harm's way.)

With five screenwriters (Cuarón included), it's impossible to give credit for the intelligent path *Children of Men* takes through James's 1992 novel, preserving while enriching her allegorical premise. Humanity is facing its own extinction—not through nuclear proliferation or global warming, but the end of fertility. Like James's book, the movie opens with the violent death of the world's youngest person (eighteen-year-old "Baby Diego," stabbed by an irate fan in Buenos Aires) and imagines what might happen if the human race were granted a miraculous second chance. Universal may have deemed *Children of Men* too grim for Christmas, but it is premised on a reverence for life that some might term religious.

The year is 2027 but the mood is late 1940. "The world has collapsed," a BBC newsreader explains. "Only Britain soldiers on"—barely. The UK is a mecca for illegal immigrants, as well as a bastion of neo-fascist homeland security. London's smog-shrouded smear of garbage, graffiti, and motorcycle rickshaws is the shabbiest of havens. Armed cops are ubiquitous, and refugees—or "'fugees"—are locked up in curbside cages. Religious cultists parade through the streets. Terrorists and looters

---

25   *Children of Men* did wind up with three nominations, for best adapted screenplay, best film editing and best cinematography, if no awards.

control the despoiled landscape poignantly dotted with long-abandoned schools.

Enormously sympathetic, as always, Owen plays a wry and rumpled joker—less an actual character than a nexus of connections. His ex-wife (Julianne Moore) is an underground revolutionary; his buddy (Michael Caine) is a scene-stealing old hippie with a secret house in the woods. He has a well-off cousin in the government (Danny Huston) who lives in what looks like a South Bank power station amid recovered artworks, including Michelangelo's David (missing a leg) and Picasso's *Guernica*, and no longer worries about tomorrow. Owen's warmth is such that everyone trusts him, including animals and a mysterious young woman (Clare-Hope Ashitey) who needs to be smuggled through the countryside.

It's a measure of Cuarón's directorial chops that *Children of Men* functions equally well as fantasy and thriller. Like Spielberg's *War of the Worlds* and the Wachowski Brothers' *V for Vendetta* (and more consistently than either), the movie attempts to fuse contemporary life with pulp mythology. The war against terror and the battle in Iraq are most powerfully present in the aforementioned set piece where Owen escapes a nightmare Guantánamo into the exploding rubble of an incipient Fallujah. *Children of Men* doesn't entirely elude a sentimental tinge. (I've heard it called a disaster film for National Public Radio listeners.) But scenes that express the solace of solidarity or the fragility of human life are viscerally bleak, when not totally brutal.

Infertility is but a metaphor that enables *Children of Men* to entertain the possibility of No Future. The only parents these days who assume their children will inhabit a better world are either those living in the gated communities of the super-rich or the immigrants imported to tend their gardens. That these 'fugees are visualized as the persecuted rabble of a crumbling empire is only one of this movie's inconvenient truths.

CHAPTER THIRTEEN

2007: WHAT WAS IRAQ AND WHERE?

By the end of 2006, it was clear that for all the Hollywood hand-wringing that followed the Events of 9/11, cinematic mayhem would be the characteristic mode of Bush-era Hollywood. The war hadn't directly impinged on most American lives, but one didn't have to look too hard to find a most Baghdadian measure of blood and chaos at the multiplex.

Two rapturously received Oscar front-runners, Martin Scorsese's *The Departed* and Mel Gibson's *Apocalypto*, practically sprayed the audience with gore. Iraq itself was largely present in docs and quasi-docs (James Longley's *Iraq in Fragments*, Michael Winterbottom's *The Road to Guantánamo*), while the war was allegorized in Alfonso Cuarón's *Children of Men* and, if we are to believe its maker, *Apocalypto*. World War II was not yet played out: Clint Eastwood released a pair of combat epics, the disappointingly conventional *Flags of Our Fathers* and its far superior dark shadow, *Letters from Iwo Jima* (a movie that lacks only a measure of sardonic humor to rival Sam Fuller's down-and-dirty Korean War flicks).

Finally, some three and a half years after the Iraq War began, Hollywood considered the Iraq narrative.

NEW YORK, JANUARY 31, 2007

The Situation, Philip Haas's deftly paced, well-written, and brilliantly infuriating Iraq War thriller is not only the strongest of recent geopolitical hotspot flicks but one that has been designed for maximal agitation. Based on a script by the Anglo-American journalist Wendell Steavenson, this gutsy attempt to dramatize the way Iraqis live now is an incitement to rage and despair—the most vivid critique of Bush's War yet put on screen.[1]

An independent production, *The Situation* was frugally shot in and around Rabat, Morocco, with a largely Arab cast and one mid-level international star: Connie Nielsen, who plays the American correspondent Anna. Nominally a romantic triangle—Anna is casually involved with a friendly intelligence officer yet increasingly drawn to her Iraqi photographer—the movie is as bluntly existential as its title. It's structured as an interlocking series of mysteries inside one very large and intractable brain-twister. What in the world are we doing (or do we think we're doing) in this incomprehensible landscape and how in the world are we ever going to get out?

Haas opens by restaging an actual incident that occurred in the mainly Sunni city of Samarra in early 2004: a group of American soldiers detained a pair of teenage Iraqis out after curfew and wound up throwing them into the Tigris, drowning one. Although the case, which Anna reports on, only intermittently surfaces in *The Situation*'s narrative, its sink-or-swim horror sets the movie's tone and provides an ongoing metaphor. Iraq itself is a morass of moral equivalence; watching the various characters flounder in its treacherous currents, the spectator, too, may be overwhelmed by emotional turmoil.

The death of a hapless innocent is but one atrocious incident among all manner of abductions, bombings, raids, arrests, murders, and random brutality. Furious, uptight American occupiers contend with conspiratorial, inscrutable Iraqis—any of whom may be regarded or revealed as a potential terrorist—and the Iraqis must also contend with each other. "Civil war" is too clear-cut a term. One of the movie's points is that there's no word for Iraq's state of being: "It's the situation."

Initially didactic, Haas and Steavenson take pains to establish the

---

1 The first Hollywood movie to depict the Iraq War, Irwin Winkler's *Home of the Brave*, opened six weeks earlier on December 15, 2006.

territory's nonexistent ground rules. Given the absence of civil society and the bewildering nexus of tribal, religious, and geographic ties, petty warlords or neighborhood godfathers command more loyalty than any political entity. The cops are ex-criminals; the insurgents are gangbangers. Fear is a constant; the desire for protection trumps all. Moreover, everyone has a history: the photojournalist Zaid (Egypt-born, Germany-raised Mido Hamada) comes from a Christian family; Saddam Hussein executed his parents because they were Communists. And everyone has their reasons: a smooth ex-Baathist diplomat (Egyptian theater professor Mahmoud El Lozy) helps the Americans because he's desperate to get out of the country and won't ask the Kurds, who now run the ministry, for a job.

The Iraqis are a diverse lot. The Americans, who can't agree on the most basic principles, are closer to parody: "I'm a soldier, give me some shit to blow up," one cartoonish officer pleads. The Army is benign compared to the civilian leadership. Haas and Steavenson nail the imperial ineptitude of the neo-con know-it-alls who theorized (and continue to theorize) this war in blissful ignorance of the facts. A bow-tied Tucker Carlson type, newly arrived on the scene, suffers a friendly Iraqi official's attempt to provide some minimal guidance before cutting him off: "I have a master's in Oriental Studies." "Oh, is this the Orient?" the Iraqi politely replies.

The big picture is that there is no big picture. Hence the double-edged meaning to the CIA station chief's complaint, "We need better intel" (delivered beneath an outsize portrait of his commander in chief in full "What, me worry?" mode). Anna's pal and sometime lover Dan (Damian Lewis) is identified as the best of the Americans because he's able to use the phrase "hearts and minds" without irony. Trust is almost impossible to establish and vanishes in an instant. Investigations are never concluded. The truth, if it is the truth, turns out to be worse—and more idiotic—than we ever imagined.

The Situation, which is concerned mainly with the fate of ex-Baathists and Sunni insurgents, is seemingly set in 2004 (when Steavenson was a correspondent in Iraq for *Slate*). If anything, the current situation, with the full flowering of Shiite militia, is worse: We will soon mark the first anniversary of the Sunni bombing of Samarra's golden-domed al-Askari Mosque, the trigger for widespread Shiite rioting and reprisal killings, which is to say the ongoing cycle of sectarian violence.

That incident aside, there's a poetic logic to setting the movie largely in Samarra. John O'Hara's novel *Appointment in Samarra* may have nothing whatsoever to do with Iraq but it has everything to do with self-destruction—the title is taken from the fable of a man who flees from death in Baghdad to discover that he was fated to meet his end in the town where he sought refuge. We're all condemned to live with the consequences of Bush's war. *The Situation* makes apparent how pitifully unintended and irrevocable those consequences are.

Iraq has been the subject of several key documentaries. Each in its way, *The Control Room, Gunner Palace*, and *Iraq in Fragments* are crucial to the representation of the war. *The Situation* is the first fictional film of note to treat the conflict, and as such, it is filled with echoes of Vietnam (and Vietnam-era) movies. Haas's Baghdad certainly doesn't look like Saigon, but it has a sickeningly familiar feel. The Green Zone's swimming pools and Chinese restaurants recall the lavish pseudo-America of *Apocalypse Now*. (Indeed, Steavenson's knowingly noirish first-person reportage owes a bit to Michael Herr.) Anna's gravity seems a subliminal evocation of the concerned expression Jane Fonda adopted in the North Vietnamese photograph Jean-Luc Godard and Jean-Pierre Gorin had so much fun analyzing in *Letter to Jane*. And like the saintly Willem Dafoe's character in *Platoon*, Anna initially supports the war, but not now.

Anna, who only nominally reports, is more of a private eye. She becomes emotionally invested when one of her sources is killed, and is amazed when (paraphrasing a line from *Chinatown*) Dan tells her to forget it, "It's just Iraq." With blindingly blond hair often concealed by a headscarf, Anna functions as a beacon in the fog of war—less because of what she knows than what she is. If the lean, willowy Nielsen is distractingly beautiful, this is perhaps intentional. Haas, after all, is a cultivated man. He began as a maker of documentaries on artists and graduated to self-consciously rarefied, upper-middlebrow literary projects —fastidiously adapting the likes of Paul Auster, A. S. Byatt, and John Hawkes. (It hardly seems coincidental that he initially encountered Steavenson's war reporting in *Granta*.)

Haas has never shied away from symbolism, and where the versatile Nielsen is nearly convincing as Anna, she's sensational as the embodiment of an abstract idea. The movie's final moments make clear that this golden woman is the meaning of the war—the hope that the American invasion released from Pandora's box.

Nor was the glamorous Anna to be Hollywood's only female soldier.

NEW YORK, JUNE 12, 2007

A skilled actor vanishes into a role; a movie star appropriates it. As presence trumps character, so the star personifies Brecht's alienation effect, and whatever its ostensible subject, the movie becomes a vehicle—the latest installment in an ongoing career or, in the case of a great star, a public myth.

Angelina Jolie is the major alienation effect in *A Mighty Heart*, although she's not the only one. The hectic pizzazz with which hired gun Michael Winterbottom directs this tale of terrifying terrorism is another distraction—and so is the movie's true-life premise. An addendum to last year's 9/11 movies and a sequel of sorts to Winterbottom's *Road to Guantánamo*, *A Mighty Heart* is based on one of the most disturbing events of the 9/11 aftermath—namely the case of *Wall Street Journal* reporter Daniel Pearl, abducted by jihadi extremists in Karachi and, five weeks later, brutally executed on video, in part because he was a Jew.

A mondo-global, insanely urgent, staccato procedural in which each shot arrives like a bulletin, *A Mighty Heart* is characterized by sensational, quasi-documentary location work in swarming Karachi and a sense of near-constant frenzy. Pearl's briskly staged abduction sends the movie into controlled chaos. The crime triggers a dense montage of flashbacks and action cuts, accompanied by head-spinning techno-babble—a manhunt with a half-dozen agencies busily tracking e-mails and cellphone calls.

After his capture, Pearl (Dan Futterman) appears only in flashback—despite a few video teases, the movie resolutely refuses to show him in captivity. A tough Pakistani cop (Irfan Khan), wholly committed to the case and willing to torture prisoners when necessary, serves as a minor hero. But the heart of the movie, of course, is Pearl's wife Mariane (Jolie), seven months pregnant and compelled to endure the torments of the damned. Based on Mariane's memoir, the movie is true to her clear-headed politics, even while refracting them once more through the media's rainbow prism and the glamour baggage that its star necessarily brings.

Oscar notwithstanding, Jolie belongs less to Hollywood than the magic kingdom of publicity—in Cannes, where *A Mighty Heart* had its world premiere, she was referred to as the planet's most photographed woman. Google serves up 358,000 wildly clashing images. Over the past decade, her persona has mutated from tattooed Goth girl to possibly incestuous cyber-dish and *Esquire*'s "sexiest woman alive" to its current, suitably contradictory state—most fully expressed by Kate Kretz's five-by-seven oil painting "Blessed Art Thou," in which, posed as the Virgin Mary, a beatific Angelina and three cherubic children float on a cloud above a Wal-Mart check-out line. Jolie is Our Lady of Humanitarian Narcissism: not we but *she* "are the world," good deeds illuminating her divine person in a blinding blaze of glory.

A *Mighty Heart*, which was co-produced by Jolie's consort, Brad Pitt, is the celluloid equivalent of "Blessed Art Thou." Jolie's Pearl is an almost mystic presence; not since Lara Croft has the actress had so apposite an avatar. Jolie plays Mariane as an icon—her complexion darkened and hair tortured into a perfect mass of ringlets. Jolie as Mariane Pearl is not as extreme a notion as, for example, John Wayne playing Albert Schweitzer, or Jennifer Aniston in the role. As striking and preternaturally poised as she is, Mariane Pearl is herself a great performer—as demonstrated when she went on TV to argue for her husband's life.

No less than Jolie, the actual Mariane ascended the red carpet at Cannes; in the movie, her character is imagined as a star. Possessed of an iron will and a miraculous presence of mind, she's surrounded by an entourage yet awesomely solitary in her tragic isolation. When the worst inevitably occurs, no one is able to hug or even comfort her—she goes off alone. The movie is fundamentally a solo, and the creepiest thing about *A Mighty Heart* is the ease with which this terrible tale becomes a meditation on divadom. A limited actress but an overwhelming presence, Jolie cannily saves all emotional fireworks for her big scene.

Has Daniel Pearl been eclipsed? Blame Brecht. As Mariane, Jolie not only thinks faster but looks better than anyone else. Whatever happens, she's never less than gorgeous. There's hardly a moment when Jolie is on-screen that you can't sense the presence of make-up artists and hair stylists hovering anxiously just off frame.

A *Mighty Heart* had its US premiere as a benefit for the French organization Reporters Without Borders, an advocate for international press freedom. Most of the news was made by the star's insistence that prospective interviewers sign a document forbidding questions

on her personal relationships and stipulating that "the interview may only be used to promote the Picture. In no event may Interviewer or Media Outlet be entitled to run all or any portion of the interview in connection with any other story [or] used in a manner that is disparaging, demeaning or derogatory to Ms. Jolie."[2]

Several more ambivalent war movies coincided with the so-called Surge, Bush's new emphasis on the war in Iraq.

NEW YORK, SEPTEMBER 19, 2007

Concluding a month that brought the sixth commemoration of 9/11, a video missive from Osama bin Laden, and a surge endorsement by General David Petraeus, *The Kingdom* is a timely—if tepid—fantasy of American vengeance on the Qutbian extremists of Saudi Arabia.

Directed by Peter Berg from Matthew Michael Carnahan's screenplay, *The Kingdom* opens by analogizing the attack on the World Trade Center. A gang of Saudi terrorists orchestrate a Sunday-afternoon assault on an American compound in Riyadh—complete with stormed checkpoint, suicide bombers, and a massive, strategically delayed explosion. The grounds are littered with civilians, but the key casualty is a visiting FBI agent.

Cut to DC, where the incensed FBI would gladly invade Saudi Arabia were it not for the timidity of craven bureaucrats—mainly the US attorney general. (In this alternate universe, the attorney general panders to the Senate, not the president.) The most gung-ho of FBI agents is Jamie Foxx, a volatile woof-machine who intimidates a stray Saudi prince into signing off on an FBI mission to solve the crime. Actually, Foxx is the movie's surrogate president; in his softer moments, he comforts fatherless boys and effects twangy New Age reconciliation.

Leading the mission to Mars (the locations mix Arizona and Abu Dhabi), Foxx is accompanied by a demographically provocative trio. There's a hard-bodied, no-nonsense chick (Jennifer Garner), a wise-guy Jew (Jason Bateman), and a good-natured good ol' boy (Chris Cooper). Can you guess which of the three will be abducted and made the subject

---

2 According to the *New York Times*, most media outlets, including The Associated Press, refused to sign (Sharon Waxman, "A Deal Too Far: Interviewers Balk at Jolie's Terms," *New York Times*, 6/15/2007).

of a throat-slit video? And here's another puzzler: Are there any good Saudis—and, if so, who are they? By their appealing looks and appreciation of Foxx's street cred shall we know them: "America is not perfect, but we are good at this. Let us help you," Foxx pleads with the local chief of police (the Arab-Israeli actor Ashraf Barhom, who played a suicide bomber in *Paradise Now*).

Should terrorism, as John Kerry suggested, be handled as a crime? Halfway through the movie, the FBI agents go Marine. United in vengeance, the combined American and Saudi forces eventually eschew dull procedure for thrilling car-chase action, ending with a firefight in a very bad neighborhood. (Call it "Black Hawk downtown.") A hand-to-hand slamming-gouging-stabbing denouement got a mild rise out of the preview audience at the Loews 83rd Street, but the movie's main satisfaction is the utopian spectacle of wounded Americans heading home, mission accomplished.[3]

NEW YORK, OCTOBER 14, 2007

Acid flashback or déjà vu? Who, having lived through the late '60s, would have anticipated re-experiencing the spectacle of an arrogantly mendacious US administration bogged down in an ill-conceived, undeclared, bungled, costly, and apparently endless counterinsurgency? (Although who, familiar with American history, could doubt its recurrence?)

Iraq isn't Vietnam. Yet, pinned down in the Mesopotamian desert rather than an Indochinese jungle, US technological supremacy is confounded, with atrocious unintended consequences. It's not surprising that Viet-vet PTSD disability-compensation cases have doubled since George W. Bush declared our mission accomplished—or that, reading about American soldiers who raped a fourteen-year-old girl and murdered her family, Brian De Palma would feel compelled to remake his 1989 Viet-nightmare *Casualties of War* under the title *Redacted*.

Powerful, polarizing, and disturbing even in the context of the war's ongoing horror stories, *Redacted* was made in Jordan over eighteen days

---

3   Saudi Arabia has no movie theaters. *The Kingdom*, which had tested favorably with Muslim audiences in London, was banned in the neighboring states of Kuwait and Bahrain (Lawrence Van Gelder, "Two Gulf Nations Ban an American Film," *New York Times*, 10/12/2007).

for $5 million, and has a credibly sun-blasted look. De Palma, however, operates at one remove: "Welcome to the oven," Baghdad-based Private Angel "Sally" Salazar (Izzy Diaz) tells the presumed audience for the video journal he's keeping in hopes it will get him into film school. Much of the action is filtered through Sally's camera and tempered by his fatuous Godardian promise of "truth 24 times a second." Everything else is played out on an assortment of blogs, security cams, YouTube rants, Iraqi news reports, and jihadist websites.[4]

De Palma is consistent in this fractured multimedia methodology, as well as in his cinematic jouissance—at one point fabricating an arty French doc, replete with symphonic music and Wild Bunch homage, to show Sally and his unit administering a checkpoint. This "professional" movie enables De Palma to establish that of the 2,000 Iraqi civilians killed at coalition checkpoints, only 60 were ever ID'd as insurgents. (Those French will say anything …)

Redacted revives *Casualties'* sense of men sent on a senseless mission to a country they'll never understand and acknowledges the conditions under which American soldiers live. The paranoia is ultra-Nam, and so is the alienation. The central atrocity is set in motion when the unit's know-it-all sergeant is vaporized by a roadside bomb. But these young Americans are not the fiercely centered warriors of Gregory Burke's dramatic pageant *Black Watch*; they are crude, less-than-sympathetic constructions that De Palma has assembled from blogs, home videos, and embedded documentaries like *Gunner Palace*. The war is pitched somewhere between reality TV and *America's Funniest Home Videos*. Put on the spot by Sally's camera, his comrades reflexively recite official talking points: "We're looking for weapons of mass destruction" cues the central crime. Sally is likable, if amoral; when he's grotesquely punished, his sentimental buddies take over the doc. ("He was our very own Private Ryan," the worst of them muses.)

De Palma is no less a wise guy than he was when he made his Viet-era indies *Greetings* or *Hi, Mom!*, and *Redacted* is filled with sophomoric shock humor. An angry questioner at De Palma's New York Film Festival press conference accused him of making a "hipster horror film." *Redacted* is hardly that reductive, but it certainly reflects De Palma's career-long interest in voyeurism and violence, implicating spectator and filmmaker

---

4   In addition to protesting the War in Iraq, *Redacted* provided a cartoon critique of the new social-real.

alike. This all figured in *Casualties of War*, but there's a difference between making a movie about a war that's fifteen years over and one happening today.

Opening amid a momentary lull in public antipathy for Bush's war—attributable to an otherwise incompetent administration's sensational ability to repress images and control the story—*Redacted* has been variously attacked as arty, cartoonish, and even overly familiar. One might similarly characterize Fernando Botero's Abu Ghraib paintings; earlier this year, Philip Haas's noir analysis *The Situation* was dismissed in comparable terms.[5]

But whatever their temperaments, Botero, Haas, and De Palma are fashioning something other than propaganda. *Redacted* wasn't made to change your mind, but to unburden De Palma's. Tense, sometimes grating, and emotionally exhausting, the movie ends with a snapshot montage of actual atrocities committed against Iraqi civilians. These bloody images, which De Palma found on the internet, are set to the stately Handel sarabande that ends Kubrick's *Barry Lyndon*, providing an in-your-face coda of the sort used to far stronger effect in Lars von Trier's hitherto abstract *Dogville*.

De Palma's distributor Magnolia has redacted these photographs, using black bars to obscure the identity of the dead and brutalized Iraqis. The filmmaker has made no secret of his displeasure, but such censorship only reinforces his point that this war has been—from the outset—profoundly and continuously misrepresented. Indeed, the coda is unnecessary, even a distraction: The movie has already assaulted us by dramatizing the absence of oversight (and De Palma actually undercuts his insistence on the real by staging the final image). The most authentic thing about *Redacted* is the rage with which it was made.[6]

---

5 Botero's paintings were exhibited at New York's Marlborough Gallery in the fall of 2006. Arguing that Botero's images were able to establish "a visceral sense of identification with the victims" in a way that photographs were not, art critic Arthur Danto cited the emotional realness that enhanced photography allowed Mel Gibson in *The Passion of the Christ*: "Visual truth is sacrificed on the altar of feeling" (Arthur C. Danto, "The Body in Pain," *The Nation*, November 27, 2006).

6 De Palma's anger spilled out during the course of a post-screening press conference I moderated at the 2007 New York Film Festival. When the director explained that the film's final photographs were redacted because financial backer Mark Cuban found them disturbing, distributor Eamonn

Even as the additional manpower and financial resources poured into Iraq seemed to arrest the debacle and stabilize American public opinion, oil, fundamentalist religion, desert violence and capitalist development came together in what many found the movie of the year.

NEW YORK, DECEMBER 18, 2007

A great brooding thundercloud of a movie, Paul Thomas Anderson's *There Will Be Blood* arrives as if from nowhere on a gust of critical acclaim, lowering over a landscape of barren mesas and hot, scrubby hills.

Anderson's epic, no less than his career, is both fearfully grandiose and wonderfully eccentric. A strange and enthralling evocation of frontier capitalism and manifest destiny set at the dawn of the twentieth century, *There Will Be Blood* recounts the tale of a ferociously successful wildcat oil driller with the allegorical handle Daniel Plainview (Daniel Day-Lewis). The telling is leisurely and full of process: from the deliberately dark and fragmented prologue to the wildly excessive denouement, this movie continually defamiliarizes what might sound like a *Giant*-style potboiler.

A terrain of instant desert settlements, conical industrial installations, and scuttling motor vehicles, Anderson's central California (actually the same stretch of Bush country that served as backdrop for *No Country for Old Men*) suggests an alien planet—but then, that's pretty much what the American West was. Plainview is introduced as a solitary miner in 1898 who breaks his leg prospecting for gold and, crawling out of the shaft on his back, manages to stake his claim. Presently, this fantastically self-willed man is seen traveling the West with a small boy (Dillon Freasier), whom he introduces as his partner and son. Attempting to convince squabbling landowners to lease their property for oil exploration, Plainview presents himself as a progressive businessman who jovially proposes to improve—as well as enrich—the entire community.

Surely the most offbeat adaptation of an American novel in the decade since Terrence Malick treated James Jones's *The Thin Red Line* as

---

Bowles sprang to his feet in the audience and accused De Palma of spreading a mistruth. During the course of a heated back and forth, Bowles maintained that use of the images risked lawsuits from the GIs or the families, an argument De Palma dismissed as "specious."

a transcendentalist manifesto, *There Will Be Blood* is taken from Upton Sinclair's panoramic 1927 novel *Oil!* (Actually, it's a riff that draws on *Oil!*'s first few chapters.) Sinclair's not-inconsequential muckraker anticipates John Dos Passos's *U.S.A. Trilogy* in its scope—beginning with the California oil boom of the 1890s, it marches through World War I, the Russian Revolution, and the development of Hollywood to the Teapot Dome scandals of the Harding administration. The amiable oilman is already rich and fixed in his ways; Sinclair's protagonist is his sensitive young son.

Anderson narrows the novel's cast as well as its chronological focus, tunneling into Plainview's backstory. Nevertheless, *There Will Be Blood* is genuinely widescreen, both in its mise-en-scène and concern with American values—God, oil, family—that have hardly receded into the mist. This story of profits versus prophets could also be articulated as a death-struggle identification between the two. The narrative proper begins when a mysterious youth named Paul Sunday (Paul Dano) appears out of the night to tip Daniel off to an unexploited oil field on his family's land back in the hills. He then disappears from the movie—or rather he reappears in those hills as his twin brother Eli (also Dano), a precocious charismatic faith healer "sucking out" arthritis from an old lady's arm the way Daniel sucks black gold out of the earth.

Plainview also turns out to have a brother (played by Kevin O'Connor as Day-Lewis's weaker double) whose surprise appearance allows the oilman to elaborate on his harsh philosophy of life. Enunciating each line with the certainty of someone engraving his words in stone, Day-Lewis projects a fearsome intensity comparable to his performance in *Gangs of New York*—for most of the movie, however, it's mercifully tempered by an equally powerful restraint. Craggy features accentuated by a wide-brimmed hat, Plainview has the glittering eye of incipient madness; midway through, around the time that his boy is deafened by an oil-well explosion, his rotund, oratorical tone turns oracular. As though providing a flash-forward to subsequent California corruption, Day-Lewis begins channeling the overripe, ineffably sinister John Huston of *Chinatown*.

Nor is that Anderson's only film reference. Whereas the impudent director challenged Scorsese and Altman with his ensemble epics *Boogie Nights* and *Magnolia*, he here seems to have Orson Welles in his sights. No less than the archetypal tycoon Charles Foster Kane, Daniel

Plainview deserves to have his name followed by the epithet "American." Plainview is a visionary materialist and the loneliest of lone wolves, not to mention a self-invented entrepreneur and the very embodiment of D. H. Lawrence's formula for our essential national character: "hard, stoic and a killer." As apocalyptic as *There Will Be Blood* is, he's also a biblical figure, although ultimately more Nebuchadnezzar than Daniel.

The past few months have hardly lacked for audacious exercises in cine-hubris—*The Assassination of Jesse James, Southland Tales,* and *I'm Not There,* to name three excellent examples—but, as bizarre as it often is, *There Will Be Blood* is the one that packs the strongest movie-movie wallop. This is truly a work of symphonic aspirations and masterful execution. Anderson's superb filmmaking is complemented throughout by Radiohead guitarist Jonny Greenwood's excellent score—at once modernist and rhapsodic, full of discordant excitements, outer-space siren trills, and the rumble of distant thunder.

There's hardly a dull moment. Digs collapse, gushers burst into flame, God metes out punishment and so does man. Revelations overturn the narrative: the last twenty minutes are as shocking in their way as the plague that rains from the sky in *Magnolia's* finale. By the time the closing words "There Will Be Blood" appear (with a burst of Brahms) inscribed in heavy gothic letters on the screen, Anderson's movie has come to seem an Old Testament story of cosmic comeuppance and filicidal madness— American history glimpsed through the smoke and fire that the lightning left behind.

The annual *Village Voice* critics poll named *There Will Be Blood* the Best Movie of 2007; Anderson's startlingly original tale of prophets and profits in the American outback opened at the last moment to top the Coen brothers' *No Country for Old Men* and David Fincher's *Zodiac.* Made by highly self-motivated mavericks operating somewhere on the frontier between indie and studio filmmaking, all three were movies about natural born killers—American even if played by foreigners (Daniel Day Lewis and Javier Bardem), and charismatic too. The never-quite-identified Zodiac killer may be all the more charismatic because, as Fincher makes amply apparent, he's as much an obsession as a person.

Why the preoccupation with homicidal sociopaths? America had been at war for the past four and a half years—with, to cite the

top-polling documentary, *No End in Sight*. Nothing like war to make you ponder the definition of murder and wonder who is enabled to commit it.[7]

---

7 Other notable films featuring murderous protagonists were *The Assassination of Jesse James by the Coward Robert Ford*, *Before the Devil Knows You're Dead*, and *Sweeney Todd: The Demon Barber of Fleet Street*. Way, way down the list of favorites was the year's most significant fiction film about Iraq, Brian De Palma's *Redacted*.

CHAPTER FOURTEEN

2008: THE ELECTION

O ur election year began with a simulated terrorist attack, advertised only by its opening date 01.18.08 and rated PG-13 for
"violence, terror, disturbing images, sublimated 9/11 fears."

Cloverfield's cryptic, untitled trailers fueled considerable online
speculation as well as a box office bonanza. The first 2008 release
to gross $100 million, the movie combined *Blair Witch*'s subjective
camera with *War of the Worlds*' use of 9/11 imagery—more amateurish
than the former and campier than the latter. Key moments include the
crowd of people using their cell phones to document the head of the
Statue of Liberty being flung by the monster onto a lower Manhattan
street, and one of the protagonists taking a call on his cell mid-
Armageddon from his mother.

Skyscrapers tumble, bridges collapse, the amateur filmmaker
remains glued to his camcorder no matter what—it's his historical
mission as well as his life-raft—while providing a running commentary that only enhances the inexplicable nature of the catastrophe.
Thus *Cloverdale* dramatizes the irresistible force of the monster's pure,
mindless, irrational destruction against the immovable object of the
filmmaker's fascination, even as the aspect of a group ordeal (including the wildly visceral, if not tortuous, camerawork) to be endured by
the audience, connect *Cloverfield* to the new disaster film. Moreover,
from a film-historical point of view, *Cloverdale* appears as one of
the key movies of the post-9/11 decade—taking a world-historical

disaster as its subject, creating an animated movie from photographic material, attempting to represent the new social-real and emphasizing film (or at least, cinema) as an object.

Nor did the high-concept blockbuster *Cloverdale* offer the season's only evocation of national trauma ...

NEW YORK, JANUARY 22, 2008

He's back—unflagging, indestructible, super-colossal. Through this epoch-defining figure one might refract American history. John Updike had his Rabbit Angstrom and Philip Roth his Nathan Zuckerman, but who are they compared to John Rambo, woken from a twenty-year sleep in *Rambo*: "A Film," as the credits had it, "By Sylvester Stallone."

A veteran now in his sixties (as well as of them), Rambo has chosen to spend his retirement in deepest Thailand, dreamily fishing with a bow and arrow or capturing cobras for a backwater snake show. He's still wearing his trademark bandanna (over a wig hat, unless the still-luxuriant coiffure is a function of the HGH that the star has admitted using) but, more to the point, he remains unreconciled, still nursing that thousand-yard stare and schlepping a cargo of resentment. Rambo's first line of dialogue is the traditional "Fuck off!" delivered over-the-shoulder at his jabbering gook boss.

What crisis disturbed the creature's slumber and brought him back to life? Iraq, Iran, North Korea, Hugo Chávez? Somewhere in the Ramboverse, there'd been a chemical-weapon attack—it's the crisis in Burma! Accompanied by newsreels too grisly for the Human Rights Film Festival, Rambo explains that Christian farmers have been singled out for extermination, their rice paddies turned into killing fields. Rambo is approached by a church-sponsored group of idealistic American doctors looking for a way to enter Burma and save a bit of the world. Will he ferry them upriver? "Fuck the world," he tells the group's wimpy leader.

The expedition's lone woman tries to reason with the Rambot: "We're here to make a difference," she insists. "What is is what is," he explains Buddhistically. But when she remarks that he must have believed in something once, Rambo relents. Naturally, his worst fears about human nature are immediately confirmed once their boat is attacked by slavering river pirates who want nothing more than to kidnap and ravish the

White Woman. Rambo liquefies the scum. The Christians are appalled ("Taking a life is never right," the group leader whines), but the mission continues.

A sort of parody *Apocalypse Now*, complete with listless coochie dancers entertaining the Burmese troops, *Rambo* finds its own heart of darkness once Rambo drops the doctors in Burma. No sooner have they begun nursing the maimed and ministering to the mutilated when ka-BLAAAAM!!!!!! The local storm troopers attack, stabbing children, blowing up houses, massacring old people, and making off with the WW—the village left looking like Jonestown after the Kool-Aid.

Rambo has the feel of a terminal Vietnam flick. The absence of choppers hovering like angels overhead only reinforces the sense of abandonment in this green hell. Smeary black-and-white clips from *Rambo: First Blood Part II* establish historical perspective, such as it is, and function as the turgid nightmare from which the hero is trying to awake—and which is, in fact, interrupted by another pastor pleading with him to help rescue the captives. Strapping on his mega-Bowie knife and leading a band of screwball mercenaries into the jungle ("Live for nothing or die for something"), Rambo penetrates the storm trooper stronghold just as the rape orgy commences and initiates his own bloodbath. It's a reasonably entertaining spectacle replete with half-animated action sequences in which CGI bodies disintegrate like breakaway bottles.

After twenty years in remission, Rambo remains tough enough to rip out a guy's throat with one hand, smart enough to assemble something like a tactical nuclear device while galumphing through the underbrush with Burmese police dogs nipping at his keister, and noble enough to pose for Mount Rushmore. He finishes the job and, his curiosity whetted by the White Woman, goes home to "the world." But this is where, twenty-six years ago, *First Blood* began—can the Rambodyssey really be over?

At once cowboy and Indian, GI and VC, Rambo was arguably the great pop icon of the Vietnam War. Or rather, this puppy-eyed, Nautilus-built killing machine was the great pop icon of the decade-after Vietnam War revisionism that characterized the reign of Ronald Reagan. It's as though the ongoing political discourse, with some politicians claiming to be the new Reagan and others denying it, had conjured his reappearance: Rambo redux.

Back in 1982, *First Blood* gave the cliché of the psychotic Vietnam vet a novel twist. Driven to run amok in the Pacific Northwest, Stallone's sweet but implacable Green Beret was misunderstood and unappreciated. He was a victim not only of the war overseas but the one at home—another longhair vagrant persecuted by the pigs. *First Blood* was constructed to appeal to hawks and doves alike and, however schematic, struck a responsive chord. It was an unexpected hit, the movie that dethroned *ET* as the nation's No. 1 box-office attraction and gave Stallone his first real success outside the Rocky cycle, returning him to the charmed circle of bankable stars.

Three years later, *Rambo: First Blood Part II* provided Stallone the muscle to elbow aside Clint Eastwood at the top of the list. Sprung from the prison where his earlier rampage landed him, the Green Beret extraordinaire was recruited to parachute back into Nam on a thirty-six-hour mission to find and photograph 2,500 MIAs (who are actually POWs). Bucking orders, he leads them to freedom. The scenario effectively reworked the previous year's *Uncommon Valor* and *Missing in Action*, with a greater body count and more explicit meaning. "Sir, do we win this time?" Rambo plaintively asks his Green Beret guru. Affirmative to the max!

New morning in America: Rambo was the fetish rattle brandished by our national medicine man. During the movie's third boffo week, Hezbollah terrorists hijacked a TWA flight en route from Athens to Rome and forced the plane to land in Beirut, holding it there for seventeen days. (After one American hostage was killed, the hijackers released the rest—followed soon after, in an implicit quid pro quo, by Israel freeing a number of Shiite prisoners.) Asked how he would deal with terrorists in the future, Reagan promised to consult his oracle: "After seeing the movie *Rambo*, I'll know what to do the next time something like this happens." The master of fantasy merged with the fantasy of mastery— Ronbo. Meanwhile, a pumped-up Bruce Springsteen was hailed as the Rambo of Rock. The Vietna-malais was over. America stood at attention.

Released in the Reagan administration's final year, *Rambo III* was necessarily anticlimactic. Vietnam behind him, Rambo was available for commando work in Afghanistan, teaming with the mujahidin to rescue a captive from the Russian occupying army. (Having fought to make the world safe for bin Laden, sending Rambo back to wipe out the Taliban would seem the least Stallone could do for us.) In September 1990, Stallone was in his kinder, gentler bespectacled phase; the star declared he would never do a Rambo movie about Iraq's occupation of Kuwait.

That was minor, "just another speed-bump in history." Instead, his never-realized *Rambo IV* would focus on "environmental concerns."

How green was my beret. Reviewing *Rambo: First Blood Part II* in 1985, I noted that its protagonist was a symbolic reminder that the Vietnam War would never be behind us: "The bitterness and resentment of the men who fought and lost there is a political time bomb, to be activated anytime between now and 2001"—which then seemed to me like the end of time. It further seemed that the Vietnam issue had been buried with the 2004 election, in which a meretricious pair of draft-evading warmongers successfully slimed a genuine anti-war war hero. But I was wrong.

Promoting the new *Rambo*, Stallone entertained a *Time* interviewer by quoting an obscure bit of 1968 acid rock as his source of inspiration, but it was hardly coincidental that as part of *Rambo*'s eve-of-release PR blitz, the star used a Fox News morning show to make a political endorsement: "There's something about matching the character with the script," Stallone explained. "And right now, the script that's being written—and reality—is pretty brutal and pretty hard-edged, like a rough action film, and you need somebody who's been in that to deal with it." Who else but Senator John McCain? (To complete the love fest, as well as the script, McCain was already using the *Rocky* theme as entrance music.)

Hooray for Hollywood: Brian De Palma was hardly the only old New Lefty equating Iraq with Vietnam. But *Redacted* was "Vietnam: The Bummer." *Rambo* was something else. Stallone knew that if the Republicans nominated action-hero McCain, Vietnam might return—with bells on. And, back on the national agenda, the war would have to be won all over again—all the more if John-bo ran against Hillary for, while he was rotting in a tiger cage, she was out waving a Vietcong flag.[1]

As the renewed obsession with the late Ronald Reagan suggested, it was back to Fantasyland! The Democrats could consider themselves lucky that Governor Arnold Schwarzenegger was born in the Austrian zone of the former Third Reich. Meanwhile, McCain's rival, former Arkansas governor Mike Huckabee cast his suitably bargain-basement Reagan-era muscleman as the embodiment of homeland security: "My plan to secure the border? Two words: Chuck Norris." But as McCain suggested, his guy

---

1   McCain enjoyed his own dramatic comeback two and a half weeks before *Rambo* opened. Having placed fourth in the Iowa caucuses, the aging Vietnam veteran effectively returned from the politically dead to revive his candidacy.

could kick that has-been's butt—and anyway, homeland security begins over there.

Stolidly slaughtering thousands to complete a dubious mission bungled by Christian do-gooders and incompetent bureaucrats, Our Rambo once again freed the captives and redeemed the nation—not just a rerun but a great second chance, history rewritten. The answer to a Republican prayer, he was economical, too: a one-man surge.

The War in Iraq was distinguished by the presence of participant-chroniclers as seen first in *Gunner Palace* and fictionalized by *Redacted*, as well as two other movies from 2007, Paul Haggis's *In the Valley of Elah*, a thriller which involves recovering video data—evidence of torture—from a dead soldier's cell phone, and Nick Broomfield's *Battle for Haditha*, in which an instance of combat was restaged with actual US soldiers. If ordinary combatants were making movies of their experiences, documentary filmmakers were inspired to draw on their own in imagining the war as motion picture simulation.

REPRESENTING IRAQ: THREE AMERICAN DOCUMENTARIES[2]

Standard Operating Procedure caps Errol Morris's atrocity trilogy. *Mr. Death* (1999) offered a disturbingly facetious portrait of a "scientific" Holocaust denier; more sober, *The Fog of War* (2004) presented that old devil Robert McNamara with an all-too-human face, albeit allowing McNamara to put his own spin on his prosecution of the Vietnam War. *Standard Operating Procedure* addresses Iraq—specifically, the infamous photographs of abused prisoners at Abu Ghraib and the so-called bad apples who took them.

Morris doesn't use voiceover; he's a master at getting interviewees to pose certain questions on their own—like why did Abu Ghraib even exist? For one thing, this prison was where Saddam's minions murdered 30,000 Iraqis. For another, it was located in a combat zone—and under frequent mortar attack. Common sense, if not common decency, would

---

2   *Standard Operating Procedure* was reviewed in the April 23rd issue of the *Village Voice*; *Operation Filmmaker* in the June 4th issue; *Full Battle Rattle* in that of July 10th.

have suggested that the US level this nightmare. Instead, as Morris's interviewees attest, Rumsfeld and his generals elected to "Gitmo-ize" the operation, torturing and otherwise brutalizing prisoners they dumped there—thus converting Abu Ghraib from Baathist hell to international symbol of American occupation.

Standard Operating Procedure is all about symbols. The Abu Ghraib images are hardly unfamiliar; Morris's mission is to interrogate them. How did these pictures come into existence? And what, if anything, do they reveal?[3]

The snapshots and videos are mainly annotated by interviews with four of the seven bad apples, all former MPs, as well as letters home written by the most diligent of the amateur photographers, Sabrina Harman. What emerges from this testimony—which also goes a bit up the chain of command to include Janis Karpinski, the former brigadier general who supposedly oversaw Abu Ghraib, and who has since been demoted—is the suggestion that whatever the CIA was doing to extract dubious intelligence, the MPs were just entertaining themselves by producing their own show.[4]

Bored, ignorant, and afraid, the bad apples were simply having fun. The prisoner photographed naked on all fours with a dog collar around his neck wasn't actually dragged by the leash. The hooded guy standing

---

3   Or not: *Standard Operating Procedure* repeatedly makes clear that the photographs have been cropped, that some actors are off-camera, and the photographer's mise-en-scène is unknowable, and that this corresponds to the nature of the prison's powers that be. Moreover, photography creates its own standards of behavior—people naturally strike poses, clown or smile. The paradox is that Morris's camera and tape-recorder similarly serve to impose their own standards.

4   Speaking of Abu Ghraib in his book *The Virtual Life of Film*, David Rodowick suggests that these digital images are "the nephews of television rather than of print journalism." Given "the quantitative accumulation of images captured cheaply and at prodigious rates, the capacity for real-time monitoring and instant random access, and the possibility of instant editing and (re)transmission," the Abu Ghraib snapshots are closer to video than photography, and as such, are readily assimilated into convergence culture— "quickly copied, recontextualized as screen savers and calendar images ... shared and transmitted within the prison via CD-ROM and, subsequently, across the globe via the Internet" (Cambridge, Mass.: Harvard University Press, 2007, 145–47). In other words, while the legal evidence these images provide may be problematic, their evidence of a social network is undeniable.

on a box, wires attached to his outstretched hands, was never really in any danger. These pictures were posed! For Morris, who seems skeptical that photographs can ever disclose anything, the issue is legalistic. Focusing only on the photographic evidence, he asks if these images prove the commission of criminal acts or simply illustrate what one MP calls "standard operating procedure"—that is, the acceptable methods of stress positioning, sleep deprivation, and the ordering of inmates to masturbate while wearing nothing but panties on their heads.

If there's a moral distinction, I must be too dense to grasp its significance. In either case, these photographs demonstrate the fascist thrill of dominating a helpless fellow human—although Sabrina says that hers were an intended exposé of prison conditions. (As evidence, however, they only served to send the bad apples to jail, while their superiors and the system that created Abu Ghraib went largely unscathed.) But whether one interprets these images as proof of torture or sadism or artistic expression, they attest to the gross objectification of the prisoners (who are scarcely less objectified in this film). The MPs may have given these men names—that's Gus on the leash and good ol' Gilligan on the box— but they were used as living props.[5]

---

5   In its witless way, *Harold and Kumar Escape from Guantanamo Bay*, released in New York the same week as *Standard Operating Procedure*, is also founded on epistemological questions. As these two Asian-American stoners (John Cho and Kal Penn) are profiled throughout, so do they consistently profile others. As the resident voice of reason tells the comic villain, a Homeland Security goon who (literally) wipes his butt with the Bill of Rights: "It's people like you who make the world think Americans are stupid!"

Unfortunately, nothing in *Harold and Kumar Escape from Guantanamo Bay* is funnier than its title. A tiresome succession of scatological gags and rote dick jokes, this sequel to *Harold and Kumar Go to White Castle* starts promisingly with Kumar busted as a terrorist while attempting to assemble a "smokeless" bong in an airplane toilet. His buddy Harold is innocent but, profiled by Homeland Security as a two-dude axis of evil—"North Korea and Al Qaeda working together"—the pair is shipped off to Gitmo. Their actual incarceration may be brief, but it's fascinating to see that the filmmakers, Jon Hurwitz and Hayden Schlossberg, imagine the worst form of torture as sexual humiliation. It's a scenario that would have made perfect sense to Sabrina and the gang.

Escape from Guantanamo Bay is a largely mind-numbing experience, but if I hadn't sat through it before seeing *Standard Operating Procedure*, I don't think I'd have appreciated how much the Abu Ghraib photos owe to dumb-ass frat humor, stupid pet tricks, and YouTube gross-outs. Despite their aggressive bad

Credit where credit is due: By arranging Gilligan's mock crucifixion, Sabrina did create a poster boy for the Iraq War. For his part, Morris fusses with the frame. He literalizes ghosts haunting the prison corridors. He introduces Gilligan with a flash of lightning. When one of Sabrina's letters makes reference to an exploding helicopter, the filmmaker obligingly visualizes it; he accentuates her account of finding a corpse in the shower with a low-angle shot of water exploding in super-slow motion from the showerhead. A description of dogs attacking naked prisoners is supplemented with close-ups of slavering hounds. This obtrusive mannerism is not only superfluous but, for a movie that aspires to be a critique of representation, bizarrely self-defeating.

Does Morris fear that the faces, voices, and photographs he's assembled are insufficiently compelling to hold an audience? A vivid description of Fallujah's nauseating stink doesn't require Smell-O-Vision to register. Is he, like his subjects, compelled to amuse? Diverting attention from the banality of his inquiry? Fielding questions after a screening at the Museum of Modern Art, the filmmaker blurted out an observation on the strength of Janis Karpinski's bladder—a non sequitur less revealing of her anxiety than his. Indeed, this admission exposed Morris's standard operating procedure: Attention must be paid—if not to the film, then at least to its maker.[6]

Another fable for our reality-TV reality, Nina Davenport's *Operation Filmmaker* is as much virus as video documentary. This essentially comic tale maps a contagion of mutual exploitation that seems to have burnished the careers of everyone involved.

In 2004, MTV's *True Life* telecast a piece on young Iraqis that devoted a segment to Muthana Mohmed, a twenty-five-year-old Baghdad film student obsessed with the idea of going Hollywood. Among those who saw the episode was Liev Schreiber, then preparing to make his suitably serious directorial debut with an adaptation of Jonathan Safran Foer's

---

taste, Hurwitz and Schlossberg are too nice to introduce Harold and Kumar to Gus or Gilligan. Why so squeamish? After all, the prisoners dehumanized at Abu Ghraib have long since assumed their position in the moral shithole of Bush-era American culture.

6 The *Standard Operating Procedure* DVD, which offers the option of Morris's explanatory voiceover, is far more revealing than the theatrical release version.

Everything Is Illuminated. Operating in full humanist mode, Schreiber decided to give Muthana a break and hired him to work on his set. The actor also reasoned that this generous act should not go unrecorded: he contacted an MTV producer, who recommended Davenport—a Harvard classmate—to document Muthana's education.

Everything is illuminated, indeed. Muthana arrives on location in the Czech Republic; it's his first time outside Iraq, and his first time in the self-contained, self-absorbed world of a movie set. An intern—and yet a star, or at least a celebrity— he is put to work as an assistant gofer. Thus humiliated—and displaying an excellent command of colloquial English—Muthana has no qualms complaining to Davenport: "What the fuck?! The most important scene was rolling on the set while I was mixing the snacks!!"

The question that courses throughout *Operation Filmmaker* is: Whose needs trump whose? Schreiber imported Muthana to feel good about himself, while his production requires the kid to prepare vegan treats. Contracted to produce a documentary, Davenport is no less needy than her subject. She wants Muthana to just be himself, naïvely expressing his gratitude ("I love George Bush—he changed my life") and preju-dices (describing *Everything Is Illuminated*, which deals in part with the Holocaust, as "a movie defending the Jewish theory"). Meanwhile, someone on the project has sent cameras to Muthana's Baghdad friends. Their video letters urge him not to even think of venturing back to Iraq. Muthana appears stunned—somehow, the job he's been given editing the wrap-party gag reel seems … petty.

Understandably, Muthana wants to get a US visa, but since he doesn't know how, the *Everything Is Illuminated* producers (anxious to rid themselves of this ungrateful pest) conclude that he's a slacker and lacks initiative. Worse: is he really in danger, or is he just manipulating them? One producer actually tells Muthana to return to Baghdad, write a screenplay, and then call him in Hollywood. Later, the same producer will introduce the high-concept notion—embraced by Davenport as her ruling metaphor—that helping Muthana has turned out to be the boon-doggle equivalent of invading Iraq.

Davenport frequently shows herself giving her subject advice—suggesting, among other things, that he be more honest and "real" on camera. Muthana does take direction, albeit in his own way. Cast as a hustler, he necessarily becomes one—managing to extend his Czech visa and get a gig on the set of the sci-fi action flick *Doom*. Davenport (who continued to film Muthana in Prague) drolly cuts from footage of Iraqi carnage to a field of zombie corpses on the *Doom* set. Confusion breeds confusion. *Doom*'s star—Dwayne "The Rock" Johnson—thinks Muthana might be a hero, like himself, and in the movie's supreme gesture (self-interested or not?), makes it possible for the young exile to pursue his dream at some dubious professional academy in London: "You're going to film school, buddy!"

It's a chaotic situation and an appropriately chaotic film, filled with Davenport's anxious asides to the camera. But no one is more invested in Muthana than she, and he knows it. ("What's your next project—a guy from Afghanistan?" he sneers.) Caught in a quagmire, Davenport keeps giving Muthana money; he accuses her of making a documentary designed to demonstrate American goodness and Iraqi weakness, then demands an additional $10,000 or he'll quit her project. (He even holds footage for ransom.) It's at this point in their mutual guilt-tripping that Davenport presents the televised image of George W. Bush promising to "stay the course."

Whereas she had originally hoped for a happy ending, Davenport tells us, she's now looking for an exit strategy. From her perspective, *Operation Filmmaker* is both. Aggravating as her experience may have been, the filmmaker has managed to have her cake and eat it, too. As a teacher at the New York Film Academy tells her, straight-faced, after viewing a video monologue submitted by the desperate Muthana: "He's very, very castable in today's market." *Operation Filmmaker* proves it.

The nature of Muthana's authenticity is the subject of *Full Battle Rattle* which documents a self-described reality TV show starring Iraqi refugees. The Iraqis are actors but, unlike those in *Standard Operating Procedure*, those in *Operation Filmmaker* and *Full Battle Rattle* have voices.

Full Battle Rattle, a combat doc once removed from combat and twice mediated by stagecraft, depicts simulated war in a theme-park reality. Part scripted, part improvised, the doings on a back-lot battlefield are experienced as the real thing—whether actual war movie or actual war. As suggested by its title (Army slang for fifty pounds of protective gear), *Full Battle Rattle* is a costume film. The set is a facsimile Iraqi village, somewhere (along with a dozen other such villages) in the National Training Center, a 1,000-square-mile chunk of the Mojave (location for countless Westerns and sci-fi films), inhabited by some 1,600 role-players, mostly Iraqi refugees hired by the military and American soldiers. The latter not only play themselves but also, as coached by Hollywood actors like Carl "Apollo Creed" Weathers, Iraqi insurgents.

Back in the day, the NTC used to be the site for Cold War games pitting the US Army against the dreaded Krasnovian invaders, rolling through a (post-nuclear?) swath of an imaginary Eastern Europe. For the past several years, this simulated, interactive Iraq—irresistibly comic and deeply disturbing—has served as an introduction for American troops to actual Iraq. We may assume that the Pentagon is pleased with the facility; otherwise the documentary could never have been made. Tracking the education of an Iraq-bound battalion and its by-the-book colonel, *Full Battle Rattle* looks just like a regular war movie. The slippage is constant. The soldiers naturally feel as if they're in a movie, even if the field hospital is populated by a mix of "wounded" soldiers and artfully mangled dummies.[7]

Given the situation that might have been conceived by Philip K. Dick (or Walt Disney), the documentary could have been devised to satirize the theses of French theorists Jean Baudrillard and Paul Virilio. "In industrialized warfare," Virilio wrote in *War and Cinema*, "the representation of events outstripped the presentation of facts." Reported as fake news, are these experiences fact or fiction? How do you document a simulation? An information officer interviewed by the filmmakers inevitably compares the setup to reality TV. And, as in life, everything that happens in the NTC is shown on TV. Call it *The True Man Show*. In their effort to train soldiers for all contingencies, including civil war, the largely invisible powers-that-be script staged executions, attacks, and, most intricately, a checkpoint accident. Afterward, the guilty soldiers hand out fake reparation money—too much, as it turns out.

Set off by sprightly graphics and shimmering with over-bright colors, *Full Battle Rattle* has a fake transparency. The movie arouses, without gratifying, a desire to see the camera—not to mention the hidden command center where the scenarios are devised, and perhaps even the real war. The documentary is somewhat too seamless, even if the filmmakers

---

7   These bloody prosthetic wounds resemble nothing so much as the zombie props in *Doom*, one of the films within the film *Operation Filmmaker*.

do break the illusion to interview American soldiers and Iraqi role-players. (Most of them seem to live in San Diego; all are, or seek to be, US citizens. One even glimpses American talismans—a bit of *South Park* merchandise—in their Iraqi home. Is that additional verisimilitude?)

Lurking around the periphery, American "insurgents" confide to the camera that they are planning to kill as many people as possible. Sure enough, in one late movie set-piece, the insurgents launch a surprise attack on a celebratory banquet attended by both the village mayor and the colonel. The latter is bizarrely cool. Assuring all that his men have the situation in hand, he turns speechless when "casualties" stagger in dressed up in newly applied zombie wounds. Having lost the game big-time, the colonel wonders if he is a failure. Cut to a staged military funeral, where the attendees cry real tears.

As well they might: The show ends with the American actors being sent to Iraq as the Iraqi performers prepare to entertain their next batch of recruits. The filmmakers alternate a few stories: American families are separated; Iraqi families are reunited in America. (One Iraqi amuses relatives by showing them the tape of his staged execution.) The movie reports that out of 1.4 million Iraqi DPs, fewer than 600 have found refuge in the US. A sizable portion of these fortunate few have made lives in the virtual villages of the NTC—speaking Arabic, wearing traditional clothes, eating traditional food, staging mock weddings and funerals. ("For real, we're family," one tells the filmmakers.) One of the many surreal aspects of this fabulously disorienting movie: its representation of an Iraqi heaven that's an American hell.

As the interminable 2008 presidential campaign moved towards the home stretch, it seemed as though we had seen this movie before— sort of. Titled "What We Learned about the Election in This Summer's Movies," the following article was the September 17 *Village Voice* cover story.

NEW YORK, SEPTEMBER 17, 2008

Once upon a time, a hugely unpopular president tied to a baffling, unpopular, and apparently interminable war halfway around the world could not run for re-election. New faces appeared upon the screen. A well-liked if elderly soldier, paired with an aggressive young partisan, took on a high-brow, highfalutin' orator from Illinois, whose undeniable eloquence and evident intelligence inspired both loyalty and suspicion. It was the election of elections. The fate of the planet hung in the balance.

Such were the parameters of the 1952 presidential contest, the first national election in which television would play a crucial role and the last one before 2008 with neither an incumbent president nor a sitting vice president in the race. Harry Truman—the Democratic president that Republicans most love to praise—occupied the White House. American boys were pinned down in Korea. And General Dwight D. Eisenhower, the Supreme Commander of Allied forces during World War II, was pitted, along with brand-new senator Richard Nixon, against Adlai Stevenson, first-term governor of Illinois. John McCain was sixteen years old; Barack Obama's mother was ten.

Those were the Latter Days. There was Communist aggression without and red subversion within; American scientists hastened to beat Stalin in developing a weapon of mass destruction a hundred times more powerful than the Model T dropped on Hiroshima. American forces subjected North Korean installations to the heaviest air attacks since World War II. Congress voted $52 billion toward a worldwide network of military bases. In late June, air-conditioned theaters in ten large American cities hooked into a closed-circuit telecast of the latest civil-defense procedures; three days later, the CBS news show *See It Now* televised a simulated nuclear attack on New York City. And on the last two Saturday nights in July, routine air traffic was directed away from the Washington, DC, airport as F-94 jets blasted off to defend the nation's capital against an armada of mysterious radar blips.

But these were also the Latter Days. Because, barring some cataclysmic cosmic intervention, either an African-American or a supposed Manchurian Candidate—held captive by the North Vietnamese for five and a half years and running with a mysterious young woman as his vice president—would be inaugurated next January.

How did we know that the end is nigh? Hollywood told us so—then and now. Tension was apparent in the titles of 1952's summer movies: *Red Planet Mars* (Commies or God broadcasting from outer space?), *One Minute to Zero* (GIs doing whatever it takes to win in Korea), *High Noon* (one man standing alone ... because he's right!). And now?

Well, according to Hollywood, a black man in the White House signifies disaster. In *The Fifth Element* (1997), with the entire universe under threat of obliteration, there was Tommy "Tiny" Lister; in the more provincial *Deep Impact* (1998), with a meteor hurtling toward earth, our leader was embodied by Morgan Freeman. Lou Gossett presided over the Christian-fundamentalist Armageddon of *Left Behind: World at War* (2005), as Danny Glover will over the multi-cataclysms of Roland Emmerich's upcoming *2012*. And who can forget Dennis Haysbert, who served two seasons as president in the nonstop terror world of *24* (2001–2003)? Certainly not John McCain. He informed *Entertainment Weekly* that Haysbert's David Palmer was his favorite fictional (heh-heh) president.

John McCain made his bones as a happy participant in the most destructive air war in human history, but he's not a product of Vietnam. His mentality was formed during the Cold War, pre-Elvis. Perhaps sixteen-year-old McCain caught *Red Planet Mars*—the movie that dared to ask the question "Is the Man from Nazareth the Man from Mars?"—when a student at Episcopal High School in Alexandria, Virginia. The most visionary of the anti-Communist films, *Red Planet Mars* was also the first Eisenhower film. Shot during the winter of 1951–52, this vision of divine intervention opened a few weeks before the world's first televised political convention nominated "the spiritual leader of our times" on the first ballot. The movie's president is a former military commander played by an actor who strongly resembled Ike. Moreover, *Red Planet Mars* anticipated Eisenhower's worldview, as had recently been reported in *Time* magazine, that America was a civilization built on religious beliefs now challenged by "a civilization built upon the godless theory that man himself has no value."

The apocalyptic fantasy that ruled the summer of 2008 was less ideological and less grandiose. Opening over the July 4 weekend, Pixar's *WALL-E* projected an unaccountably optimistic vision of human extinction in which a solitary robot trash compactor—its name an acronym for Waste Allocation Load Lifter Earth-class—single-mindedly organized the endless detritus of an abandoned world. For much of the movie, this endearing protagonist is the earth's last vestige of humanity. The descendants of the planet's former inhabitants drift through space in a giant shopping mall, too bloated to do anything other than drink their Happy Meals and watch TV. Could that be us?! *New York Times* columnist

Frank Rich saw the movie with an audience of innocent children and was impressed by their rapt attention: "The kids at *WALL-E* were in deep contemplation of a world in peril … They seemed to instinctually understand what *Wall-E* was saying [and] at the end they clapped their small hands. What they applauded was not some banal cartoonish triumph of good over evil but a gentle, if unmistakable, summons to remake the world before time runs out."

A week after Rich proposed *WALL-E* for president, candidate Obama got the message and took his daughters to see the movie as part of Malia's tenth birthday celebration. "I really enjoyed it," he told reporters. "And the girls had a great time." A month later in Minnesota, Obama spontaneously plugged *WALL-E* as "a great flick." Did he identify with the weird little Waste Allocation Load Lifter—community organizer for an extinct community?

Forty-odd years ago, Obama's coming was imagined by Frank Capra in an unproduced script for *The Best Man*, not as Mr. Smith gone to Washington but as the young multiracial governor of Hawaii who seizes the nomination in a deadlocked convention by appearing dressed as Abraham Lincoln and reciting the Gettysburg Address. But Obama's otherness is not simply racial. He is a singular being: WALL-E, E.T., or, as the McCain campaign jealously characterized him, the World's Biggest Celebrity.

McCain's acceptance speech aside, the big combat movie that summer—displacing *The Dark Knight* atop the box-office chart and reigning for the three weeks preceding and following the DNC—was a comedy. *Tropic Thunder*'s parody *Rambo* had something to offend everyone, including one actor who uses blackface and another who played "mentally challenged" in pursuit of an Oscar. Inducing audiences to laugh at the spectacle of American–Indochinese combat as self-serving fraud (and perhaps even consign it to the dust bin of history), its success seemed to bode well for Obama. But would it also prompt audiences to reflect upon the degree to which show business permeated every aspect of our public life?

Apparently not: The Republicans produced their own (American) idol as Alaska governor Sarah Palin burst forth from the dream life. The uncanny popularity enjoyed by last year's indie smash *Juno*—in which a feisty sixteen-year-old decides to keep her baby—predicted the political plus inherent in Palin daughter Bristol's teenage pregnancy. The columnist Maureen Dowd immediately spotted Palin as a chick-flick action diva—Sandra Bullock in *Miss Congeniality*—but she's also Reese Witherspoon in *Legally Blonde 2: Red, White, and Blonde*, Julia Roberts in *Erin Brockovich*, a sassy combination of Shelly Marie and Sgt. Semanski in the Alaska-set sitcom *Northern Exposure*.

To paraphrase the popular reality show: America's got talent! Palin, however, had no particular summer movie unless it's *Mamma Mia!*—as in, "Mamma mia, didja see that hair, that speech, that baby?" But then, Palin was not a summer blockbuster. She was a September surprise.[8]

As the 1952 election was the first to use television to privilege a candidate's image over his positions, Ike would be the first national leader sold as a product. His handlers blitzed TV nation with twenty-second spots projecting him as a friendly, folksy, God-fearin' warrior. Although the 1952 election was ultimately a referendum on Korea, Americans enjoyed no consensus on what they wanted to do about the war. They only knew that Ike was the man to do it. (Adlai Stevenson, who campaigned under the poignantly inappropriate slogan "Let's talk sense to the American people," was perceived as an egghead elitist sissy.) The key movie during the summer of 1952 would be America's leadership film for the next half-century: *High Noon*. Certainly, Eisenhower was far easier to imagine as Gary Cooper, the marshal who, pusillanimous allies notwithstanding, went back to war, and thus embodied the template for the post-televisual presidency.

The weary loner's brave posture of prescient and courageous certainty in the face of public (or foreign) cowardice is the American politician's ego ideal—or so the viewing preferences of American presidents would suggest. Eisenhower screened *High Noon* three times at the White House. According to White House logs, *High Noon* ranks as the movie subsequent presidents would most request—none more than Bill Clinton, who watched his favorite film some twenty times and told Dan Rather that he'd recommend the Western to his successor as a text. Unfortunately.

John McCain would dearly love to cast himself as Gary Cooper, the lone marshal who created the "Surge" and declared victory in Iraq, or as the first to recognize the threat to post-Soviet Georgia. But the Western, these days, is a quaint anachronism. Our post-9/11 moral landscape isn't

---

8   Palin resigned as Alaska governor after Obama's election and, for several years thereafter, enjoyed the status of America's greatest media star, political or otherwise, since Dead Elvis.

populated by good guys and bad guys, but by comic-book superheroes and cosmic evildoers.

Anticipated by *X-Men*, surprise blockbuster of the 2000 campaign, and initiated two years later with *Spider-Man*, the big-screen comic book was the characteristic Bush-era action genre. America auditioned a number of superheroes this summer and liked more than a few. (Four of 2008's top-ten grossers were superhero films.) There was the rakish *Iron Man*, supposedly inspired by the young Howard Hughes, and his struggle against the Taliban. There were the reconfigured *Hulk* and a kinder, gentler *Hellboy*. There was Will Smith's pissed-off, dissolute *Hancock* (an original character!) and the kill-machine protagonist of *Wanted*. And then there was the creature John McCain identified as his favorite superhero: Batman. (Obama agreed, but qualified his enthusiasm by also mentioning Spider-Man, a character he might have well appreciated as a lonely eight-year-old.[9])

Batman had been newly incarnated in *The Dark Knight* which, as its title suggested, was less movie than worldview. *The Dark Knight* projected a recognizable dystopia ruled by the threat of terror, in which the rich live in gated communities and the economy is controlled by the Chinese. Basically one hostage situation after another, the movie's lugubrious doomsday scenario opened with preparations for what might be a skyscraper attack and continued through two and a half hours of stylish nonstop brutality to end with a crescendo of moral confusion. The 9/11 references ran rampant, but even more insistent was the meditation on civic responsibility, the nature of due process, the legitimacy of torture. The crusading D.A. recognized Batman as our Caesar—and Batman recognized no limits. *High Noon* had given way to darkest night. As the ads put it: "Welcome to a World Without Rules."[10]

While reviewers could not help but detect a critique of the war on terror in *The Dark Knight*, right-wing pundits gratefully embraced the movie as a glorification of their fantasy. Writing in *The Wall Street Journal*, Andrew Kavan praised *The Dark Knight* as "a paean of praise to [George Bush's] fortitude and moral courage." The movie justified a president "vilified and despised for confronting terrorists in the only

---

9 This equivocating qualification, as Americans were to subsequently learn, was typical of Obama's conciliatory consensus-driven style.

10 *The Dark Knight* grossed $158,411,483 on its opening weekend (July 18–20), a new record, en route to worldwide grosses in excess of $1 billion.

terms they understand." Then CNN commentator Glenn Beck waxed even more enthusiastically specific: "Batman goes into another country and with a C-130 snatches a guy out, and then throws him back here into Gotham. So there's rendition … One of the ways they find the Joker is through eavesdropping. I mean, the parallels here of what's going on is to me stunning!" *The American Spectator* further personalized the allegory: Batman's capacity for action, his love of risk and maverick indifference to public opinion, were pure McCain.[11]

A vulgar Marxist might have noted that as Batman is the alter-ego of the richest man in Gotham City, his "law" was the protection of capital. (Smeared lipstick notwithstanding, one of the scariest things about the Joker is that he has no respect for money.) In any case, the film's ongoing discussion as to whether Batman is the hero we deserve or the hero we need was trumped by the villain's funhouse-mirror dialectic. The Joker (secret star of the movie, played by Heath Ledger, an actor from beyond the grave) argued that, operating from somewhere outside of the law, Batman was the real agent of terror while he, on the other hand, embodied a particular logic: "I try to show the schemers how pathetic their attempts to control things really are." Like bin Laden, the Joker has the power to drive Gotham City mad. This criminal is Al Qaeda squared, Katrina personified, the Wrath of God run amok. And so *The Dark Night* was illuminated by two choices: chaos or fascism.

Sarah Palin may get to make her Checkers speech, or, scheduled for early October, Oliver Stone's supposedly scabrous Bush parody *W* might constitute an intervention. But all things being equal, the choice is *Wall-E* versus *The Dark Knight*. The 2008 election comes down to absurd hope (a funny little dingbot can redeem this blighted planet) or the miserable fear of that damnable, fascinating, scary clown.[12]

---

11   Beck would leave CNN Headline News for the Fox News Channel shortly before Obama's inauguration, in January 2009, and quickly became a leading critic of the new president—indeed, some rightwing Republicans imagined Beck as a vice-presidential candidate on a dream ticket with Sarah Palin (who had been among the first guests on Beck's new show). While *Glenn Beck* enjoyed high ratings and no small controversy during the first two years of Obama's presidency, it was cancelled by Fox early in Obama's third year.
12   Although Batman did not emerge as a mascot for American oligarchy in the aftermath of the September 2008 stock market crash, a poster applying Heath Ledger's Joker make-up to President Obama began appearing at Tea Party rallies during the summer of 2009 and was considered useful

"We have seen that our product is, at worst, recession-resistant," DreamWorks Animation CEO Jeffrey Katzenberg assured a conclave of Hollywood studio execs and Wall Street investors, hosted by Goldman Sachs, amid the din of falling stock prices in September 2008. The movie industry had already endured a year-long credit crunch—two days later, Universal would back away from DreamWorks's $130-million 3-D animation *Tintin* and within a week, Goldman Sachs ceased to be an investment bank—but, according to Katzenberg, time was on their side. "More optimistically and historically," he recalled, the motion-picture product "has actually been recession-proof." Optimistic? You bet. Historical? Not entirely. Back in 1930, Hollywood had considered itself Depression-proof, too.[13]

In October, Hollywood studios began terminating franchises and buying out employees. The audience was constant, but revenues declined. Despite the colossal success of *The Dark Knight*, Warner Bros. saw a 9-percent fall in its third-quarter earnings. Stock prices

---

ammunition by the Republican Party during the run-up to the 2010 election (Ben Smith, "Exclusive: RNC document mocks donors, plays on 'fear,'" *Politico. com*, 3/3/2010).

13   Busily rewiring their theaters for newly developed "talking pictures," the Hollywood studios initially ignored the stock market crash. The crash, however, did not ignore them: the novelty of sound soon faded. By the end of 1931, the record motion-picture audience of the previous year was down by a third and falling. So were ticket prices. Production costs, however, had doubled. Warner Bros., the studio that led the initially profitable shift to talking pictures, was now hemorrhaging money. Universal terminated hundreds of employees and would soon join RKO in receivership—followed by Fox and, in what was then America's second largest bankruptcy to date, Paramount.

By the time Franklin Roosevelt took office in March 1933, theaters were empty, production slates slashed, cash-flow dried up. The industry was near collapse. Hard times pushed desperate producers toward sensationalism. Crime paid, so did sin. Not since the days of the nickelodeon had audiences been so encouraged to identify with the destitute and the desperate. Class warfare was rife. As the 1932 election neared, with nearly half the nation's labor force out of work or marginally employed, the call resounded for "strong" leadership. In early 1933, Warner Bros., the studio most identified with FDR, declared its own "New Deal in Entertainment": in *42nd Street*, Warner Baxter's tyrannical stage director demonstrates that one might defeat the Depression by making a Broadway show. The US suffered through three and a half years of economic misery before the New Deal arrived; by contrast, the Obama administration came to power only three and a half months after the crash of '08.

were down, but far more ominous, from the industry's point of view, was the drop in DVD sales. October 13, a week after the Dow suffered a five-day 1,874-point decline, 20th Century Fox announced that Oliver Stone would direct a sequel to his 1987 *Wall Street*. And then, less than three weeks before the election, Stone's portrait of the president, *W.*

NEW YORK, OCTOBER 15, 2008

Oliver Stone's bio-pic of America's soon to be ex-president is less frenzied than the usual Stone sensory bombardment, but in revisiting the early '00s by way of the late '60s, his psycho-historical portrait of George W. Bush has all the queasy appeal of a strychnine-laced acid flashback.

Hideous recreations of the shock-and-awful recent past merge with extravagant lowlights from the formative years and early career of America's most disastrous maximum leader (crudely played by Josh Brolin, often in tight close-up). Familiar faces seem to deliquesce before our eyes. It's unavoidably trippy, but did anyone, other than the perpetrators, really need to relive this particular purple haze?

W., which is as much edited as it is directed, working from a script by Stone buddy Stanley Weiser, has a patchwork chronology that takes as its central pattern the run-up to the Iraq War and ensuing search for the missing weapons of mass destruction, while pushing two theses regarding the nature of its eponymous antihero.

The more heavy-handed of these dramatizes Dubya's tormented relationship, alternately worshipful and rebellious, with his disapproving father (James Cromwell). "What do you think you are—a Kennedy?" Poppy thunders when confronted with his wastrel son's latest drunken indiscretion. "You're a Bush!" It's the Oedipal saga that *New York Times* columnist Maureen Dowd, for one, began recounting during the 2000 election, and which reached its climax when the son corrected his father's error by re-invading Iraq to depose Saddam Hussein.

In this scenario, the younger Bush becomes president to take revenge on the elder. Stone has Dubya watching the 1992 election returns with his family. As defeated Poppy chokes back tears, Dubya trumps even the bilious, class-fueled anti-Clinton rage expressed by mother Barbara (Ellen Burstyn) in ranting about H.W.'s failure to go all the way to Baghdad. This

W. is the saga of a tormented, father-obsessed asshole who manages to play out his family drama on a world-historical stage.

The second thesis—implicit in Kevin Phillips's chronicle of the Bush family's ascent, *American Dynasty*, and developed elsewhere—credits Dubya with a powerful insight into American politics. Having checked his alcoholism with a regimen of fundamentalist Bible study and consequently served as Poppy's liaison to the Christian right, the younger Bush assimilated Christian values rhetoric and successfully organized an evangelical base which would enable him to pulverize John McCain in the 2000 primaries and win re-election in 2004.

Although *W.* dramatizes neither of these campaigns—generally eschewing the public Bush in favor of his presumed backstage persona—Stone and Weiser go so far as to cast their antihero as the real Lee Atwater, suggesting that it was his canny appreciation for dirty tricks and not Atwater's that got Poppy elected in 1988, years before self-identified "fairy" Karl Rove taught him his political catechism. But undermining his own theory, Stone also presents Dubya as an idiot savant who believes his own bullshit, warning Poppy that too much thinking screws up the mind and bragging that he's decided to run for president because God told him to.[14]

Although personality regularly trumps political process in the world of Oliver Stone, *W.* seemed most deeply concerned with the run-up to the Iraq war, thus working the same territory as David Hare's play, *Stuff Happens*. Each given a presidential nickname to wear like a baseball cap, Bush's enablers—Dick "Vice" Cheney (Richard Dreyfuss, having evident fun), Donald "Rummy" Rumsfeld (Scott Glenn), Condi "Girl" Rice (Thandie Newton, looking as though about to gag), Karl "Boy Genius" Rove (Toby Jones), and "Brother" George Tenet (Bruce McGill)—confound the cautious and rational Colin "Colin" Powell (Jeffrey Wright) to lead the republic toward disaster.

Not fair (not a problem) and definitely not balanced: The least-nuanced performance in a film full of cartoon characterizations is Brolin's Bush. A simian slob, modeled on Andy Griffith's raucous run-amok in *A Face in the Crowd* and given to bad-tempered pronouncements while stuffing his

---

14   *W.* was evidently "normalized" before it was released, most significantly by the removal of several dream hallucinations featuring Sadam Hussein and Bush's magic carpet ride over Baghdad. (Richard L. Berke, "Throwing Incaution to the Wind, Stone Paints Bush," *New York Times*, 10/12/2008.)

face, Brolin uses stupidity as a crucifix. He wards off sympathy as though it were a vampire. In directing Brolin, Stone is disinclined to give the devil his due. Bush's mean-spirited charm is nowhere evident—despite the devotion he inspires in wife Laura. What exactly is this sweet young hottie (Elizabeth Banks) supposed to see in him?[15]

What were we? *W.* can't decide whether its aspirations are Shakespearean tragedy, political critique, or cathartic black comedy. The emotionally reductive Stone really only had a shot at the latter. At its best, *W.* suggests *Stuff Happens* reconfigured for the cast of *Saturday Night Live*. Running through Bush's greatest bits—choking on a potato chip, confusing Guantánamo with "Guantanamera," calling himself "the decider," complaining that he's always been "misunderestimated" by Saddam Hussein—*W.* begs the question posed by its two theses. Like, how did this stunted creature, who considers his greatest mistake to have been trading slugger Sammy Sosa from the Texas Rangers, the team he briefly owned, become our king?

Released early in the 1992 campaign, *JFK* did its modest part to destabilize the first Bush's Republican nation and contribute to Bill Clinton's Kennedy-identified juggernaut. To the degree that *W.* is able to make itself present in the hurly-burly of the election's final weeks, it could prove mildly helpful to the Democrats. But if *W.* opens at a good time, it doesn't exactly promise one. Although Stone omits the stolen 2000 election, stops short of the 2004 campaign, and spares us the second term, *W.* is a painful movie to endure. It's a shame that when Stone contemplated the nature of imperial hubris four years ago, the gods decreed he should unleash *Alexander* rather than this. Back then, *W.* might actually have made a difference.

Hung up on Bush's psychology, *W.* was completely unable to read its subject as a process while, as sentimental political docudrama, his movie was largely overshadowed by Gus Van Sant's *Milk*, starring Sean Penn as the martyred gay activist and San Francisco supervisor, Harvey Milk.

***Milk* opened in the aftermath of the 2008 election, thirty years and a day after Milk and San Francisco mayor George Moscone were**

---

15   Brolin played Ronald Reagan in the 2003 miniseries *The Reagans*, forced by conservative pressure groups from telecast over CBS to the cable channel Showtime.

gunned down in City Hall by another supervisor, ex-cop Dan White (Josh Brolin, who, better directed here than in *W.*, had the distinction of playing the year's two pre-eminent real-life villains). *Milk* was so immediate that it became impossible to separate the movie's historical moment from its actual one: The 1978 victory over Proposition 6, asserting the principle of equal protection under the law, merged with the current struggle against California's Proposition 8, overturning the State Supreme Court's affirmative ruling on same-sex marriage. (Sound bites from the movie's staged demonstrations were near-identical to those culled from those held two weekends ago.)

Milk positions Milk as both a gutsy civil rights leader and creative community organizer—not to mention a precedent-shattering politician who, it was very often reiterated, presented himself as a Messenger of Hope. And also Change. The ecstatic reception accorded *WALL-E*'s visionary *tikkun* (and the president-elect's strategic non-support for same-sex marriage) notwithstanding, *Milk* appeared as the first openly Obama-iste movie.[16]

---

16   Late 2008 releases like Darren Aronofsky's *The Wrestler* and Clint Eastwood's *Gran Torino* also profited from the current mood of anxious Obamoptimism—as did Kelly Reichardt's evocation of hard times, *Wendy and Lucy*. Danny Boyle's rags-to-riches romance *Slumdog Millionaire* was another prime beneficiary, although the thirteen Oscar nominations accorded $150-million bummer *Benjamin Button* suggested Hollywood's touching vote of confidence in itself.

PART III:
NOTES TOWARD
A SYLLABUS

CHAPTER FIFTEEN

IN PRAISE OF LOVE (JEAN-LUC GODARD, 2001; FRANCE)

Jean-Luc Godard's *In Praise of Love* is tactile yet elusive—its tragic grandeur is as graspable as running water and as shifty as smoke. Like the earliest motion pictures, Godard's new feature appears like a fact of nature. There's a narrative—and an argument—but what's initially moving, and ultimately as well, is the movie's mournful celebration of its sensuous being.

The images are punctuated by bits of black leader and gnomic intertitles, the action propelled by sweetly pulverized music and an effortlessly layered soundtrack of enigmatic conversations. Poetry is really the only word for it: "When I think about something, I'm really thinking about something else," Godard's protagonist Edgar (Bruno Putzulu) says twice in a film that is forever talking about itself (or its audience).

Not quite a filmmaker, Edgar is auditioning actors for a project that will, he explains, trace the four phases of love (meeting, passion, loss, and recovery) as played by three couples of various ages. This "trinity of stories" may also have something to do with the romance of the French resistance during World War II. There's a shadowy young woman (Cécile Camp), typically seen with her back to the camera but recognizable by her voice and long hair, to whom Edgar is attracted and whom he seems interested in casting, but when he gets around to asking "her" (as she is known in the credits), he discovers that she is dead. Indeed, the movie's French title translates as "Elegy for Love."

There are many things that *In Praise of Love* laments and a few in which it rejoices. The motion picture medium is associated with history and historical memory. Edgar's associates are concerned that their movie on the French resistance will become a Hollywood substitute for history. The movie itself is in part a sustained immersion in street photography and casual portraiture. It's been over three decades since Godard last shot a movie on the streets of Paris, and doing so seems to provide him with an elemental pleasure. (According to Godard's biographer Richard Brody, the filmmaker selected locations for their personal significance but did not personally supervise the shooting; the crew was sent to film without him.) Studied as they are, these unprepossessing, sometimes harsh images of the city and its inhabitants—many of them dispossessed —feel as newly minted as the earliest Lumière brothers' views; they evoke the thrill of light becoming emulsion. Much of the movie is a voluptuous urban nocturne with particular emphasis on the transitory sensations that were the essence of the first motion pictures.

More specifically, the coordinates of Godard's free-ranging cinephilia are mapped by his allusions to such modest and personal statements as teenage Samira Makhmalbaf's docudrama *The Apple*, a movie about twin girls who spent their first eleven years confined to their house, and recently deceased Robert Bresson's *Pickpocket*, which people trip over a beggar to line up for and which was shot on location in Paris the same summer that Godard made *Breathless*. At the same time, the industrial simulations of *The Matrix* and particularly *Schindler's List*—which, in its totalizing re-creation of World War II and the Holocaust—serve as Godard's prime negative object. America, it's several times maintained, has no history of its own and hence must appropriate history from others. Europe—visualized as Paris's timeless "there," but really a stand-in for Godard's own cinema—is nearly helpless before this voracious totalitarian appetite. "The Americans are everywhere, aren't they, sir?" a Vietnamese chambermaid asks Edgar, adding, "Who remembers Vietnam's resistance?" Resistance, for Godard, is a factor of memory.[1]

Edgar's project remains unmade; Godard's is a-chronological (and indeed, having been planned for over four years, required the longest

---

1   Richard Brody, who considers *In Praise of Love* to be Godard's response to the anti-representational challenge of Claude Lanzmann's *Shoah*, notes that like *Shoah*, *In Praise of Love* is "a film of history in which the past is revealed to live in the present" (*Everything is Cinema: The Working Life of Jean-Luc Godard*, New York: Henry Holt, 2008, 588).

shoot of Godard's career). The first two-thirds is filmed in an achingly rich black-and-white; then Godard rescues Edgar from his sorrowful stupidity by going back in time for a lengthy coda shot, in luridly over-saturated video, on the Brittany coast. (Reversing the logic of *Schindler's List*, Godard represents the past in color and the present in shades of gray.) Edgar, in the midst of composing a cantata for Resistance heroine Simone Weil, pays a visit to a celebrated old Resistance couple who are themselves negotiating to sell their story to the Hollywood company Spielberg Associates. There, by chance, he meets their granddaughter. It is "Her," encountered for the first time. Or is it again?

I can't recall another flashback in a Godard feature—his movies have all been resolutely present-tense, and with good reason. The first film-maker to recognize that cinema's classic period was over, Godard took film history as a text. But the liberating energy with which his early movies mixed genres and collaged the old has long since been co-opted. The Spielberg Associates scenario has something to do with engaging William Styron to rewrite the Resistance romance as a Tristan and Isolde vehicle for Juliette Binoche. Godard bases his own resistance on another sort of memory. One way to look at *In Praise of Love* would be as a frag-mentary remake of Jean Cocteau's *Orphée*—a movie about the attempt to retrieve a lost love that haunts *Alphaville* and is itself haunted by France's German occupation. Another way is as a loop or even a film installa-tion—a paradox in that the movie demands to be projected as film.[2]

A movie with a circular structure, *In Praise of Love* is designed so that a memory of the future guides us through the past. Toward the end, events start to decompose into flaming pools of color—an electric blue

---

2   Rodowick discusses this at length: "Not only is resolution lost in the black and white sections [when *In Praise of Love* is digitally shown] … the video images appear less color saturated and somehow more 'natural' …

Video may be the future of cinema, but, ironically, the palette achieved in the second part of the movie is best accomplished when video is printed on film. And so, while the black and white scenes suggest a present that may be passing out of existence—the disappearance of film as a medium—the color sequences may never again achieve their impres-sionistic vibrancy and luminosity when and if these video images are no longer presentable through 35mm projection.
                              (D. N. Rodowick, *The Virtual Life of Film*,
                        Cambridge, Mass.: Harvard University Press, 2007, 90.)

haze, a golden smear of sun, a blur of traffic—and then pure jumbled light. Since he embarked on his late, painterly period some twenty years ago, Godard has made physically beautiful movies—*Passion* and *Nouvelle Vague* in particular presented themselves as substantial celluloid rivals to the canvases of the old masters. *In Praise of Love* is something else. The old masters here are the impressionists. The image feels as fragile and fleeting as a reverie. This is a movie that disappears before your eyes—leaving only an elegy for itself.

CHAPTER SIXTEEN

AVALON (MAMORU OSHII, 2001; JAPAN–POLAND)

The missing link between *Blade Runner* and *The Matrix*, Mamoru Oshii's 1995 anime *Ghost in the Shell* evoked a noirish total-computer world where cybernetic-organism agents interface online or download simulated memories into hapless humans. With *Avalon*, a live action film made in Poland, Oshii attempted a new sort of cyborg entity, namely a digital-photographic fusion.

"I wanted to create characters in the same way that I do animation," the filmmaker told an interviewer. The actors' facial expressions were reworked during a post-production period that lasted longer than the actual shoot—Oshii explained that he felt enabled to animate his actors in part because they were foreign and speaking a foreign language. Thanks to this procedure, *Avalon* defamiliarizes its performers. The movie is being enacted not by humans but by their traces, played out in an a-chronological mash-up of twentieth-century East European history.

The presence of history is one thing that distinguishes the world of *Avalon* from that of *The Matrix* (and connects it to Godard's *In Praise of Love*). *Avalon* opens with World War II-era tanks rolling across a desolate battlefield. The CGI effects are sensationally evocative—explosions freeze and then separate out into two-dimensional layers. The action, sepia-tinted and somewhat smeared by soft focus, shifts to Warsaw where casualties similarly stop dead, shatter, and atomize. When the fireworks end, a soldier's helmet goes up to reveal the face of the comely young protagonist Ash (Malgorzata Foremniak). "You're not ready for Class A," she remarks to the player she's just incinerated.

A lone gamer on a solitary quest, Ash is a grave, elegant creature with a strong resemblance to the warrior maids of Japanese animation and manga, as well as the protagonist of Luc Besson's 1990 *La Femme Nikita*. (Film history is present in *Avalon* as well.) Ash is addicted to this apparently illegal virtual reality game which she plays solo after the implosion of her old championship team—it fell apart when someone called for a "reset." She is, however, spooked when she discovers that an old teammate with the Beckettian name Murphy has gone "unreturned" from the game (and is catatonic in a mental hospital) after chasing a mysterious phantom child who is the portal to the game's "realer than real" ultimate level, Special A—and, as she is transparent, often appears as though projected onto the movie.

No less than the characters in *The Matrix*, Ash spends considerable time gazing at her computer screens, and like *The Matrix*, *Avalon* suggests that the game Ash plays is a compensatory cyber illusion, providing distraction from an otherwise intolerable reality as well as a means of financial support. Some games, or movies based on game structure, are essentially narrative and implicitly character driven; others, considered ludological, are appreciated less in terms of the storyline or protagonist identification they furnish, than for the world they create. The virtual reality game in *Avalon* is one of the latter, but it is not a civilizing game like *Second Life* (introduced in 2003) or *The Sims* (2000). Indeed, rather than Baudrillard, the French philosopher whose ideas are embodied in *Avalon* is Paul Virilio, who has argued that the motor of history is military technology. *Avalon* parallels the development of America's so-called military-entertainment complex.[1]

The exciting computer-generated dream life in *Avalon*, as in David Cronenberg's *eXistenZ* (1999), is a form of utopian entertainment, as well as a source of simulated memories (mainly of war trauma), from which

---

1   In 1996, a group of US Marines hacked and reconfigured the commercial video game *Doom II* to create their own version, *Marine Doom*. This so impressed a West Point professor who had two teenage game-playing sons, that he persuaded the Pentagon to develop online games as recruiting tools. The first *America's Army* appeared in 2000 and has since served as a platform for dozens of training applications as well as "virtual soldier" experiences for state fair and amusement park patrons.

(like history) there is no escape. Trying to solve the meaning of eXistenZ, Ash has almost no life outside the game. Nor, in a sense, does *Avalon*—that is, there's a possibility that everything in the movie takes place in the game world. While the combat scenes combine actors with obvious "2-D" CGI, the oppressive "real world" is no less digitally sweetened. (The height of "realness" is the exaggerated intensity with which Oshii treats Ash's domestic preparation of food for her pet dog.)

In *Avalon*'s final movement, Ash makes a breakthrough from her drab, near-monochromatic environment into Class Real, a defamiliarized urban world of contemporary Warsaw—all street crowds and advertising—only to discover that she is still in the game. In a manner that anticipates the punch line of Lars von Trier's *Dogville* (2003), Oshii's live action anime uses the documentary realness of the ordinary photographic image as the ultimate special effect.[2]

---

2   Shortly after *Avalon* had its international premiere at the 2001 Cannes Film Festival, Paramount opened *Lara Croft: Tomb Raider*, eventually to become the top-grossing movie ever based on a video game. Oshii returned to animation for *Ghost in the Shell 2: Innocence* (2004). Even more visually spectacular than its precursor, *Ghost in the Shell 2* draws significantly on the surrealist artist Hans Bellmer to posit a lovingly wrought world in which a hard-boiled robot treasures his pet beagle as much as a possibly human child does her doll, and a cabal of unscrupulous industrialists peddle sex-toy "gynoids" with stolen souls. Batou, a hard-luck robocop with a near-human sidekick, is nearly blown up by a suicidal gynoid. This incident sends him through an urban labyrinth where, by the time Batou follows the trail into the baroque mansion that houses the Locus Solus corporation (named for one of Raymond Roussel's narrative machines), it's clear—or not—that the scary mannequins and frozen holograms he encounters are, as another cyborg helpfully notes, "a tangle of virtual experience hacked into your brain." Oshii's cinema is itself a programmatically hybrid form. The "innocent" pathos here is not that of cyborgs seeking to be human—it's of animated beings striving for life. Where the cyborgs look like dolls, the backdrops are hyper-real and Oshii typically devotes as much care to reproducing the impossible play of light reflected off the sleek surface of a slow-moving auto or a close-up of water sloshing down the dish drain as to his set pieces—like the fantastic pageant of crypto Hindu gods and pagodas floating to lugubrious Bulgarian choral chants, amid spiraling snow flurries, through the concrete canyons of some reinvented New York. For all its graphic splendor, fluid action, surrealist attitudes, and self-aware cyber-philosophizing, *Innocence* was indifferently received when shown in competition at the 2004 Cannes Film Festival. Was it a cartoon trying to pass for something real?

CHAPTER SEVENTEEN

AVANT-GARDE GOES DIGITAL: *CORPUS CALLOSUM (MICHAEL SNOW, 2002; CANADA), COTTON CANDY (ERNIE GEHR, 2002; USA), AND RAZZLE DAZZLE: THE LOST WORLD (KEN JACOBS, 2007; USA)

Cyborgs abound in Michael Snow's *Corpus Callosum. Part old-fashioned Renaissance man, part hardcore avant-gardist, the Canadian painter-photographer-filmmaker-musician gives full vent to his genius in this exhilarating perceptual vaudeville, titled for the "central region" of tissue that acts as a conduit between the brain's two hemi-spheres. Programmatically hybrid, Snow's piece similarly bridges the gap between film and video, nature and artifice, sound and image, art and entertainment.

*Corpus Callosum is a bonanza of wacky sight gags, outlandish color schemes, and corny visual puns that can be appreciated equally as an abstract Frank Tashlin comedy and as a playful recapitulation of the artist's career. From the opening reverse zoom through the series of 360-degree pans to the final line animation created by Snow in 1956, this ninety-three-minute feature is a self-curated retrospective, but with a twist. Four years in the making, *Corpus Callosum* was shot and edited on video, and reworked with custom software. Everything is stretched, squeezed, or flipped—the bodies of Snow's large cast not the least. Zapped by all manner of gross and subtle digitalized distortions, human actors are transformed into cartoon characters. (At one point, one guy ties another in a knot.) Space is similarly malleable. Is the camera panning, or is the image being subjected to some sort of digital taffy-pull?

Although *Corpus Callosum* might be considered underground state-of-the-art, technology is not fetishized. (In some ways the contemporary filmmaker to whom Snow here seems closest is the obsessive super-8 cut-and-paste animator Lewis Klahr.) Having marked out his conceptual grid, Snow uses—or rather accepts—unpredictable static or bleached-out colors as formal elements. Some of the effects, like the mad pixel dance created by throwing the movie into rewind, are ridiculously simple.

Scarcely divorced from (post)modern social reality, *Corpus Callosum* is largely set in a generic information-age office and the cast members costumed as "workers." (Often the costume is the actor—as in the blond wig, hot pink blouse, and micro miniskirt ensemble that circulates among the players.) Situated atop a Toronto skyscraper, Snow's workplace is a Skinner box of wildly unstable identities, bodies, and (at times) genders—an arena for erotic fantasies and grotesque physical distortions. (These suggest a dialogue with his countryman David Cronenberg.) In one of the most spectacular transformations, a man and woman crammed together in a doorway fuse into a single entity, carrying on as a rectangular slab of digital humanity. The office is a theater of cruelty, although, a few moments of globalized epilepsy aside, the artist's most sadistic ploy is to roll *Corpus Callosum*'s long (but not uninteresting) credits two-thirds through the movie.

Snow is judicious in his tricks, but *Corpus Callosum*'s visual pyrotechnics can distract one from its superb soundtrack—a silly symphony of hums, bells, buzzes, sirens, foghorns, gargles, chirps, and boi-i-ings that recalls the vulgar modernism of Raymond Scott's electronic commercials for Hostess Twinkies and Auto-Lite sparkplugs. Snow's laconic directions are heard throughout, drawing attention to the degree to which *Corpus Callosum* has been post-produced. The artist casually emphasizes his conjuring act by directing his actors against the special effects that transform them.

Snow is conscious of art history, as well as his own. *Corpus Callosum*'s second major location is a living room whose pop clutter recalls Richard Hamilton's 1956 collage manifesto, *Just What Is It That Makes Today's Homes So Different, So Appealing.* In addition to an apparent family of three, the furnishings include an eye chart, an electric guitar, a Ming vase, a model airplane (that may or may not allude to a similar craft in Jacques Tati's *Playtime*), a muscle-man calendar, a crutch, a stuffed fox, two Snow paintings, and a television broadcasting blue sky. The only continuously "real" aspect of the scene is the camera's reflection in a mirror. The family watches TV, impervious to their own transformations or the visual cacophony going on about them as, in a paroxysm of Bugs Bunny formalism, the objects begin to dance, implode, and otherwise act out.

Corpus Callosum is not only funny but remarkably generous as well. (There are more ideas in any single minute than in the entirety of an overwrought 57th Street yard sale like Matthew Barney's *Cremaster*.) Among other things, Snow's movie is a feast for film theorists. A brief sequence in a classroom notwithstanding, it's in no way didactic. Still, *Corpus Callosum* is that rarest of things—a summarizing work. Like Chantal Akerman's *Jeanne Dielman* or Chris Marker's *Sans Soleil*, it could be used to conclude Motion Pictures 101.

History doubles back on itself. *Corpus Callosum* ends in a screening room with the presentation of Snow's crude cartoon of a weirdly elastic, waving human with a twisty foot kick. Rigorously predicated on irreducible cinematic facts, Snow's structuralist epics—*Wavelength* and *La Région Centrale*—announced the imminent passing of the film era. Rich with new possibilities, *Corpus Callosum* heralds the advent of the next.

Avant-garde master Ernie Gehr's first foray into DV is innocuously titled *Cotton Candy*—although given the piece's implications, he could have easily gotten away with something as weighty as "Montage of Attractions," "The Myth of Total Cinema," "Carnival of Souls," or "That's Entertainment."

Gehr uses a mini-digital recorder to look back on the Machine Age in the form of San Francisco's beleaguered Musée Mécanique, located on the site of the city's former resort zone on Ocean Beach. For slightly more than an hour, *Cotton Candy* documents this venerable collection of coin-operated mechanical toys—including an entire circus—mainly in close-up, isolating particular details as he alternates between ambient and post-dubbed (or no) sound. By treating the Musée's cast of synchronized figures as puppets, the artist is making a show—but is it his or theirs? Gehr's selective take on the arcade renders it all the spookier. There's a sense in which *Cotton Candy* is a gloss on the moment in *The Rules of the Game* when the music-box-collecting viscount unveils his latest and most elaborate acquisition. (It also brings to mind the climax of *A.I.*: the DV of the future tenderly regards the more human machine of the past.)

The Musée's assortment of space-bending, raucously interactive video games is shown only obliquely, and relatively late in the film. Gehr prefers to focus on the outmoded and archaic. Thus, *Cotton Candy* pays particular attention to the old-fashioned, hand-cranked photographic flip-books known as mutoscopes. In what could be a movie from the 1890s, a secretary fights off a masher; later mutoscopes have a cowboy belly up to the bar, a boat drift toward the rapids, and Harold Lloyd dancing on a skyscraper girder. How many nickels have dropped in the slot? How many times have these images flickered? Crumbling before our eyes, the worn-out motion pictures still work!

In addition to the persistence of Persistence of Vision, *Cotton Candy*'s other main concern is the effect of sound, synchronous and otherwise, on the moving image. Gehr extracts a wry pathos from having his puppets "sing" the *Fox Movietone Follies of 1929* hit, "If I Had a Talking Picture of You," and even manages to wring a degree of defamiliarization when the mechanical band appears to strike up a melancholy passage from Erik Satie. A frequently heard player piano appears onscreen for a "sync event" closer—the mindless reiteration of a melody programmed perhaps a hundred years ago, by someone long dead.

Gehr has always been interested in the ephemeral, and *Cotton Candy* could well be his most preservationist film. Also the most epic—the automata provide the filmmaker with his largest-ever cast. (This is also the first time he's ever had to pay his actors.) Appropriately, the Museum of Modern Art, which commissioned the work, is projecting it straight from disc—it's not really a film, but a "film" about film.[1]

*   *   *

---

1   Less than a year after *Cotton Candy* had its world premiere at the Museum of Modern Art, the Musée Mécanique was relocated to a temporary home in heavily touristed Fisherman's Wharf where, as the *New York Times* noted, "the games will be neighbors with businesses that sell San Francisco snow globes and 'Your Face on Time Magazine' gimmick photos" (Matt Richtel, "Coin-Operated Nostalgia with an Uncertain Future," *New York Times*, 8/17/2002).

The early twentieth-century amusement park and its attractions provide the basis for Ken Jacobs's exploration into the ground zero of cinematic representation, *Razzle Dazzle: The Lost World*. Jacobs's digitally produced video projection takes its evocative title and much of its imagery from a minute-long 1903 Edison *actualité*, which documented the circular whip-like amusement-park ride known as the Razzle Dazzle. Edison's image spins in and out of grainy abstraction, accompanied by a combination of old-timey carnival music and solo-piano waltzes. Jacobs complicates the footage through stroboscopic cutting, invented close-ups, and some meticulous digital colorization. The effect is precise without being slick, as when the artist contrives to have the whole once-photographic image pivot and float away. Later, the picture plane will swell and throb, or take the form of a spinning cube.

Despite such digital razzamatazz, Jacobs's video is largely predicated on the rhythm of projected film. The same impulse can be found in Stan Brakhage's late abstractions—but, unlike Brakhage, Jacobs is never a-historical. He annotates the amusement-park footage with a series of nineteenth-century stereopticon images, with domestic scenes shifting to more spectacular photographs of mid-air leaps and crashing waves. The rapid oscillation of two slightly different points of view produces a shimmering frozen moment, while inducing a shallow 3-D effect.

Using his computer with the enthusiasm of a teenager, Jacobs slices the image like a sausage; he introduces new colors and creates floating vapors to further complicate the spatial ambiguity. *Razzle Dazzle* is all about decoding depth perception. As the amusement park ride warps space, so the movie itself is warped. The image buckles and disintegrates; an invented storm is imposed over the bunting-bedecked ride. As Jacobs focuses ever more closely on the original material, however, this excavation becomes a *memento mori*. Traces of traces, faces of the Lost World start to resemble skulls; Old Man Edison himself materializes, or rather his voice, talking about the "Great War." The stereopticons obligingly provide images of soldiers, battlefields, and Jesus hovering in the sky. Ultimately, these are compressed into a planet of skulls and bones, spinning mid-screen like a Buddhist mandala.

In a sense, *Razzle Dazzle* is a continuous loop. The amusement park merges with the film machine; these long-vanished children are riding the celluloid ribbon through the projector. Despite its defined ending, the piece projects an eternal Now as the artist ponders the infinite possibilities that photography (and re-photography and post-photography) afford to reconstitute the moment—a digital example of film after film.

CHAPTER EIGHTEEN

RUSSIAN ARK (ALEXANDER SOKUROV, 2002; RUSSIA)

The ultimate trip, a post-*2001* space odyssey, Alexander Sokurov's *Russian Ark* is the longest continuous take in the annals of motion pictures, a single ninety-six-minute tracking shot in which the invisible narrator (Sokurov) and a historical figure, the nineteenth-century French Marquis de Custine (Sergey Dreiden), accompany a lively group of dead souls across several centuries and through thirty-three rooms of the Hermitage museum in St. Petersburg.[1]

The narrator wonders if this unfolding pageant has been staged for him, as well he might. Some 2,000 costumed actors and extras, including a full symphony orchestra, rehearsed this unparalleled stunt for seven months before it was shot, on high-definition digital video saved to disc on a custom-built hard drive. A participant in the action, Tilman Büttner's camera peers into windows and swims among the artworks. The terrarium effect is enhanced as people slip and fall on cue, sidling through the slightly wide-angle field of vision. One can only imagine the crazy minuet going on behind the Steadicam. (There were evidently three short false starts, then the entire movie was shot straight through, in late December with only four hours of sufficient daylight.)

A kind of human arabesque, arms folded behind his back, Custine

---

1 Custine's 1839 *Letter from Russia* is to Sokurov's homeland as de Tocqueville's more or less contemporary *Democracy in America* is to the United States—although Custine's book, banned both before and after the October Revolution, might well have been titled *Despotism in Russia*.

skips and strides through the whispery corridors, recalling his previous visit to the Winter Palace and commenting on the half-baked state of Russian culture. The narrator mildly contradicts—and at times, defensively corrects—the caustic marquis's remarks as they wander together through history's backstage, glimpsing Peter the Great beating one of his generals and Catherine II watching a performance in rehearsal (and then frantically searching for a pot to piss in).

By its nature *Russian Ark* emphasizes the forward flow of time, yet the movie is blithely anachronistic and slyly a-chronological. The walls are hung with images of frozen tumult. A blind woman—later identified as an angel—explicates a Van Dyck painting of Madonna and child. The marquis meets the Hermitage's current director and complains that there's an aroma of formaldehyde. Eluding an attempt to close the museum on them, Custine and the narrator stumble upon a royal presentation—emissaries sent by the shah of Persia to apologize to Nicholas I for the murder of some Russian diplomats—and catch sight of Alexander III *en famille*. When the pair open a forbidden door, a custodial worker reproaches them for treading on the corpses of World War I. (The Nazi siege of Leningrad goes tactfully unmentioned.)

Although the viewer may be only intermittently aware of the ongoing tour de force, *Russian Ark* builds in hypnotic intensity toward a suitably mind-boggling finale of the Hermitage's last royal ball. (Although nominally occurring in 1913, the event follows Custine's description of a Hermitage ball as a procession "proceeding from one immense hall to another, winding through galleries, crossing the drawing rooms, and traversing the whole building in such order or direction as the caprice of the individual who leads may dictate.") For eight minutes or so, the camera circles around and threads between hundreds of courtiers dancing the mazurka in the huge Nicholas Hall. (The marquis joins in.) Sokurov can be forgiven for the inscribed applause as the last chord sounds in this crescendo and a sense of pleasurably exhausted melancholy descends.

"Everyone can see the future but no one remembers the past," somebody remarks. In a final flourish, Sokurov's camera cavorts behind and—coming off the grand staircase—pirouettes ahead to gaze back at the exiting throng, revealing more and more people. History disappears into the Petersburg mist. The long day closes and the long take becomes its own meaning in this dazzling dance to the music of time. The narrator murmurs his farewell to Europe and yet, suddenly nostalgic, the marquis has decided to stay with the revelers. What, besides the movie, is ending? Is it modernism or museum culture, socialism or czarism, authentic Russia or bogus imitative Russia? Is it preservation or transcendence or the end of photographic cinema—which both preserves and transcends?

Does *Russian Ark* embody or derange a "progressive" notion of history? And where does Sokurov's movie end? Does it leave us on the eve of the October Revolution (after a mysterious flash forward to the "forbidden room" of World War II) or in the Now floating on a digital sea of eternity?

CHAPTER NINETEEN

TEN (ABBAS KIAROSTAMI, 2002; IRAN)

I t's been a century since the violent, fast-moving pulse-pounder *The Great Train Robbery* left the nickelodeon audience agog. To their credit, motion pictures are still looking for, and sometimes even producing, new sensations—be they gross or subtle. Abbas Kiarostami's *Ten* is something of a cerebral cool breeze.

Like Kiarostami's first-person documentary *ABC Africa* (2001), *Ten* is a movie made possible by new digital video technologies. This is the Iranian director's most form-minded experiment since his 1990 hall-of-mirrors staged doc *Close-Up*. A small digicam planted on the dashboard of a moving automobile records either the vehicle's driver or its passenger. The first of ten numbered sequences begins when a boy of twelve or so (Amin Maher) climbs into the car and immediately begins browbeating the unseen motorist—who, it soon becomes apparent, is his mother.

Their family quarrel escalates as they navigate Tehran. The mother has divorced the boy's father and remarried; the child is upset. He dislikes her new husband even more than her feminist rationale for ending her marriage. Plus, he feels that his father's honor has been besmirched. (In order to get a divorce, his mother had to testify that her husband took drugs—a swipe at Iran's clerical laws.) Ignoring her placating offer of ice cream, the boy petulantly hectors his mother while loudly complaining that she lectures him. He is, in every sense, a little man, elaborately refusing to listen to what she says and then—when she raises her disembodied voice—grandly informing her that "a woman doesn't shout in the street."

The sequence, which lasts around ten minutes and feels like a single take (it isn't), ends with the kid dismissing his mother as an idiot and disembarking for soccer practice. Only then does Kiarostami cut to the driver as she waits for a space and parks her car. The mother (Mania Akbari, who may or may not be a professional actress) proves unexpectedly glamorous in lipstick, shades, and a fashionable white chador. For the rest of the movie, which extends over several days, this unusually independent Iranian woman serves as our Virgil, driving through Tehran in the company of various other females, as well as her never less than irate offspring. Subsequent passengers include her sister, an old woman on her way to pray, a hooker who jumps into her car (reasonably assuming it to be driven by a man), a recently deserted wife, and a younger woman who is having difficulties with an unwilling fiancé.

Every ride is a conversation—although the somewhat stilted trip with the unseen, disconcertingly snickering prostitute—is more of an interview. (She too calls the driver an idiot, although not for the same reasons that her son did.) These sometimes banal discussions of men and women or God and fate take on an unexpected poetry for unfolding in the street—all manner of traffic glimpsed outside the moving car—and yet on such an intimate scale. The only time the camera leaves the automobile is to show the hooker getting into another. The movie's forward velocity is so constant that there's a narrative jolt at one point when the car stops so that the driver can turn around and look at her passenger.

Ten is conceptually rigorous, splendidly economical, and radically Bazinian. Despite certain intimations of allegory and several ongoing storylines, the movie has no dramatic ending—or, rather, it ends as it begins, with the child shouting at his mother as they journey through the midst of life. From a perceptual point of view, the movie is extremely modern. *Ten* is suffused in urban overstimulation and filled with the stuff of the photographic unconscious: fugitive expressions, haphazard compositions, and chance occurrences. Neither fiction nor documentary, it operates in the gap between the two—even as it prompts a certain fascination as to just how it was produced.

Auditioning a number of non-actors, Kiarostami evidently determined what they would talk about in a given scene, and then removed himself when the movie was lensed—at a most generous shooting ratio of 15:1. Thus, one of the few filmmakers since Andy Warhol to rethink the nature of onscreen acting, Kiarostami has called *Ten* a movie made without a director. In fact, the notion of "director" is redefined as the one who plots the course and sets the vehicle in motion. Paradoxically, Kiarostami's own absence serves to push his style to its limit. The more minimal the movie, the more it is recognizably his.

CHAPTER TWENTY

GOODBYE, DRAGON INN (TSAI MING-LIANG, 2002; TAIWAN)

The poet and critic Parker Tyler once described the movie theater as the "psychoanalytic clinic of the average worker." Tsai Ming-liang's *Goodbye, Dragon Inn* puts one such clinic under analysis, examining the inner life of the Fu-Ho theater, a since-demolished poured-concrete cavern in the heart of Taipei. "It is really a film about the memory of this movie theater, which is the 'character' of the film," Tsai has said. "When we go into a movie theater to watch a movie, it's a kind of timeless space, time is in suspension."

As Jack Smith's *Flaming Creatures* is set in a haunted movie studio with various undead movie archetypes at play, so the Fu-Ho is filled with ghosts. This shabby temple is unspooling its last attraction to a handful of devotees: an old *wuxhia* flick—namely, King Hu's 1966 *Dragon Gate Inn*. *Goodbye, Dragon Inn* puts the history of popular cinema in Taiwan between brackets. *Dragon Gate Inn* was the first movie Hu produced after breaking with the Hong Kong–based Shaw Brothers and relocating to Taiwan. Among the most influential martial arts films ever made—enriching the genre with a number of new tropes, including sword-wielding maidens and evil eunuchs—it also put Taiwan's popular cinema on the international map. *Goodbye* consigns that popular cinema to the crypt, along with the audience it attracted, even while receding further in time to evoke the increasingly archaic motion picture apparatus itself.

In one sense, the movie is a superimposed double feature, or a sort of gallery installation, with Hu's wildly kinetic movie collapsed into Tsai's programmatically static one. The action is entirely confined to the Fu-Ho theater and Hu's classic runs throughout—if sometimes present only as reflected light, overheard music or the whir of the projector. At times, the big screen (within the screen) opens a glorious chasm of deep space in the gloomy Fu-Ho bunker. More often, the screen is glimpsed through curtains or severely angled. Always, however, *Dragon Gate Inn* provides *Goodbye* with a variety of shadows to contemplate—in some shots, the internal movie registers only as patterns of light shifting on the empty seats. Meanwhile, Tsai's trademark monsoon allows for the contrapuntal pitter-patter of water leaking through the theater's roof.

The movie is characterized by a pervasive, sometimes comic, sense of loneliness, isolation, yearning and ungratified desire. The patrons include a little boy attending the movie with his nostalgic grandfather, and a lonely Japanese tourist, who alternates between watching the movie and hopefully cruising the largely empty theater. Tsai's characters include a young woman with a severe limp who takes tickets at the box office and cleans up after the show; in a way, she's the spirit of the Fu-Ho theater, the Hunchback of Notre Dame or Phantom of the Opera. The movie ends when she goes home. It's pure movie-movie, a long shot of the ticket-taker receding into the distance to the strains of an old pop lament: "So much of the past lingers in my heart / Half is bitter / Half is sweet / Year after year I can't let it go."

While Tsai's long, static takes are basic Lumière, his narrative evokes the lost world of silent cinema. A prolonged gag is derived from a specta-tor's efforts to retrieve her fallen shoe. A wordless scene in the men's toilet is a small masterpiece of comic timing. The action is a dance of simple activities: The ticket-taker eats her steamed bun and then makes an arduous journey from the box office, leg brace clanking, down an endless corridor and up the narrow stairs to the booth where she leaves a portion of her meal as an offering for the unseen projectionist, mysterious object of her adoration.

The movie-within-the-movie aside, the first line of dialogue occurs midway through: "Do you know this theater is haunted?" someone asks the Japanese tourist. Indeed it is. Poltergeists noisily gobble their sunflower seeds. A pair of feet suddenly materializes over the tour-ist's shoulder. Lights flicker, doors creak, two of *Dragon Inn*'s actors, Miao Tien and Shih Chun, are in the audience watching their young, phantom selves on-screen: "No one goes to the movies anymore. No one remembers us." Tsai, however, is less concerned with nostalgia than a sense of cosmic ritual or what might be called the "cinematic uncanny." (In this sense, *Goodbye, Dragon Inn* is a version of Pat O'Neill's *Decay of Fiction* or a minimalist cousin to Olivier Assayas's *Irma Vep*.)

Goodbye, Dragon Inn has its metaphysical aspect—are the phantoms on the screen or in the audience; is cinema spiritual or material; does the projectionist really exist? In a witty inside joke, the man in the booth rewinding *Dragon Gate Inn* turns out to be Tsai's axiomatic protagonist and alter ego, Lee Kang-sheng. He's the prime mover and it's his story after all.

CHAPTER TWENTY-ONE

DOGVILLE (LARS VON TRIER, 2003; DENMARK)

A beautiful fugitive named Grace (Nicole Kidman) is harbored, exploited and nearly martyred by the denizens of the eponymous small American town until, in a convulsive finale, she brings down God's wrath upon them. The movie has countless echoes—both filmic and literary—and yet is immediately recognizable as something new.

An austere parable of failed Christian charity and Old Testament payback, its action divided into nine chapters and infused with the fathomless sarcasm of John Hurt's rich, insinuating voiceover, *Dogville* is less a narrative movie than the blueprint for a movie given form by the mind's eye—it is entirely filmed, *vérité* style, on an obvious schematic and highly minimalist set and although described as filmed theater, feels more like filmed radio.

Von Trier stipulated that most of the cast had to be present on the set for most of the shooting—six weeks at close quarters in a giant hangar somewhere in Sweden: "The team of actors will be on stage all the time, because there are no walls between the buildings. We are going to live together." No boundaries, everyone together: von Trier, the former communist, is always dreaming of a utopian collective. He is also dreading its realization—see *The Idiots* (1998), a movie about acting ... out, and, even more, see Jesper Jargil's documentary of its making, *The Humiliated*. (*The Humiliated* makes clear that *The Idiots* was a pretext to make something happen in life as much as on film.)

Dogville is a tour de force of ensemble acting. (The oddball cast includes Ben Gazzara as a solitary blind man in proud denial; Lauren Bacall as an acerbic shopkeeper; and Philip Baker Hall as the hypochondriac town doctor, along with Patricia Clarkson, Chloë Sevigny, Stellan Skarsgård and Paul Bettany, as the nominal hero, a smug do-gooder and writer manqué.) Kidman delivers yet another remarkable performance—acting "natural" in an almost absurdly diagrammatic setting and even playing a character who seems "naturally" good. Albeit a gangster's daughter on the lam, Grace is direct, honest and above all positive, her thoughtful formulations framed as sunshine clichés. Is she an illegal immigrant? A political refugee? A fallen angel?

Dogville is set in an America one might abstract from Hollywood movies. Like *Bonnie and Clyde*, *Dogville* evokes the Depression era with a few cloche hats, Model Ts and a bit of FDR over the radio, while von Trier populates his isolated Rocky Mountain community with stock figures ranging from the boy inventor and the black mammy to the town doctor and the big-city gangster. Its tale of martyrdom and hypocrisy could hardly seem un-American to anyone familiar with Nathaniel Hawthorne's *The Scarlet Letter* or Theodore Dreiser's excoriating *Sister Carrie* or the corrosive late Mark Twain of *Letters from the Earth* or the prophetic scolding of Bob Dylan's *John Wesley Harding* or the resentment of Clint Eastwood's *High Plains Drifter*. The famously agoraphobic von Trier has never been to the United States, but like that other mental traveler Franz Kafka, he's imagined an Amerika that, in its iconography and concerns, seems almost a contribution to American literature—in this case, to the specific genre of the jeremiad. (This angry sermonizing is amplified, of course, by *Dogville*'s visual puritanism.)

Dogville's fascination with the sin of pride—or "arrogance" as it's usually called—has, for some, a particular resonance, and not only because von Trier himself is often so characterized. His imaginary Rocky Mountain town exhibits more than its share of confident self-deception. *Dogville*'s main drag is nostalgically named Elm Street, although, as Hurt notes, it is a thoroughfare "on which no elm had ever cast its shadow." The silver-mine may be abandoned, but some sort of cosmic drama is about to unfold at the dead end of the Rocky Mountain road. Grace's first day of work, doing odd jobs for the townspeople, is the spring equinox; the Fourth of July marks her glorious integration into Dogville's polity. Blossoms fill the air as the townspeople hold their Independence Day picnic and together sing Irving Berlin's patriotic hymn "America the Beautiful": "God shed his grace on thee." Speaking for the town, the blind man thanks Grace for showing them who she is—by which he means sharing her innate goodness. Then the appearance of a police "wanted poster" precipitates Dogville's moral crisis: Will these good folks believe authority or their own eyes?

Even though the townspeople may think Grace innocent, they feel guilty for not reporting her presence—guilty and, somehow, self-righteously entitled. Sentiment builds to drive out the fugitive. Grace offers to leave, but Tom intervenes. He persuades her to stay and his fellow citizens to assuage their fears by exacting greater evidence of her gratitude, giving Grace additional work for less pay. As the town sins by its exploitation of Grace, a malicious child precipitates her inevitable downfall. By now it is autumn. Fog rolls across the set. Grace is raped in the apple orchard. Hurt's narration assumes a tragic tone. The fugitive is punished—not least for her various good deeds. At this point, the movie does become painful. Grace is enslaved and chained like a dog to be used at will by the town's men and is betrayed even by her self-appointed protector Tom (although he alone fails to take sexual advantage). When the townspeople turn on him for, however insipidly, defending Grace, and Grace finally questions what Mark Twain would call his "moral sense," the petulant writer drops a dime and summons her pursuers.

Five days later the convoy of black sedans arrives in Dogville. God shed his Grace and now He has returned—in the form of gangster king James Caan. *Dogville* builds in suffering to the apocalyptic conclusion (the town's nightmare on Elm Street). America, as we are often told, is the most Christian nation on earth; *Dogville* creates a space within which to wonder what exactly that means. Grace is unwillingly reunited with her (God)father and, as the fate of the hapless town hangs in the balance, these two Hollywood deities sit in the back seat of a chauffeured automobile pedantically debating the definition of arrogance, discussing the quality of mercy and parsing the nature of human nature.

Dogville has a horrifying denouement, but the movie saves its catharsis for the end credits—a devastating juxtaposition of pop music and photographic evidence. David Bowie's perky disco anthem ("A-a-a-ll-ll night, she was a young American!") provides the contrapuntal soundtrack for the most wrenching images of human misery, many of them culled from Jacob Holdt's *American Pictures*. It's a nasty joke, but the music is so stirring and—who could laugh at these images of naked distress? The town's hitherto unseen dog turns "real" at the end, and so does von Trier's America.

CHAPTER TWENTY-TWO

THE WORLD (JIA ZHANGKE, 2004; CHINA)

The amusement park has served filmmakers as a ready-made set, if not a found allegorical landscape, at least since Edwin Porter's 1903 *Rube and Mandy at Coney Island*. In both F. W. Murnau's *Sunrise* (1927) and Pál Fejös's *Lonesome* (1928), the urban amusement park functions as the nexus of freedom and modernity; nowadays, as in *The Truman Show* (1998), movies are more likely to posit imaginary theme parks as sinister manifestations of un-freedom and post-modernity. But few films have been as confined to the location as Jia Zhangke's *The World*, and few amusement parks offer the Beijing World Park's hermetic totality.

A 115-acre tract southwest of the city, the World Park opened in 1993, with "scenic areas" devoted to Asia, Africa, Europe, the United States, and Latin America. Trains and motorboats traverse the park, simulating a trip around the world. Attractions include scale models of the Cheops Pyramid, the Eiffel Tower, and the White House; the Statue of Liberty, Copenhagen's Little Mermaid, and the Venus de Milo are among the featured statues. Jia compounds the site's geographical delirium by merging the World Park with its sister attraction, the Shenzhen World Window, hundreds of miles to the south, while blurring the distinction between onstage and backstage. *The World* opens with a prolonged SteadiCam tour of a chaotic dressing room as the dancer Tao (Zhao Tao), in a gauzy green harem outfit, noisily solicits her comrade showgirls for a Band-Aid before she goes out to perform on the stage adjacent to the mini-Taj Mahal. Despite her apparent brashness,

Tao will remain throughout the movie alone in the World and seeking emotional solace.

Jia's previous films peered behind the facade of the Chinese economic miracle; *The World* makes that facade its subject. As metaphor—not to mention as documentary backdrop—the film's hyper-globalizing, oppressively ersatz location is almost too powerful. In its dedication to social organization, including the rationalized pleasure principle, the theme park has long been recognized as an ideological happy hunting ground that is both an achieved Utopia and a form of soft totalitarianism—and this is particularly true in East Asia where, as Ian Buruma noted in the *New York Review of Books*, themed environments like the Beijing World Park "are to East Asian capitalism what folk dancing festivals were to communism."[1]

The World Park's slogan is "Give us a day, we'll show you the world"; its theme music is Beethoven's "Ode to Joy." (The lone trace of Communism may be the atmosphere of enforced optimism.) Tao and her boyfriend, Taisheng, a security guard, as well as the other workers of the World, are diligent, docile consumers—highly media-trained, well-adjusted to ongoing upheaval, and thoroughly privatized in their aspirations. All have come to Beijing from someplace else; only one is seen to have any family. Although more socially integrated than the protagonists of Jia's previous films, they are even less rooted in a recognizable social reality.

Hardly McLuhan's global village, their milieu is a social illusion. It might as well be cyberspace. Cell phones figure in nearly every scene, providing characters with instant updates on their paramours and thus combining a private existence with a generalized sense of total surveillance. One is seldom more conscious of words bouncing off a satellite than while watching this film. To dramatize the web of spurious communication, *The World* is punctuated with perky, animated versions of the

---

1   Where folk-dancing pageants demonstrated joyous social cohesion, however, the World Park is designed to dramatize social cohesion and showcase economic growth. American theme parks are typically repositories of a sanitized or substitute national history (and in the former East Germany and the Czech Republic, the *mentalité* of the lost Communist order, known in German as *ostalgie*, has been preserved in the form of ironic or cautionary theme parks). Asian theme parks, Buruma suggests, have no particular interest in history—save for its obliteration. Ultimately, all China will become "a continent-sized Singapore" where "constant fun and games will make free thought redundant."

text messages that Tao regularly receives—stand-ins for her inner life. A techno-pop score, the first unmotivated music in any Jia film, provides a sense of voluptuous anomie, while shots of an empty highway add to the sedated sci-fi quality. It is never entirely clear when the working day or where the World Park ends.

Happy tourists practice tai chi by the Tower of Pisa and pose for photos in front of the Vatican. This People's Xanadu provides a sort of canned Marco Polo experience—although its extravagantly costumed employees are themselves unable to travel. A planet without borders for a land without passports: the park's attractions include a tour of a grounded jetliner. One scene, recalling the visit to the photographer's studio in *Sunrise*, has Tao and Taisheng make a souvenir DV in which their images are matted into an imaginary magic-carpet ride. Tao is fascinated by a troupe of Russian dancers who seem less guest workers than slave laborers—they embody the exotic otherness that she enacts. (Over the course of the movie, she appears as a Hindu princess, a stewardess, an African, a geisha, and a Western bride.) Tao befriends one of the Russian women; because they lack a common language, they each imagine the other to be free.

The World's world has its share of scams and crimes, fatal injuries and romantic betrayals. (Taisheng cheats on Tao with a seamstress-entrepreneur who, in keeping with the theme of total simulation, specializes in inexpensive copies of European fashions.) The various lies and deceptions are appropriate to those of the World Park. And yet all these plot developments feel curiously muted, even irrelevant. Has the melodrama been rendered absurd by the spectacle of young people quarreling in spangled Elizabethan doublets, or subdued by the seductive emptiness of China's brave new World? The facade feels impervious, and is an unavoidable part of the movie itself. *The World* may well be a sort of anti-infomercial for the World Park, but it celebrates the park nonetheless.[2]

Just as a stray water cooler blocks the view of the miniaturized Taj Mahal in one of *The World*'s picture-postcard panoramas, so documentary overshadows the movie's narrative (while leaving an overwhelming sense of loneliness and alienation). The exits are closed and time stands

---

2   As pointed out by Valerie Jaffee, a visiting scholar at the Beijing Film Academy, in an onset report for the online journal *Senses of Cinema*, this critique of "sham cosmopolitanism" will be the movie that facilitates Jia's transition from international film-festival star to domestic success.

still. As in socialist realism, life has improved, comrades—which is to say that, in this materialized fantasy, the fake trumps the real. History, too, has been banished, personal and otherwise. The World Park's mini-Manhattan, Taisheng proudly informs visiting homeboys, still has its Towers.[3]

---

3 The Beijing World Park was one of three authorized "protest zones" during the 2008 Beijing Olympics, an event for which *The World* offers a prescient critique. Would-be demonstrators were obliged to obtain police permits and provide detailed information on the nature of the protest and identity of the expected protestors. According to the BBC (8/18/2008), seventy-seven applications were received, seventy-four of these were "withdrawn," two "suspended" and one "vetoed"—and some would-be protesters appeared to have been arrested after making their applications.

CHAPTER TWENTY-THREE

BATTLE IN HEAVEN (CARLOS REYGADAS, 2005; MEXICO)

M ade forty years ago, Andy Warhol talkies like *Vinyl* and *Beauty #2* remain the *reductio ad absurdum* of behavioral direction— non-actors coping with minimal instruction and a camera guaranteed to grind relentlessly on until it runs out of film.

Going beyond Warhol is never easy but ambitious directors have intermittently experimented with this form of situational performance. Each in its way, Lars von Trier's *Idiots* and Abbas Kiarostami's *Ten* is predicated on a set-up designed to cue on-camera improvisation. With *Battle in Heaven*, Mexican filmmaker Carlos Reygadas established himself as a Warholian impresario who, working without a screenplay, creates existential conditions where non-professional actors are compelled to expose themselves—sometimes cruelly—on camera.

The designated outrage of the 2005 Cannes Film Festival, *Battle in Heaven* appeared in competition amid rumors of earlier rejected versions. The audience was primed for graphic sex and indeed Reygadas began his second feature by quoting Warhol's *Blow Job*: a leisurely close up of a middle-aged man's face, impassive yet noticeably responding to some form of stimulation happening outside of the frame. Accompanied by saccharine string music, the camera pans down his portly frame to reveal that he is being serviced by a young woman with an extravagant bird's nest coiffure. The camera slowly zooms in, pivots and re-zooms. A reverse angle reveals the fellatrix in close-up. Her closed eyes open, each dropping a single, jewel of a tear as though she were the Virgin of Guadalupe—which, in a sense, she turns out to be. Reygadas has called this opener an overture. Like the complementary scene that postscripts the action, it functions like the famous close-up of the bandit firing at the camera in *The Great Train Robbery*—an attraction that is about, but not of, the narrative which, in addition to providing the occasion for explicit sex, almost incidentally desecrates Mexican militarism, religious piety, and love of soccer. Indeed, having thus commandeered the audience's attention, Reygadas cuts to a sequence of Mexican soldiers marching in formation as they prepare to raise the nation's flag above its capital city. The equation between the two rituals is clinched by the presence of the man we've just seen, tagging along as the general's chauffeur.

Battle in Heaven details the mortal, if not mythological, combat between Marcos, played by Marcos Hernández, an actual driver (for Reygadas's father, no less) and his general's daughter Ana played, under the name "Anapola Mushkadiz," by the actual, and then teen-aged, daughter of a wealthy Mexican media mogul. No less than Warhol superstars, they essentially impersonate themselves—a connection reinforced by Mushkadiz's uncanny *Poor Little Rich Girl* resemblance to the well-bred, ever-poised, throaty-voiced Factory ingénue Edie Sedgwick.

Co-conspirators in Reygadas's film, each of these class antagonists has a criminal secret. Seeking to make a quick score, Marcos and his wife have orchestrated and botched the kidnapping of a neighbor's baby; Ana, like the protagonist of Buñuel's *Belle de Jour*, amuses herself by working in a brothel, euphemistically referred to as "The Boutique." Marcos, naturally, is acquainted with Ana's other life and, offering a confession she scarcely knows what do to with, he tells her about his. In the enigmatic universe of Reygadas's cinema, this leads first to sex and then death; the movie's title has the effect of locating a cosmic struggle amid everyday life. During the central scene of Ana and Marcos fucking, the camera simply wanders off, drifting away to observe workers putting up a satellite dish, the hazy skyline, kids at play, and other apartment windows, before circling back to the unlikely lovers.

This is actually the most conventional of the movie's sexual interludes. To judge from the response at Cannes, audiences were far more disturbed by a scene of stolid, not untender, conjugal relations between Marcos and his thick-necked, rotund, señora. (Mrs. Marcos is played by Bertha Ruiz;

not surprisingly, Regyadas maintains that he wanted Fernandez's actual and he's said, even more obese, wife.) Meanwhile, the hovering presence of a household religious shrine allows for the comparison of these all too real human bodies to Christ's mortified flesh.

With its rigorous camera placement, *Battle in Heaven* suggests Warhol by way of Fassbinder, presenting ordinary people in de-eroticized erotic situations with an uninflected stylization based on head-on compositions and long static takes. As a good post-Warholian, Reygadas makes effective use of fixed camera and off-screen sound throughout. Marcos and his wife have a long introductory scene shot in close-ups and staged in a crowded subway underpass. (Like the non-actress who plays her, she sells jellies in the metro.) The surreal detail of a gas station blasting classical music through its loudspeakers is resolved once one realizes that the proprietor is attempting to drown out the chanting of the penitents wending their way to the Basilica of Guadalupe: "We're going to heaven and you hold the key."

At the movie's climax, bare-chested Marcos joins the religious procession, face hidden inside a blue hood, crawling blindly forward on his knees. In an extended quasi-documentary passage, Reygadas takes advantage of Our Lady's festivities, planting actors amid the crowd—presumably including the two young, ice cream-eating police women, who cast a bored eye on Marcos as he struggles past them towards his date with eternity.

Ritualistic as it is, *Battle in Heaven* suggests a new sort of ceremonial cinema at once dauntingly local and boldly universal. Certainly, Reygadas seems closer to Arturo Ripstein's extravagantly feel-bad melodramas—particularly the 1997 cine-cult extravaganza *Divine*—or the sado-surrealistic showbiz mysticism of Alejandro Jodorowsky's counterculture sacraments *El Topo* and *The Holy Mountain*, than with the movies of Mexico's current new wave. Unlike the more conventionally insolent Carlos Carrera, Alfonso Cuarón or Alejandro González Iñárritu, the precocious Reygadas has found a way to insert himself into an ongoing discourse in cinema history. *The Sin of Father Amaro, Y Tu Mamá También,* and *Amores Perros* represent; *Battle in Heaven* is.[1]

---

1 As a postscript to Reygadas's would-be outrage, I witnessed a small real-life drama involving its principals. The filmmaker and his stars had just left a press conference where the poised Mushkadiz held forth charmingly on her dilettantism, and were ascending Cannes's fabled *tapis rouge* to their

public screening. Suddenly, seemingly out of nowhere, jury member Salma Hayek descended from celebrity Olympus to greet her countryman. Abashed and publicly snubbed, blinded by the material presence of a real movie star, Mushkadiz broke character and simply seemed ... really lost: *Battle in Heaven* to be sure.

CHAPTER TWENTY-FOUR

THE DEATH OF MR. LAZARESCU (CRISTI PUIU, 2005; ROMANIA)

If there's a tougher sell than a Romanian movie by a hitherto unknown director, it's a Romanian movie by an unknown director that takes two and half hours to tell the tale of a sixty-two-year-old pensioner's final trip to the hospital—a journey to the end of the night (and "a grinding ordeal" per *New York Times* critic Stephen Holden) uninvitingly called *The Death of Mr. Lazarescu.*

The second feature by thirty-nine-year-old ex-painter Cristi Puiu is an ode to mortality, albeit not without a certain grim humor. (Call it deadpan.) Puiu's everyman Dante Remus Lazarescu, a retired engineer, living alone with his cats and the bottle, wakes with an unfamiliar headache and a bad stomach and, after a day of futile self-medication, calls the local equivalent of 911. Time passes; the sound of the TV news mixes with the reverberating boom box upstairs. Lazarescu consults the couple living across the hall. "An ambulance on Saturday—do you think they will bother?" the husband wonders. It's fun to talk symptoms; hanging out in the hallway where the light flickers on and off, they discuss various remedies. The neighbors, themselves a pair of heart attacks waiting to happen, are not uninterested in the old man's case but totally self-absorbed. (When he vomits a bit of blood, he's offered a plate of homemade moussaka.) Life goes on: intense self-preoccupation amid teeming social existence is the heart of this movie.

After forty-five minutes (film time), the ambulance arrives, and from the limbo of his squalid flat, our Dante enters the first circle of hell, presided over by a medic so ferociously angry he might be named Dr. Cerberus. For the remainder of the movie, he will be transported from hospital to hospital, to be variously diagnosed, ignored, browbeaten, humiliated, and finally processed by a harried succession of brilliantly acted doctors and nurses. Sympathy is in short supply. "Why did they bring him here?" the first of these medical professionals demands, even going so far as to order Lazarescu off the gurney. (He promptly falls.) It's a running joke that everyone immediately assumes the patient is simply drunk. Maybe so, but even drunks can have symptoms. Indeed, before long, the increasingly objectified Lazarescu does begin to babble incoherently, alone amid the gossipy hubbub, in the pitiless illumination of the harsh fluorescent lights.

The Death of Mr. Lazarescu is highly scripted but shot like a documentary. As filmmaking, it's a tour de force, with Puiu successfully simulating—or rather, orchestrating—the institutional texture of a Frederick Wiseman *vérité*. (According to the director, the movie was shot over a period of thirty-nine nights on location in various Bucharest hospitals.) The ensemble is constantly talking; when not squeezed into an impossibly tight corner, the camera is in near continual motion. Puiu claims his inspiration was the NBC warhorse *ER*: "When you watch the American TV series, there's movement in every direction, the choreography of the characters is amazing ... In my country, doctors and everyone else live in slow motion, as if they were on Valium and still had 500 years to live." Of course, *ER* manages to successfully resolve three or four cases over the course of an hour and *The Death of Mr. Lazarescu*, well ...[1]

Among other things, the movie's staged hyper-reality offers a stunning dialectic between drama and artifice—where did Puiu find these actors? Ion Fiscuteanu in particular demonstrates an astonishing absence of vanity in the title role. Puiu's movie also oscillates between naturalism and allegory. The endlessly patient paramedic (Luminita Gheorghiu)

---

1   Subsequently asked by interviewer Christoph Huber to clarify his feelings about *ER*, Puiu replied: "Actually, 'inspired' is the wrong word. I'm revolted by it! The way they treat the patients is completely unbelievable ... What disgusts me about *ER* is how the doctors are portrayed, their level of involvement [with their patients]." Allowing that *Lazarescu* was in part a representation of the institution, Puiu told Huber that the movie was "not so much about the social level, but the metaphysical level," namely "the extinction of a human being" (*Cinema Scope*, Spring 2006).

who initially fetched Lazarescu from his flat is obliged to wait with him in various emergency rooms and then escort her charge to successive hospitals as his diagnosis becomes increasingly dire. She would be his Virgil except that the movie already has a character named Virgil who is never actually seen. (Virgil is married to Eva; their resonant names, like Lazarescu's grandiose, oft-reiterated moniker, give the movie the sense of unfolding on some grotesque kitchen-sink Olympus.) In any case, the paramedic becomes Lazarescu's surrogate in that the hospital workers tend to see his case as her problem: "Doctor, can't we help her?" a colleague pleads by way of asking him to admit Lazarescu.

By the movie's end, with the unconscious protagonist lying shaven and prepped at his fourth hospital, he will have lost everything. *The Death*—or should we call it *The Passion?—of Mr. Lazarescu* is nothing if not visceral, at times recalling Stan Brakhage's avant-garde morgue documentary *The Act of Seeing With One's Own Eyes*. All the talk about smells, beginning with the stink of Lazarescu's cat-ridden apartment, inspires gratitude that the movie's verisimilitude doesn't extend to aroma-rama. We are spared the issue of pain as well—Lazarescu may complain, but at least he isn't screaming in agony. Nevertheless, his ordeal is our spectacle as well as our fate. Life is for the living; however large the crowd or busy the ward, the dead and the dying are on their own.[2]

Puiu's 2010 *Aurora* is a murder mystery in which the killer's identity is known but his motives are not and, like *The Death of Mr. Lazarescu*, something of a test. The premise is absurdist (and ultimately humorous), but, despite the probing of a documentary-style camera, little is immediately apparent. The near-total absence of establishing shots and abundance of seeming non sequiturs renders every cut a jolt. The compositions are typically underlit or obstructed; the movie's characteristic setup has the action glimpsed through a half-open door. As confounding in its way as *L'avventura* must have seemed in 1960, *Aurora* piques curiosity and provokes hyper-vigilance. That the protagonist's expression rarely changes, that he never quite understands what anyone says to him, and that he appears in nearly every shot, becomes even stranger if you know that this furtive yet compulsive character is played by the movie's director. Less a

---

2 *The Death of Mr. Lazarescu* is in some way also about the death of Romania's revived cinema. Although the most popular Romanian language film shown in Romania in 2005, its total audience was 30,000 people.

psychological case study than a philosophical treatise, *Aurora* embodies the "shame of self" that Sartre describes in *Being and Nothingness* as the disconcerting recognition that one is "the object which the Other is looking at and judging."

CHAPTER TWENTY-FIVE

DAY NIGHT DAY NIGHT
(JULIA LOKTEV, 2006; USA)

A frail-looking young woman, outfitted with a bomb, wanders through Times Square—finger on the switch, searching for the moment to blow up. That, in a sentence, is the premise of Julia Loktev's outrageously abstract *Day Night Day Night*.

Terror is existential in this highly intelligent, somewhat sadistic, totally fascinating movie. Identified in the manner of a French "new novel" only as She, the teenaged *suicidiste* (Luisa Williams) is introduced on a cross-country bus en route to her fatal rendezvous. "Everybody dies," she chants in an accent-free whisper, then addressing an otherwise Higher Power, adds, "My death will be for You."

As its title suggests, *Day Night Day Night* has two halves. The first is devoted to the preparation. She gets off the bus and contacts her handlers, is taken for a quick ramen dinner, and dropped at a nondescript New Jersey motel. Awaiting further instructions, She bathes, shaves her armpits, clips her toenails, and washes her clothes—anxiety mounting despite, or perhaps because of, these banal, yet final, activities. Before her hooded handlers arrive, She blindfolds and handcuffs herself—becoming, in effect, her own victim. Her handlers give her instructions and invite her to ask questions (which they ignore). Treated gently, as if not quite human, She touchingly invites her comrades to share the pizza that's been ordered. She doesn't want to eat alone.

The Russian-born, thirty-something Loktev has an extremely dry sense of humor. The three ski-masked palookas suggest that She might want to record a video for her parents. "My parents are dead," the girl timidly offers. No matter, She's dressed up in vaguely military garb and posed, holding a carbine, before a generic militant backdrop. As a costume for the mission, She models a bunch of Kmart outfits. (Finally, the handlers nix the pink Baby Girl zippered sweatshirt in favor of a striped sweater.) She's given an identity to memorize and interminably drilled. Process is all: She is evidently a woman of faith but her cell has no obvious politics, no apparent religion, no overt nationality.

The mission is all about directing a performance—as is the movie. Williams, a neophyte actress who Loktev says she chose from 650 candidates (perhaps because, as the press notes maintain, the actress developed a tween crush on Anthony Perkins's Norman Bates), has Mediterranean coloring, a tentative little voice, and a not-quite crucifix around her neck. Her character is obedient, fastidious, and dutiful; her sharp features are squeezed together, large eyes sunk deep within the heart-shaped, bony face that frequently fills the screen. It's a great turn—a virtual solo. (Not since Bresson's *Trial of Joan of Arc* or the Dardennes' *Rosetta*, two movies that anticipate Loktev's strategy, has an actor been so closely and continuously observed.) Williams's intense focus may mirror that of her director; Loktev's first feature *Moment of Impact* was a disturbingly intrusive documentary on the daily life of her severely disabled father.

Day Night Day Night's second half begins with She's emergence from the Port Authority outfitted with a lethal backpack ("It's about 50 pounds, but most of the weight is in the nails," She's been told) into the sensory bombardment of midday Eighth Avenue. It's documented street theater. Walking through the crowd, She resembles the Professor in Joseph Conrad's *The Secret Agent*, although Loktev's model is more likely Hitchcock's *Sabotage*—the grandfather of all suicide-bomber flicks, including Hany Abu-Assad's more politically "responsible" *Paradise Now*.[1]

---

1   Telling the tale of two West Bank auto mechanics whose mission in Israel goes unexpectedly awry, *Paradise Now* (2005) was a heroic undertaking; the movie was shot on location in Nablus, as well as Abu-Assad's hometown, Nazareth, with the filmmakers dodging near daily firefights and missile attacks while walking a cautious line between the Israeli occupying army and various Palestinian armed factions. The politics are similarly ambiguous or, rather, complex. Audaciously as well, Abu-Assad imbues *Paradise Now* with a measure of dark absurdism. The youthful mechanics—Said (Kais Nashef) and Khaled (Ali Suliman)—receive their assignments only a day in advance. The most

Real surveillance has become more virtual. The camera runs free, and over-stimulation reigns: She seems dazed, asking the way to Times Square and proceeding down the Deuce with a big mustard-slathered pretzel in each hand. Someone slams into her, tourists ask her to take their pictures, police sirens blare, unwelcome suitors appear. She ducks into a huge candy emporium for a jelly apple. (Food is an issue throughout.) Free-floating anxiety gives way to fear and trembling, being and nothingness, curiosity and impatience. She pees her pants. A public toilet must be negotiated—as well as a pay phone. She panhandles a quarter; the donor wishes her a nice day.

So what's the game plan? Where's the moment of impact? Will there be an epiphany? At key moments, the crowd is reduced to extreme close-ups of individual gestures, the sound cutting in and out like waves pounding the beach as the scarily sympathetic terrorist's finger trembles over the iPod switch that will trigger the bomb in her childish yellow backpack. Time stands still; the wait is interminable. However low-budget and minimalist, this digitally shot, quasi-guerrilla production is a new-style disaster flick—as experiential in its way as the ritual ordeal provided by *United 93*. But, here however, there is catharsis neither for the terrorist nor the audience.

Were it not for its durational aspect, Loktev's concept might also have been realized as a performance piece or a gallery installation. Unlike *Paradise Now*, *Day Night Day Night* has no interest in mapping the prime mental terra incognita of contemporary politics. The movie

---

elaborate preparation involves the videotaping of their farewell statements. (Later we discover that local video emporiums do a brisk business in the sale and rental of such martyr tapes—as well as their opposite, tapes that document the execution of Palestinian "traitors.") A true filmmaker, Abu-Assad does not resist the temptation to restage the tawdry mise-en-scène, amateurish overdirection, and maladroit camera operation involved in the making of the tape. He's less specific regarding the nature of the cell that has recruited Said and Khaled—it seems too secular to be Hamas, insufficiently ideological for the Al Aqsa Martyrs Brigade. Newly shaved and anointed, the human time bombs are sent off, amid a hubbub of prayers, to cross the green line (with surprising ease) into Israel. It is in this sequence, with the terrorists wandering in their "wedding suits" through a landscape that they have never before seen, that *Paradise Now* packs a powerful existential wallop. The friends are separated. Lost amid his potential victims, Said experiences disorientation, doubt, and the stolid acceptance of his fate.

has nothing to do with the psychology of the suicide bomber and everything to do with the psychology of the spectator: "My death will be for You."[2]

---

2   Some days after a car bomb was found in the Times Square area on the evening of April 30, 2010, the Sundance Channel suspended scheduled telecasts of *Day Night Day Night*. Alluding to *Saturday Night Live*'s comic sketch spoofing the confessed bomber, Pakistani-born US citizen Faisal Shahzad, broadcast on May 8, Loktev told *indieWIRE* that "it says a lot that we've reached a point where something like that can be shown now. So, was the problem that *Day Night Day Night* wasn't funny?" (Anthony Kaufman, *Cannes Winner Cut: Sundance Challenged for Pulling Bomb Plotline Picture*, 5/11/2010: www.indiewire.com/article/sundance_channel_suspension_director_decries_day_night_day_night_decision/.)

CHAPTER TWENTY-SIX

SOUTHLAND TALES
(RICHARD KELLY, 2006; USA)

A doom-ridden pulp cabalist with a dark sense of purpose as well as humor, Richard Kelly shoots the moon with his rich, strange, and very funny sci-fi social satire, *Southland Tales*.

Kelly's debut, *Donnie Darko*, was the first post-millennial cult hit; his second feature achieved *film maudit* status long before the credits rolled during its disastrous press screening at the 2006 Cannes Film Festival. (Kelly might have lost half the audience two minutes in by simply quoting T. S. Eliot's sonorous "This is the way the world ends ..." in the context of a suburban barbecue.) *Southland Tales* recognizes the protocols of the National Entertainment State, but, flirting with sensory overload and predicated on a familiarity with American TV, political rhetoric, corporate trademarks, and religious cant, it's a movie without a recognizable genre or readymade demographic. The French hated it (some things don't travel); so did the Americans (too much information can breed resentment).

Kelly's fever dream premiered at two hours and forty-five minutes; subsequently trimmed by twenty minutes—subplots dropped and explanatory voice-over added—it remains a gloriously sprawling, over-stimulating, and enjoyably unsynopsizeable spectacle. (Indeed, as demonstrated by the *Donnie Darko* director's cut, Kelly is actually better when his cosmology remains obscure.) Fictions breed and conspiracies multiply in this self-aware pop object, alternately over- and under-explicated by cartoonish characters speaking in agitated tele-clichés.

Every aspect of this convoluted narrative is monitored, scripted, and directed from within the movie. Half the characters are watching the other half or else producing their own self-promoting video vehicles. The news cycle spins merrily out of control, along with something that Kelly is pleased to term a rift in the space-time continuum.

History in this alternative universe was changed not by 9/11 but a July 5, 2005 nuclear terror attack on Abilene, Texas. Introductory home video footage of the mushroom cloud, as seen at a suburban barbeque, yields to a gaudy political phantasmagoria unfolding mainly around Venice, Hermosa Beach, and the Santa Monica pier. Where *Donnie Darko*, which opened in New York just before Halloween 2001, uncannily anticipated the city's post-9/11 mood, *Southland Tales* sets out to evoke what Sasha Baron Cohen's Borat called Bush's "War of Terror" and, no less than Baron Cohen, Kelly pushes a particular logic to comic extremes.

Oil prices have spiked and an absurd German multinational has figured out how to produce energy—along with a new psychedelic drug—from the ocean. The draft is back; war has spread from Iraq and Afghanistan to Syria. Thanks to the Patriot Act, cyberspace is under government control, leased to a corporation called USIdent that's visualized as a war room of multiple video monitors. Every phone is tapped; any public activity may be taped. Even the bathroom stalls at LAX are monitored. USIdent deploys SWAT teams at will while army snipers are positioned offshore, their RPGs trained on the heedless beach. (It's one of the movie's jokes that the populace insists on its right to party.) Plus, it's an election year. The Republicans have nominated the poetic team of Eliot and Frost (many invocations of the "road not taken"). In a throwaway gag, it's noted that the Democrats are running Clinton and Lieberman. Local leftwing terrorists have a fish bowl of severed thumbs used to manufacture bogus votes.

Former wrestler Dwayne "The Rock" Johnson heads the large cast of familiar icons—many recruited from *Saturday Night Live*—playing an anxious, amnesiac celebrity, action-hero Boxer Santaros. He's paired with TV's diminutive vampire-slayer Sarah Michelle Gellar, here a socially conscious porn queen with a business plan who, mirroring the movie's desire to embody the present moment, calls herself Krysta Now. Working with this unlikely pair, Kelly contrives two memorable comic performances as well as a convincing tabloid love story. Fingers nervously aflutter, the Rock projects a poignant blankness—he's always trying to comprehend the Now. Gellar, by contrast, is a briskly determined, humorless firebrand. "All the Pilgrims did was ruin the Indian orgy of freedom," she snaps to a sex-star-posse roundtable during the course of her *View*-like "topical discussion chat-reality show."

Having been abducted and brainwashed, no longer remembering his marriage to Madeline Frost (sunny pop star Mandy Moore, here superbly petulant), the daughter of Republican VP candidate Bobby Frost (Donnie Darko's dad, Holmes Osborne), Santaros is shacked up with Krysta. Together they've written a screenplay titled *The Power* that, among other things, serves to program the dithering hero as well as Kelly's movie. Rival blackmailers—a self-described "international documentary filmmaker" (Nora Dunn) and a volatile urban guerrilla (Cheri Oteri)—strive to exploit the Santaros–Now liaison as a means to intervene in the election, variously employing a troubled cop whose twin brother is an Iraq veteran (both Seann William Scott) and a slam poet (Amy Poehler) who boasts that "all your regulation can't stop this masturbation." The secret controllers, however, are the Baron von Westphalen (sinister gnome Wallace Shawn), inventor of the alternative energy psychedelic drug Liquid Karma, and Nana Mae Frost (Miranda Richardson), the candidate's wife, who spends all her time in the USIdent control center.

Southland Tales begins *in media res*, bombarding the audience with chunks of back-story. (Like *Donnie Darko*, *Southland Tales*—originally imagined as a nine-part extravaganza of movie, interactive website, graphic novel—is an example of convergence cinema: Kelly provided MySpace pages for his characters and a website for USIdent, while Gellar released Krysta's song "Teen Horniness is Not a Crime" under her own name.) The narrative is one element in a mash-up of literary citations, TV texts, pop music references, and movie quotes. Boxer's role in *The Power* is Jericho Cane, the Arnold Schwarzenegger character in *End of Days* (1999); Nana Mae Frost is made up to resemble Angela Lansbury in *The Manchurian Candidate*; the action is more or less framed with quotes from the apocalyptic LA noir, *Kiss Me Deadly*. As the specter of Karl Marx surfaces in various guises, including as the namesake for the last remnant of the Democratic Party, so do refugees from the world of David Lynch.

Kelly's narrative structure is something like a continuous media flow that, as with Brian DePalma's *Redacted*, frequently changes register by shifting to home (or surveillance) video, going online, or interpolating cable news feeds. Ads disrupt the action as the narrative takes a commercial break from itself. In one spot, a pair of SUVs mate; in another, an irate householder asks, "Do you think your personal privacy is worth more than my family's safety from terrorist attack?" Music videos insinuate themselves into the flux, most elaborately when the artfully scarred Fallujah survivor who narrates the movie (Justin Timberlake) lip-syncs the Killers' "All These Things That I've Done" in a pinball arcade populated by a chorus line of vinyl-clad babes.

Attention is divided rather than directed. The frame is filled with and split into multiple screens. Everything happens twice, at least. Yet, even as the narrative arc, which might be compared to advancing from one level to the next through a video-game topography, turns to scribble-scrabble, events do come together as the surviving characters converge for the launch party for the Baron's new dirigible—interiors modeled on Kubrick's *2001*. An earthquake erupts. Riots break out. It's just like *Titanic*, except Rebekah Del Rio is singing the national anthem, solemn little Krysta is previewing her new video, and a levitating ice-cream truck serves as the fatal iceberg.

For all its willful, self-involved eccentricity, *Southland Tales* aspires to be something other than what is conventionally termed a movie. This cinema might have been made to be seen on a laptop—it's a YouTube epic. Kelly's new social realism is addressed less to his characters than the spectator, inducing the as yet unnamed mental state—a mix of distracted concentration and obsessive behavior—that anyone might experience in living online or manning the USIdent panopticon under the influence of Liquid Karma.

CHAPTER TWENTY-SEVEN

INLAND EMPIRE (DAVID LYNCH, 2006; USA)

No director has ever worked closer to his unconscious than David Lynch, and, facilitated by the use of amateur digital-video technology, his three-hour *Inland Empire* takes this blandly enigmatic filmmaker as far inland as he has ever gone.

Inland Empire is all but free-associated—Lynch shot scene to scene without a script beyond a fourteen-page monologue for Laura Dern (recorded in a single seventy-minute take and interspersed throughout the finished film), working off and on this way for three years before enlisting French television to underwrite the completed work—and, however cryptic, it's as personal as a diary film. Lynch shot whatever and whenever he felt like it. This method, Dern told *New York Times* interviewer Dennis Lim, was "unbelievably freeing. You're not sure where you're going or even where you've come from. You can only be in the moment."

The sense of present-ness is contagious. A movie about Lynch's obsessions, *Inland Empire* is largely a meditation on the power of recording: the first image is a shaft of projected light; the second is a close-up of a phonograph needle dropping on a record's groove. Familiar tropes include a movie-within-the-movie and the notion of Hollywood as haunted house. But nothing in Lynch's work is truly familiar, as when a TV sitcom (also within the movie) is enacted by a cast of humanoid rabbits. For most of *Inland Empire*, sinister Eastern Europeans are, as is said, "looking for a way in"—whether to the movie industry or the narrative or the empire itself. (And is this to be, per Neal Gabler's history of Hollywood, an "empire of their own"?)

Reality is first breached when a ditzy, sinister gypsy diva (Grace Zabriskie) traipses into the vintage, disconcertingly empty Hollywood mansion that belongs to actress Nikki Grace (Dern). Spooking the star with her wolfsbane accent and aggressive prophesies, hissing that evil is a form of reflection, she casts a spell of weirdness that lasts throughout the movie. Suddenly it's the next day and Nikki has the role she covets, working with an over-eager director (Jeremy Irons) and acting opposite young rapscallion Devon (Justin Theroux), who's been touted by a nasty TV gossip (Dern's mother, Diane Ladd) as the biggest womanizer in Hollywood. An adulterous affair seems over-determined, particularly as that's the premise of *On High in Blue Tomorrows*, the unlikely title of the movie that Nikki and Devon are making. Script inevitably merges with life. "Hollywood is full of stories," someone remarks, referring to the rumor that the *Blue Tomorrows* screenplay is itself haunted. Haunted? A previous version was abandoned when "they discovered something inside the story ... The two leads were murdered."

They discovered ... Something or someone is lurking in the recesses of the set—and as Nikki's character fissures, it turns out to be her. (Dern is in nearly every scene, and pondered by Lynch's DV camera, her long, angular face is taffy-pulled by wide-angle close-ups into a mask of anguish.) As in a dream, Nikki is both spectator and protagonist. At one point she is trapped by a mysterious spotlight and spooks herself; at another, she climbs a shabby stairway somewhere in Poland and, suddenly another character altogether, launches into an outrageous, tough-girl confession that might be the world's most preposterous screen test.

Inland Empire is Nikki's world, but she really doesn't live in it. She's variously threatened by characters out of *On High in Blue Tomorrows*—taunted, for example, by a lascivious girl gaggle who break into a choreographed version of "The Loco-Motion," thus providing Lynch's obligatory burst of '60s pop. Nikki's mansion devolves into a squalid dump, and a scary Pole known as the Phantom appears next door. Blood mixes with ketchup at a backyard barbecue. Nikki plays her biggest scene at 4 a.m. on the intersection of Hollywood and Vine; having been stabbed with a screwdriver, she staggers bleeding across the star-spangled Walk of Fame to collapse on the pavement amid the homeless. Hollywood is haunted by itself.[1]

It's an understatement to call *Inland Empire* Lynch's most experimental film in the nearly thirty years since he completed *Eraserhead*. But unlike that brilliant debut (or its masterful successors, *Blue Velvet* and *Mulholland Drive*), it lacks concentration. It's a miasma. Did the price of film keep Lynch focused? Cheap DV technology has opened the artist's mental floodgates. *Inland Empire* is suffused with dread of … what? Sex, in Lynch, is a priori nightmarish. But there's a sense here that film itself is evil. Movies are all about editing and acting—which is to say, visual lies and verbal ones—and *Inland Empire* insures the that viewer is cognizant of both.

Lynch's notion of pure cinema is a matter of tawdry scenarios and disconcerting tonal shifts. Everything in *Inland Empire* is uncanny, unmoored, and out of joint. The major special effect is the creepy merging of spaces or times. Do the characters travel through wormholes from Los Angeles to Lodz and the sad, shabby rooms of the *On High in Blue Tomorrows* set? Are these memories or alternate worlds? Is Lynch looking for some sort of movie beneath the movie? (His long search for closure may be turgid and unrelenting, but it hardly lacks for conviction.) The heroine's persistent doubling and Lynch's continuous use of "creative geography" reinforce the sense that he assimilated Maya Deren's venerable avant-noir *Meshes of the Afternoon* at an impressionable age. And like *Meshes*, *Inland Empire* has no logic apart from its movie-ness.

After three hours, Nikki is transfigured (by the "power of love") and her fearful trip is done. But given its nonexistent narrative rhythms, *Inland Empire* doesn't actually feel that long. (In fact, it doesn't feel like anything but itself.) It's an experience. Either you give yourself over to it or you don't. And if you do, don't miss the end credits.

---

1 Thanks to Hollywood, Los Angeles is the world's most photographed metropolis and hence the most apparitional. As film historian Thom Andersen points out in his 2003 cine-essay, *Los Angeles Plays Itself*, this is a metropolis where motels or McDonald's might be constructed to serve as sets and "a place can become a historic landmark because it was once a movie location." The whole city is haunted by an imaginary past. See my essay "A Bright, Guilty World," *Artforum*, February 2007.

CHAPTER TWENTY-EIGHT

BETWEEN DARKNESS AND LIGHT (AFTER WILLIAM BLAKE) (DOUGLAS GORDON, 1997/2006; UK)

The desire to couple movies most likely derives from the Depression-era gimmick of the double feature. The imperative, though, is much more than more-for-your-money—it's yin-yang, thesis-antithesis, right brain versus left brain. That's why it's fertile to write about movie pairs, and natural to program or teach them. Juxtaposed, films cross-pollinate; they talk to each other, especially when screened simultaneously.

Ken Jacobs has been treating movies as objects for years, inventing multiple forms of multi-film projection; Andy Warhol favored double images, shown side by side. James Benning has matched one movie's soundtrack with another's images. More recently, Luis Recoder developed a method for projecting two movies through the same projector. For his 2006 retrospective at the Museum of Modern Art, Scottish artist Douglas Gordon devised another sort of double bill—an empty room where *The Song of Bernadette* (1943) and *The Exorcist* (1973) are shown together on a centrally suspended translucent surface.

Gordon calls this piece *Between Darkness and Light (After William Blake)*, and it's hard to imagine a more Manichaean bill. It's a Hollywood vision of Catholic good and evil, a match made in heaven or hell: A black-and-white inspirational, starring Jennifer Jones as the simple-minded God-intoxicated peasant girl of Lourdes, shares the screen with the color horror flick featuring little Linda Blair possessed by Satan (which was itself once denounced by the Reverend Billy Graham as the embodiment of evil). It's all happening at once, although, depending on which side of the room you choose, the sound from one movie will be slightly dominant.

Simultaneous projection creates a ghostly, ambiguously flattened pictorial space (Rauschenberg depth with a Rosenquist scale). Certain effects are generated automatically—the bizarrely (in)appropriate reaction shots, the strange face grotesquely attached to foreign shoulders. From a narrative point of view, such mutually haunted movies naturally break down into isolated phrases, gestures, and free-floating symbols. Double projecting is inherently experimental. As with human couples, paired movies can mutually liberate repressed aspects and unconscious desires. (I recently had the good luck to simul-show *Fahrenheit 9/11* and *The Passion of the Christ*—the latter imbued the former some cosmic gravitas, the former gave the latter a bit of documentary grit, the suffering Gold Star mothers complemented each other.)

However much *The Song of Bernadette* and *The Exorcist* may crash each other's parties, they emerge as essentially the same movie—lit by candles, filled with crosses, endlessly talking about God and faith. Bernadette will never exorcize *The Exorcist*, but united as *Between Darkness and Light*, they constitute a pageant: anxious mothers fuss over their divine daughters, who take their orders from invisible presences and are regularly harassed by unsympathetic clusters of mainly male unbelievers. Agitated priests discuss faith as miracles erupt into daily life with the force of projectile green vomit.

Because *Bernadette* is half an hour longer than *The Exorcist*, *Between Darkness and Light* is not a simple loop but a relationship—maybe even an altarpiece—that changes over the course of a single day's several projections. During the hour I spent in rapt contemplation, I witnessed Bernadette's humble mother sweep out Regan's suburban palace and a grime-encrusted subway rattle through the streets of Bernadette's village. I saw one possessed child undergo a brutal hospital examination while the other was interrogated by an exceptionally nasty Vincent Price.

Between Darkness and Light is only one of Gordon's cine-manipulations. His famous *24 Hour Psycho* (1993) slows down Hitchcock's thriller to a majestic, pulsating crawl; his proposed *5 Year Drive-By* (1995) would be a site-specific projection of John Ford's *The Searchers* that would not only incorporate one of the movie's locations in Monument Valley, but, shown at an approximate speed of one frame every fifteen minutes would extend over five years, the same period of time the movie encompasses. The visceral and disorienting *left is right and right is wrong and left is wrong and right is right* projects alternate frames of Otto Preminger's *Whirlpool* simultaneously side by side, with one image flipped, to create a kaleidoscopic action flicker film. (*Whirlpool* is a melodrama about hypnosis; *left is right* is an installation designed to induce a hypnotic state.)

Unlike *24 Hour Psycho* and *left is right*, both of which were installed as part of Gordon's MOMA show, *Between Darkness and Light* invites sustained viewing—at least in its current form. (Gordon premiered the piece some years ago in the dank, if not foul, precincts of a pedestrian underpass beneath a busy intersection in Münster, Germany—an environment bound to evoke the spiritual ambience of *The Exorcist* as well as the garbage dump where Bernadette saw the Mother of God.)

Watch any simultaneous projection and, at a certain point, another miracle will occur. The two movies will begin to flow in chaotic sync— everything will make sense. *Between Darkness and Light* has no beginning or end, only an eternal cycle spinning off stray phrases: "She's an angel of God ... How do you go about getting an exorcism ... To think that such a thing could happen in the middle of the nineteenth century ... Your mother sucks cocks in hell ... You're playing with fire, Bernadette!"

CHAPTER TWENTY-NINE

LOL (JOE SWANBERG, 2006; USA)

All in their mid twenties, the three male protagonists of, and collaborators on, Joe Swanberg's ultra-low-budget, semi-improvised, collectively written satire *LOL* are more involved with various cyber-relations than with any human at hand. *LOL* maps a system based on cell phones, instant messaging, websites, and YouTube, to suggest a virtual world more compelling than the real one.

The movie's first shot is of a computer screen with a moving mouse scampering about until it clicks on a link where some boor has posted his girlfriend's private (albeit suspiciously professional seeming) striptease. As she dances and disrobes, eyes never leaving the camera, Swanberg intercuts close-ups of a half-dozen, notably unattractive young guys home alone and comically transfixed by the performance. Could there be hundreds, even thousands, of them enjoying this secret performance? To add to the embarrassment, one spectator—the aspiring musician Alex (Kevin Brewersdorf)—receives an unexpected visit from his friend Tim (Swanberg) and is nearly caught with his pants down. "Have you ever met any of your internet girlfriends?" Tim will later ask Alex.

Alex is seriously infatuated with an image named Tessa, a feature of the website "Young American Bodies," to whom he sends regular (unanswered) emails in hopes of arranging a meeting. Chris (C. Mason Wells) argues with his girlfriend (Greta Gerwig)—who is only present in visual or audio recordings, since she is currently living in another city—complaining that the naked pictures she emailed him, at his request, are too "cold." Tim, who has a flesh-and-blood girlfriend, sits on the couch sending cyber-messages to his buddy over her head and, even in bed keeps one eye on the computer screen in case an email arrives.

While *LOL* is a form of neo neo-realism, it's also an attempt to make a contemporary new wave film. Swanberg's production is characterized by primitive jump cuts and all manner of sub-Godardian sound/image disjunction. A panicky voicemail message is heard over a montage of faces, email messages function as silent movie intertitles. Alex, the most serious as well as the most deluded of the protagonists, is a musician composing a montage of people making mouth noises—as "if MySpace could sing" per the commentary included on the movie's DVD release. This reference is only one of the things identifying *LOL* as a near-instant period piece. Smart phones and Skype for Mac were introduced barely six months after *LOL* was completed. Social networking is primitive. The protagonists are compelled to use cumbersome email and cell phones—rather than Twitter—to report on the minutiae of lives. Even the notion that Alex compulsively checks his email twenty times an hour seems quaint. Stranded without access to the internet, having gone home with a young woman who doesn't have a working computer (and only checks her email once a week), he panics. Still hoping to hear from Tessa and failing to get an ancient PC belonging to the girl's mother online, Alex is forced to call Tim in the middle of the night to get his messages.

Posting on the website PopMatters, Jake Meaney described *LOL* as "an eighty-minute commercial for the pernicious effects of the contradictory bifurcation and conflation of the real and cyber," making the point that the "proliferation and ubiquity of cell phones, Blackberries, computers et al has done more to drive people apart and garble communication than bring them together and make connections easier." But Swanberg celebrates, even as he satirizes the brave new world of cyber-communication. Ancillary material on the *LOL* DVD, the movie was "born out of ideas batted back and forth via computer, cell phone etc and then filmed in the same manner that people use webcams or their cell phones ... but for a few chance non-meetings or unhappy accidents, a much different film could have emerged." Even the filmmaker's unflattering self-portrait has a techno utopian component. If he could make this movie, you could too.[1]

---

1   A particular movement of micro-indie New Talkies (aka Generation DIY, aka Cine Slackavetes, aka MySpace Neo-Realism, aka Mumblecore) coalesced in 2005 when Andrew Bujalski's *Mutual Appreciation*, Swanberg's *Kissing on the*

Mouth, and the Duplass Brothers' *The Puffy Chair* premiered at the SXSW film festival. Over the next eighteen months, these home-made, low-key comedy-dramas of twenty-something angst, along with related films like Aaron Katz's *Dance Party USA*, began turning up in New York, mainly at Two Boots Pioneer, the same East Village venue that incubated the *Donnie Darko* cult.

Bujalski's 2002 *Funny Ha Ha* established the template. Set in a post-graduate milieu, the movie drew heavily on Bujalski's college confreres, using nonprofessionals to portray a small galaxy of awkwardly diffident young people—the most obnoxious loser played by the filmmaker himself. While following Bujalski's lead in constructing narrative and characterization out of constant chatter and a succession of uninflected moments, subsequent Mumblecormedies—disarmingly pragmatic, full of abrupt cuts and choppy inserts and typically running a compact eighty minutes—eschewed 16mm for DV, became even more documentary-like in their reliance on close-ups and presented themselves as collectively scripted enterprises with cast and crew often being identical. Thriving on the modest truth of clumsy mishaps and incoherent riffs, fueled by a combination of narcissism and diffidence, Mumblecore reflects sensibilities formed by MTV's *The Real World* (our life is a movie) and *Seinfeld* (constant discourse), as well as *The Blair Witch Project* (DIY plus Internet). Of course, Mumblecorps members prefer to cite Dogma or Gus Van Sant, who cast his mega-Mumble *Paranoid Park* (2007) through MySpace.

Acting is mainly a coping mechanism. The characters alternate between unconscious and self-conscious. Embarrassment rules. The denizens of Mumblecordia are often failed musicians or would-be writers. Their world is demographically self-contained: straight, white, and middle class. There are no adults, which is to say anyone over thirty. Given the compulsive navel-gazing, paucity of external references, and narrow field of interest, Mumblecore is not for every taste. These movies may be self-absorbed—but what else could a self-portrait be?

CHAPTER THIRTY

FLIGHT OF THE RED BALLOON (HOU HSIAO-HSIEN, 2007; TAIWAN–FRANCE)

In the early 1990s, I made the truculent, unprovable assertion that if Chinese grandmaster Hou Hsiao-hsien were French, he'd be the darling of Manhattan's Upper West Side. The moment of truth arrived with Hou's *Flight of the Red Balloon*—set in Paris, starring Juliette Binoche, and inspired by Albert Lamorisse's classic kid flick about the friendship between a lonely boy and a curiously sentient crimson inflatable.

Spielbergism avant la lettre, *The Red Balloon* was the art-house *E.T.* of 1956. *Flight of the Red Balloon* is something far more baffling—a literal-minded movie with an amiably free-floating metaphor. Hou, who only screened *The Red Balloon* after he was commissioned to remake it by the Musée d'Orsay, has said the Lamorisse film shows the "cruel realities" of childhood. His own version begins as fantasy—as seven-year-old Simon (Simon Iteanu) addresses the otherwise unnoticed scarlet sphere drifting overhead—and then casually naturalizes, tracking the boy over the roofs of Paris to contemplate the untidy existence he shares with his mother Suzanne (Binoche).

Almost immediately, the balloon's role is assumed by the Chinese film student Song (Song Fang) hired to look after Simon. A would-be guardian angel, she hovers in the boy's vicinity before locating the studio where Suzanne is rehearsing her new, Chinese-inspired puppet show. Like the balloon, Song is round-faced and benign, a preternaturally calm, solitary, self-contained observer. She is also like Hou in that she, too, is a foreigner remaking *The Red Balloon*, albeit in DV. Unlike him, however, she's fluent in French.

Is admiration for the balloon a modest form of globalism? Launched at the same Cannes Film Festival that premiered Wong Kar Wai's first non-Chinese-language movie, *My Blueberry Nights*, *Flight of the Red Balloon* was as tepidly received by French critics as *My Blueberry Nights* was by Americans. But where Wong facilely filtered the alien terrain of Soho and Reno through his own distinctive lens, Hou appears to have accepted his distance from the material—and worked with it. *Flight of the Red Balloon* is explicitly an outsider's movie, full of odd perspectives and founded on dislocation.

As though shooting a silent, Hou wrote a script without dialogue—then discussed each scene with his actors, who had to invent their own lines. This surely accounts for Simon's diffidence as well as Binoche's splendiferous eccentricity. Where actual film student Song Fang essentially plays herself, Binoche was compelled to invent the theatrical character Suzanne. The movie is animated not only by the hide-and-seek antics of the red balloon but by her extravagant turn as a frazzled performance artist. Played with total self-absorption and a corresponding absence of vanity, Suzanne is a harried composition in frowsy blonditude, filmy scarves, and mad décolletage—the most dynamic female protagonist in the Hou oeuvre.

Let's call her the spirit of the place. Paris apartments are cluttered, Parisian lives are messy, the city is shown so congested you can smell the exhaust fumes. To cope, Hou himself has adapted a looser, more lyrical style—using window reflections, some of which seem digitally sweetened, and shallow focus to layer and otherwise complicate the image. A movie that encourages the spectator to rummage, *Flight of the Red Balloon* is contemplative but never static, and punctuated by passages of pure cinema. A medley of racing shadows turns out to be cast by a merry-go-round. A long consideration of the setting sun as reflected on a train window that frames the onrushing landscape yields a sudden flood of light. There's a relaxed interest in backstage technique—the yet-to-be-erased techie visible in Song's film, a puppeteer's hidden "dance" in Suzanne's performance, the use of the end credits as a coda to the movie.

Suzanne's interest in Chinese marionettes links Hou's *Red Balloon* (as well as the original) to his 1992 masterpiece, *The Puppetmaster*. The mode can be off-handedly self-reflexive, as when Hou's camera ponders the virtuosity of two movers maneuvering a piano up an impossibly narrow stairway, or in the melancholy juxtaposition of archaic 8mm home movies with Suzanne's voiceover characterizations. Her vocalizations are crucial: Not only does she provide the voices for her puppets, but also much of the back story, explicated over the course of two emotional telephone solos—one brilliantly staged behind the light-struck windshield of a moving car, the other played in total domestic chaos, complete with a blind piano tuner going about his business. Typically, Hou's narrative rhythms allow for long periods in which nothing much happens, followed by a cascade of overlapping information. Abruptly it's revealed that Suzanne, who has inherited two tiny flats, wants to get rid of her deadbeat tenant so that her grown daughter can move in downstairs.

Suzanne's situation may be an emotional jumble but, untethered by mundane reality, the balloon is free to roam—variously appearing as an image on the side of a building, a painting at the Musée d'Orsay, a character in Song's movie, and itself, suddenly visible through a skylight, "watching" Song learning how to make crepes. In her last scene, Song—or rather her reflection—shares the screen with the balloon's shadow, its mirrored image, and finally its fleeting presence as it soars up and away, out of the story. *Flight of the Red Balloon* is no less free. In its unexpected rhythms and visual surprises, its structural innovations and experimental performances, its creative misunderstandings and its outré syntheses, this is a movie of genius.

CHAPTER THIRTY-ONE

HUNGER (STEVE MCQUEEN, 2008; UK)

stablished artists who've made mid-career leaps from gallery to movie
house have not easily found their footing. Julian Schnabel's first
feature was a flop; Robert Longo, David Salle, and Cindy Sherman never
got any further than theirs. British video artist Steve McQueen is the
exception that proves the rule. *Hunger*—which won the prize for best first
feature at the 2008 Cannes Film Festival—is a superbly balanced piece of
work, addressing the passion of Irish Republican martyr Bobby Sands,
who starved himself to death in Belfast's Maze prison in 1981.

Perhaps because of McQueen's experience making video installations, *Hunger* is a compelling drama that's also a formalist triumph. The
opening close-up of prisoners rhythmically banging their cups is held
long enough to establish the movie as something percussive, deliberate, cool, and object-like. McQueen is not just remarkably sensitive to
duration, structure, and camera placement, he brings those issues to
the forefront without mitigating the power of the situation being represented. In a way, the movie is also an installation—as intensely visceral
as it is rigorously detached. (In his review, *Nation* critic Stuart Klawans
described *Hunger* as "a sensory recreation—'re-enactment' is too weak
a word.")

Early on, Prime Minister Margaret Thatcher is heard declaring that
"there is no such thing as political murder, political bombing, or political
violence—there is only criminal murder, bombing, and violence." This
is not something McQueen chooses to push further. As its title suggests,

Hunger is concerned with existential situations—imprisonment, punishment, faith in history (if not God). One never knows the precise crimes the prisoners may have committed, and the jailers, too, are shown locked into their social roles. The emphasis is on procedure. *Hunger* is less a narrative than a cycle of stories or a series of routines: A new prisoner is brought in and stripped—*ecce homo*—then thrown into a literal shit-box with a naked, hirsute madman who has apparently been decorating the cell walls with fecal mandalas.

This excremental environment is a vision of hell, but it, too, is a sort of installation—as well as a tribute to human ingenuity. The prisoners construct dams with mashed-up food in order to flood the corridor with urine; they pass messages through bodily orifices, cope with sensory deprivation by befriending flies. Having refused to wear the prison uniforms, the naked men suggest medieval hermits operating under obscure vows. The guards cope with disobedience by bashing the prisoners' heads against the walls, forcibly shearing their hair, and, at one point, making them crawl a gauntlet. The latter event is comparable in its brutality to the scourging sequence in *The Passion of the Christ*—a movie McQueen may have found useful, not least in its choreography of violent ensemble scenes.

Hunger, too, is essentially contemplative. (It can be bracketed with such other "experiential," post-Gibson passions as *The Death of Mr. Lazarescu, 4 Months, 3 Weeks and 2 Days, United 93*, and *Day Night Day Night*.) The takes are long; the camera is mainly static, moving only to map out some confined space. The emphasis is on the individual setup. The piss-drenched corridor is scrubbed in real-time, with a guard working his way toward the viewer. The mode is materially Christian. The prisoners may use their Bibles for stationery or cigarette paper and exploit mass as a meeting place, but Sands (Michael Fassbender), who only appears midway through the movie, is an explicitly religious martyr. Even the Brits are into self-mortification—one cop compulsively washes his hands in scalding water. One of the few scenes outside the Maze is a cold-blooded execution, resulting in a savage *pietà*, the victim face-down in his mother's blood-spattered lap.

The heart of the movie is an extraordinary twenty-minute conversation between Sands and a tough, far from unsympathetic parish priest (Liam Cunningham), much of it shot in a single take. Sands has requested a meeting to inform the priest of his planned hunger strike.

The hardboiled banter (playwright Enda Walsh's main chance to riff out) is suffused in bleak Irish humor. All argument is stymied, however, by the prisoner's stubborn determination to fast unto death; the priest's irate "then fookin' life must mean nothin' to you" cues a close-up in which Sands answers with a story—or rather a long story within the story. It's not quite "The Grand Inquisitor," but I can't recall a movie with a more powerful priest–prisoner dialogue. (It also offers a discomfiting parallel to the confessional martyr videos produced by devout suicide bombers.)

Hunger's harrowing final movement is informed not only by scripture, but by a thousand years of religious art—with Thatcher, or at least her voice, brought back to play Pontius Pilate. The subject is now exclusively Sands—or rather the physical state of his emaciated body—as he lies on a prison-hospital cot covered with running sores and stigmata lesions. One can barely watch this living cadaver or the bedside food tray that is his constant temptation. I've seen Hunger three times, and with each screening, the spectacle of violence, suffering, and pain becomes more awful and more awe-inspiring.

CHAPTER THIRTY-TWO

OPENING CEREMONIES, BEIJING OLYMPICS (ZHANG YIMOU, CHINA; AUGUST 8, 2008)

Nearly two years in the making, the opening ceremony for the Beijing Olympics was the most elaborate and expensive in Olympic history—with a cast of 15,000 performers and a reported cost of $100 million that may or may not have included the construction of the new National Stadium designed according to the show's requirements or the 1,014 rain dispersal rockets fired to intercept and disperse a rain belt heading toward the stadium—as well as the most-watched telecast in human history. Far surpassing spectatorship for the moon landing, the Obama inauguration, and Princess Diana's funeral, the estimated audience was placed between one and four billion viewers.[1]

Conceived and directed by Zhang Yimou, the live spectacular was characterized by Bob Costas, the NBC sportscaster who provided voice-over commentary for American viewers, as a "cinematic blockbuster in real time." As a technological spectacle and demonstration of cinematic might, the Olympic ceremony belongs to the innovative sci-fi tradition of *2001*, *Close Encounters of the Third Kind*, *Tron*, and *The Matrix*. As a technical tour-de-force historical pageant and real-time performance

---

1   Nick Harris, "1,000,000,000: Beijing sets world TV record," *Sunday Times*, 5/10/2009; Edward Cody, Maureen Fan and Jill Drew, "A Spectacular Opening to the 29th Olympiad," *Washington Post*, 8/9/2008. The numbers are unknowable: Roger Ebert put the show's audience at 3 billion and its budget at $300 million in his review ("Zhang Yimou's gold medal," *Chicago Sun-Times*, 8/9/2008).

preserved by the camera, it begs comparison with *Russian Ark*. As the projection of a national ideology, the Olympic ceremony is only comparable to the cinema of Leni Riefenstahl, sharing an aesthetic previously developed by Zhang with his 2002 *Hero*.[2]

---

2   *Hero* reinvents China's founding myth—attributing the success of the third-century BC king of Qin and China's first emperor to an anonymous warrior (Jet Li) who, recognizing Qin's national destiny, martyrs himself for the empire to be. (In addition to creating an administrative model for Chinese government that would last over 2,000 years—and then providing an ideal for Mao Zedong—the First Emperor standardized Chinese writing, currency, and measurements, built roads and canals, consolidated the Great Wall and introduced the practice of book-burning with a state-sponsored conflagration of Confucius's writings.)

Although Zhang's homage to *Star Wars*'s famous *Triumph of the Will* swipe is surely a nod to George Lucas rather than Leni Riefenstahl, *Hero*'s vast imperial sets and symmetrical tumult, decorative dialectical montage and sanctimonious traditionalism, glorification of ruthless leadership and self-sacrifice on the altar of national greatness, as well as its sense that this might stoke the engine of political regeneration, are all redolent of fascism. Zhang's insistence that he is uninterested in politics is further reminiscent of Riefenstahl. The movie is proudly two-dimensional (heroic Jet Li has no name and less personality, particularly as surrounded by the charismatic likes of Tony Leung, Maggie Cheung, and Zhang Ziyi) and the action is highly aestheticized, with swordplay variously compared to music, calligraphy, and theater.

The degree to which *Hero* is a paean to the authoritarian state informed a number of interesting analyses. (See, for example, Evans Chan, "Zhang Yimou's Hero and the Temptations of Fascism," *Film International* no. 8, 2004; Jenny Kwok Wah Lau, "Hero: China's response to Hollywood globalization," *Jump Cut* no. 49, Spring 2007.) *Hero*'s US release was also controversial. Having acquired China's most costly and top-grossing movie, distributor Miramax kept it on the shelf for eighteen months, diddling with the running time until other forces came into play. Zhang wrote an angry letter to Miramax head Harvey Weinstein: "If you insist on doing nothing to support the film but keep on delaying and cutting down the movie, and eventually destroying it, I cannot imagine how the Chinese government and the whole Chinese population will think of you and Miramax. I truly believe no one could stop their anger! You will be hurting not only me, but also the whole Chinese population." Quentin Tarantino persuaded his padrone Weinstein to restore the movie to its original length and Weinstein's estranged padrone Disney CEO Michael Eisner provided additional funds to facilitate its release as a Tarantino presentation, hoping to facilitate a proposed Shanghai Disneyland—a project finally approved in November 2009.

At $31 million, the most expensive production that had ever been produced in China, an impeccably crafted, all-star martial arts extravaganza, clearly intended to surpass Taiwanese director Ang Lee's 2000 *Crouching Tiger, Hidden Dragon* as an international blockbuster, *Hero* established Zhang as the nation's leading official artist—not just a director but a member of the Chinese People's Political Consultative Conference. *Hero*, which was submitted for Oscar consideration before its Chinese premiere (at the Great Hall of the People!), was praised by government officials as "a new starting point to China's new century." The Olympic ceremony confirmed China's ascendance—and not simply because the nation's GNP had nearly tripled between the two cinematic events.

As with the Nuremberg rally Riefenstahl documented in *Triumph of the Will*, Zhang's stage show was designed to be seen on the screen. Extensive aerial camerawork fully revealed the complex choreographed patterns as field-level close-ups introduced individual participants; effects such as the waterfalls projected on the scrim above the stadium seats or the magical elevation of the Olympic "dream rings" from the stadium floor and into the air, were best enjoyed on television. A dramatic sequence of twenty-nine firework "footprints" marching through Beijing to the stadium was, in fact, digitally enhanced for the live telecast.[3]

For American TV viewers, the Olympic ceremony was further filtered through the consciousness of Bob Costas. Although evidently spooked by the 2008 drummers pounding out a primal beat with a precision he called "intimidating," as well as "awe-inspiring," while suggesting that they smile more, Costas mainly served as a mind-blown cheerleader. He expresses amazement at the skill with which the performers dance on a giant LED video screen or hit their marks in impossible circular

---

3   Steven Spielberg, then working on his own Olympic movie *Munich*, had been asked by Zhang to serve as a consultant on the opening ceremony in 2005. In late 2008, he celebrated Zhang as a *Time* Person of the Year and hailed the Olympic ceremony as "arguably the grandest spectacle of the new millennium." Every movie in Zhang's career was a "luminous precursor" to this "personal journey of destiny … In one evening of visual and emotional splendor, he educated, enlightened and entertained us all. In doing so, Zhang secured himself a place in world history."

To Zhang's embarrassment, Spielberg withdrew as an advisor in February 2008, citing China's support for the Sudanese government and the ongoing violence in Darfur (Rachel Abramowitz, "Spielberg drops out as Beijing Olympics advisor," *Los Angeles Times*, 2/18/2008).

formations while repeatedly using the term "harmonious" to describe what he saw without linking it to Chinese president Hu Jintao's notion of a "harmonious society." When not benignly patriotic, the sentiment is pure "We-Are-The-World" with British soprano Sarah Brightman singing the Olympic theme song "You and Me" with Chinese pop star Liu Huan as dancers run around in real time slow motion, joined by the children of the world. "Benetton could not have done it better," noted the *New York Times* reporter Jim Yardley of this dramatic Global Village.[4]

---

4   The big story, reported on the *Times*'s front page, was the synthesized youngster who became the Olympic ceremony's de facto star. The adorable Lin Miaoke, whom Bob Costas identified by name and who briefly became a planetary celebrity, was, according to a last-minute Politburo directive, actually lip-synching "A Hymn to the Motherland"—another child was deemed to have a better voice but thought insufficiently cute (Jim Yardley, "In Grand Olympic Show, Some Sleight of Voice," *New York Times*, 8/13/2008).

CHAPTER THIRTY-THREE

CARLOS (OLIVIER ASSAYAS, 2010; FRANCE)

The terrorist act by itself is next to nothing, whereas publicity is all. But the media, constantly in need of diversity and new angles, make fickle friends. Terrorists will always have to be innovative. They are, in some respects, the superentertainers of our time.

—Walter Laqueur, *Terrorism: A Study of National and International Political Violence* (1977)

C*arlos*, the widescreen telefilm epic directed by Olivier Assayas, from a script co-written with Dan Franck, gives Ilich Ramírez Sánchez, aka "Carlos the Jackal," his cinematic apotheosis and Assayas an aesthetic breakthrough.

In the fifteen years since *Irma Vep* put the neo in new wave, cine Assayas established two poles: terror and *terroir*. Assayas movies have alternated between essentially callow multi-cultural meta-pop globalizing genre flicks (*demonlover*; *Clean*; *Boarding Gate*) and their antithesis, overly genteel, borderline dull, talk-driven, *très, très* ensemble dramas (*Late August, Early September*; *Les Destinées*; *Summer Hours*). An epic international thriller of many airports, with scenes set in at least fifteen different countries, *Carlos* clearly belongs among the former. But the movie is not without its own sense of *terroir*.

Carlos uses half a dozen or more languages, with almost every actor playing a character of his or her own nationality. The movie's aim is total you-are-there immersion. Despite some jarringly anachronistic dialogue seemingly derived from Hollywood action flicks, *Carlos* evokes the intense craziness of the era itself. This period piece has tremendous immediacy; indeed, the most contemporary thing about *Carlos* is its authentic sense that the nation-state is in some ways helpless. Carlos's twenty-odd-year run was enabled by the complicity (and incompetence) of many, many governments. His career, like the movie, was an international co-production.

Part I follows Carlos around Western Europe as he organizes a series of not always successful bombings and airport attacks, then makes his bones by shooting his way out of a Latin Quarter party full of guitar-strumming Latin American lefties, gunning down two (unarmed) French secret policemen and a PFLP snitch point blank. Reporting on the Rue Toullier massacre, next morning's *Libération* ran the headline MATCH CARLOS 3-0. His pseudonym in the papers! Now in Yemen, his mentor Wali Haddad (Lebanese actor Ahmad Kaabour) disapproves: "You have become a star for the Western media."

Word comes that Saddam Hussein is impressed with Carlos and requests that he head up an operation he's bankrolling to hijack the upcoming OPEC summit meeting in Vienna and punish America's Middle Eastern allies by offing the Saudi and Iranian oil ministers. Part I ends with Carlos and his posse, dressed like Black Panthers (leather jackets, berets, shades) and carrying their weapons in gym bags, setting off down the Ringstrasse to storm the Texaco Building. The extended treatment of the OPEC mission that takes up much of Part II would make a terrific movie in its own right. After a lengthy shoot-out, Carlos and his gang take control, allowing the team's showboat leader to preen and posture on the world stage—most famously the tarmac of the Algiers airport. In Assayas's account, Carlos bonds with some of his captives and threatens others, makes extravagant demands on the Austrians, and generally gives his greatest performance. (Assayas can't resist having one of the lesser oil ministers request an autograph.)[1]

---

1   *Carlos* is privy to the nature of the mission although, back in the day, the world was dumbfounded. ("The terrorists seemed to have only a hazy notion of what they intended to achieve," Walter Laqueur would write. "They induced the Austrian radio to broadcast the text of an ideological statement which, dealing with an obscure topic and formulated in left-wing sectarian language, might just as well have been read out in Chinese ...") This daring stunt dominated headlines for several days before Christmas 1975 and soon after became a non-event—or rather, an event named "Carlos." Carlos entered

Heralded by an incongruous bit of Hawaiian music as he returns to Yemen, Carlos finds a grim-faced Haddad. As punishment for reneging on the OPEC contract, which stipulated that he terminate the Saudi and Iranian oil ministers, Haddad takes him off the next big job, hijacking a Tel Aviv–bound Air France Airbus to Uganda. Lucky break, as it turns out. The German radicals Haddad used to replace Carlos were killed by Israeli commandos at Entebbe. When the press eagerly credits him as the mastermind, Carlos is outraged and self-righteously quits the PFLP: "I won't go on with them, my brand image suffers from it too much!"

Now in business for himself, the "jet-set terrorist" lines up a new backer, Syria, and even takes a wife, the ultra-sulky revolutionary feminist vixen Magdalena Kopp (Nora von Waldstätten). Business seems promising: Colonel Qaddafi (and, so the movie suggests, Soviet spymaster Yuri Andropov) award Carlos the contract on Egyptian president Anwar Sadat. In Part III, the Jackal appears as the de facto King of Budapest, ensconced in a Rózsadomb villa, using the local cops for target practice, throwing himself a birthday bash at the Grand Hotel on Margitsziget. For excitement, Carlos carouses in East Berlin with Stasi-agent hookers and contemplates blowing up Radio Free Europe on behalf of Romanian dictator Nicolae Ceausescu. His sense of omnipotence suffers when a rival outfit beats him to the Sadat hit, but when Magda gets busted in France, he orchestrates a petulant, if deadly, series of retaliatory bombings—mildly Carlossal.[2]

---

the Dream Life; he was now Carlos the Jackal. The nickname, never used in the Assayas film, came when British police found a paperback copy of *The Day of the Jackal*, Frederick Forsyth's 1971 bestseller about a plot to assassinate French President Charles de Gaulle, in what they assumed were Carlos's belongings; but his emergence as an international star coincided almost exactly with the widespread popularity of the Thomas Harris thriller *Black Sunday*. A vision of pro-Palestinian terrorists hijacking the Goodyear blimp in order to bomb the Super Bowl in Miami and obliterate 80,000 fans, including the President of the United States, *Black Sunday* was published the same month as Carlos's Rue Toullier shootout. By the time John Frankenheimer's movie version appeared in April 1977, "the most celebrated and sought-after terrorist abroad today" was the subject of an English-language biography with "all the ingredients of a fictional espionage novel" per the *New York Times*.

2   Meanwhile, the legend grew. Most famously, Carlos would appear as the arch villain of Robert Ludlum's eighties Bourne trilogy. The new Secret Agent of History, he's credited with even masterminding the Kennedy assassination— as a fourteen-year-old Caracas schoolboy!

When the Berlin Wall comes down, Carlos's racket falls apart. "Things have changed," his Syrian patron hisses. Having already lost his East European bases to perestroika, Carlos is kicked out of Damascus and ping-ponged around the Arab world until he finally finds refuge, *sans* Magda and their child, in Sudan. The movie ends on a definite diminuendo with the overweight playboy contemplating liposuction and then getting nabbed dancing the frug with his final concubine at the last disco in Khartoum. Carlos is kidnapped and returned to France to stand trial for the Rue Toullier shootings, twenty years earlier.[3]

While it's hardly surprising that political terrorism would be a major preoccupation of the early twenty-first century, only a few small movies— notably Hany Abu-Assad's *Paradise Now*, Julia Loktev's *Day Night Day Night*, and Paul Greengrass's *United 93*—have pondered the nature of contemporary terrorism. Meanwhile, the ghosts of bombings past have paraded across the screen. Two American documentaries, *The Weather Underground* and *Guerrilla: The Taking of Patty Hearst*, initiated the cycle, as did a revived interest in *The Battle of Algiers* among Pentagon theorists and cineastes alike. Steven Spielberg's *Munich* planted Hollywood's flag; the cycle then went international with Koji Wakamatsu's *United Red Army*, Uli Edel's *The Baader Meinhof Complex*, and Barbet Schroeder's *Terror's Advocate*, a documentary portrait of rogue lawyer Jacques Verges, which devotes a substantial amount of time to Carlos and even features the still-stylish Magda in a supporting role.

For all their mayhem, these movies provide an odd sort of comfort. However crazy, misguided or evil, seventies terrorists had a comprehensible rationale and even a social agenda. The fanatics of the '00s are far more frightening, and not just because suicide bombings are a near-daily occurrence in Iraq, Afghanistan, and Pakistan, or because the combined

---

3   Brought to justice, Carlos became an even more fantastic creature. His capture was fictionalized in *The Assignment* (1997), with Aidan Quinn playing both the terrorist and his CIA-trained double; the Bruce Willis vehicle *Jackal* (a remake of the 1973 *Day of the Jackal*, by now widely assumed to have been inspired by Carlos) was released shortly after. British journalist John Follain published a new Carlos biography in 1998; the same year, Carlos had a cameo role in Tom Clancy's novel *Rainbow Six* and in *The Last Inauguration* by Charles Lichtman, hired by Saddam Hussein to wipe out the entire US government by sabotaging the inaugural ball, and either the book's arch-villain or, according to one reviewer, its "most appealing character."

body-count produced by Baader-Meinhoff, the United Red Army, the Symbionese Liberation Army, and Carlos was considerably less than the 3,000 casualties reaped by Al Qaeda in a single day. The conventional wisdom of the seventies held that urban terrorism was incapable of effecting political change and remarkable mainly for the attention paid to it. "Terrorism ultimately aims at the spectator," psychiatrist F. Gentry Harris told the US Congress in hearings held in early 1974, at precisely the time that Patty Hearst was captive to the SLA, and Carlos chucked a bomb into the London branch of an Israeli bank. "The victim is secondary."

A generational audience is inscribed when giddy *Baader Meinhof* opens with plaintive Janis Joplin fanfare, while *Munich* features a key sequence founded on the universality of Motown. *Carlos* taps into an even more active nostalgia. Watching this bizarre saga, it is difficult not to tsk-tsk the amazing innocence of the pre-9/11 world—the astounding absence of embassy security, the incredible possibility that militant crazies might simply bring their rocket launchers to the airport and attempt to blow up El Al planes on the runway.[4]

The latest and the longest cine-spectacularization of seventies terrorism made since 9/11 changed the world, *Carlos* pays relatively little attention to terror's casualties. They are collateral damage—sacrifices on the altar of celebrity. As much as any reality-TV hopeful, Carlos's true interest is fame. Bustling around the world on a perpetual adrenaline high, suitcases full of firearms and pockets stuffed with fake

---

4 This appreciation of disorder is something quite different from a yearning for lost ideals (Carlos has none), although, as an epic docudrama constructed around a dangerously dashing Latin Lover of action, *Carlos* has been inevitably bracketed with Steven Soderbergh's *Che*. *Carlos* and *Che* are both technical achievements but the filmmaking is quite different. Soderbergh engages Rossellini; Assayas is closer to Fritz Lang. (As *Les Vampires* was to *Irma Vep*, so *Dr. Mabuse* is to *Carlos*.) Soderbergh's protagonist is a martyred saint; Assayas's is a publicity-seeking celebrity. Where *Che* is high-minded, emotionally distant, and ascetic, *Carlos* is low-down, up close, and sensationalist. This is as it should be. Despite his jaunty beret and taste for Cuban cigars, Carlos was the anti-Che; in Castro's Cuba, the "urban terrorism" that came to supersede guerrilla warfare was, in fact, a derogatory term. As cinema, *Che* aspires to be an objective meditation on the process of "making history." Less rigorous and more fun, *Carlos* is an outrageous political gangster film, full of cheap thrills and unburdened by even a hint of German philosophy. Carlos's interest is less in making history than simply making up his story.

passports—confidently arrogant yet desperate for approval—Carlos is a show-business hyphenate, a would-be producer-director, the wannabe star of a self-written scenario. Even in jail, he attempted to sue Assayas's producers for the right of final cut.

CHAPTER THIRTY-FOUR

THE STRANGE CASE OF ANGELICA (MANOEL DE OLIVEIRA, 2010; PORTUGAL)

The most existential of filmmakers, Manoel de Oliveira has, for decades now, been making each movie as though it were his last. *The Strange Case of Angelica* is one more unique sign-off—drily comic, intentionally stilted, deliberate yet digressive, at once avant-garde and retro.

An amateur who made a silent documentary, *Working on the River Douro*, in 1931, then spent decades managing his father's lighting-fixture factory—as well as racing cars—and who only managed to make two features before 1970, Oliveira is an artist with a unique career trajectory: he hit his stride in his late sixties, soon after Portugal's "Revolution of the Carnations," and became ever more prolific as he aged—making over half of his movies since turning eighty.

Although technically another one of Oliveira's frustrated love stories, *The Strange Case of Angelica* is also sui generis. As funny and peculiar as its title promises, it's a modestly serene and sublime meditation on the essence of the motion-picture medium, glimpsed in the half-light of eternity. One rainy night, the amateur photographer Isaac (Oliveira's grandson Ricardo Trêpa) is rousted from his boarding house in the northern Portuguese town of Régua and brought to an estate where he is commissioned to create a last image of the family's beautiful daughter, dead but a few days after her wedding. The family treats Isaac with a touch of suspicion—he's immediately been identified as a Jew and hence an uncanny presence. (There may be only a thousand Jews in all of Portugal, but the country is haunted by the thousands of Sephardim who, like the parents of Baruch Spinoza, were driven from the country or forced to convert.)

Gathered in the parlor, the bereaved family solemnly watches as Isaac sets about photographing their beatifically smiling Angelica, laid out in her wedding dress on a fainting couch. For his part, Isaac is taken aback when, studying his subject through his viewfinder, she appears to open her eyes and widen her smile ... just for him. O muse of photography! (Or, as an unidentified poem, twice cited in the film puts it, *Time, stand still ... Angels open the gates of Heaven, for in my night is day, and God is in me.*) Angelica's family, we note, lives surrounded by the framed photographs of their ancestors. For his part, Isaac is forever seeing the representation of angels—creatures of light—engraved in books, carved in ceilings.

Angelica's time is splendidly indeterminate. Despite some topical references and recent vintage automobiles, the fashions and the ambiance suggest the early 1950s—when Oliveira wrote his first version of the script—while the social protocols, and the narrative development, could be those of the late nineteenth century. Technology is similarly timeless: Isaac makes his images the old-fashioned way, by exposing photographic film to the light. One miracle leads to another; after Isaac develops and prints Angelica's portrait, the girl in the picture broadly grins at him. (Her playful gesture recalls the luridly blinking images of Jesus Christ once sold in neighborhood *botánicas* and Times Square novelty stores.)

Having thus produced a motion picture and, like more than one filmmaker, fallen in love with the image his camera has brought back to life, Isaac repeatedly returns to Angelica's family church, surreptitiously attending her funeral, photographing the nave, or pondering her crypt— each time encountering and ignoring the same halfhearted beggar. He delays delivering the finished photographs, perhaps afraid that this will end her nocturnal visits. By night, smiling Angelica materializes to transport the photographer through the air; together they fly over the roofs of Régua and the River Douro and into the starry sky.

The effect is pure Méliès, as is the joke when Isaac falls from heaven to wake with a start in his bed. In the great avant-garde tradition, *Angelica* is programmatically anachronistic. Although Oliveira here uses CGI for the first time (in the service of his first-ever dream sequence), the movie's special effects might have seemed quaint a hundred years ago—albeit no more obvious than the rain machine Oliveira employs to atmospheric effect in several scenes. It's striking that the morning after his first flight, Isaac awakens to a world grounded in ambient noise.

The reclusive photographer's evident preoccupation and odd behavior becomes an object of concern for his landlady and the subject of some discussion among his fellow boarders. The mock philosophical symposium is one of Oliveira's favorite forms of narrative digression. Gathered around the breakfast table, the landlady bustling in and out, these gentlemen of leisure hold forth on Ortega y Gasset's notion of "man and his circumstance," discuss the economic crisis, bridge construction, climate change, anti-matter and the "seven mosquitoes of apocalypse." During the conversation, a distracted Isaac makes his taciturn appearance, standing off to the side to nurse his cup of coffee.

Oliveira has not spoken to his movie's allegorical aspect—or rather, he has steered his interlocutors in another direction. *The Strange Case of Angelica* is based on a script the filmmaker prepared in 1952. (Had it been filmed then it would have been his second feature, after the proto neo-realist *Aniki-Bóbó*, made under the sign of Jean Vigo and shot mainly around the Oporto waterfront; as it was, his second feature *O Acto de Primavera*, completed in 1963, documented the village of Curalha's annual passion play.) The Ur-*Angelica* may have been intended as a response to the massacres of World War II although now, it would seem, the meaning of the story lies in the pleasure of the telling. (At once matter-of-fact and fantastic, it might be a subplot in Ben Katchor's comic strip "Julius Knipl, Real Estate Photographer.") Feinting this way and that as he prepares his endgame, Oliveira advances the narrative with the expertise of a chess master pushing his pawns.

Every camera angle and foley effect seems precisely calibrated. The filmmaker seems to savor each set-up without ever clinging to the moment. No less than *Vertigo* or *Solaris*, *The Strange Case of Angelica* is a variation of the Orpheus myth (Isaac, like Cocteau's poet, derives inspiration from static-garbled radio transmissions) but Oliveira's version of the myth is playfully prosaic. After a night spent with Angelica floating over his bed, Isaac wakes to the clamor of the morning—his landlady is mourning her dead canary. One of the boarders suggests that she preserve it through taxidermy. Isaac believes the bird's death is connected to Angelica's resurrection; rather, it presages his own fate. Inevitably, the obsessed photographer joins his beloved in death.

If Angelica is the essence of photography, Isaac is the medium's humble servant. He even lives in a sort of camera—his rented room is a darkened box, illuminated only by the window overlooking the Douro, subject of Oliveira's first movie. In addition to thinking about Angelica, or perhaps as an antidote, Isaac makes photographs of the world, specifically a group of laborers, singing as they work the olive grove across the river, disdainfully indifferent to his attention. (Again, all times coexist: the workers are repeatedly described as "old-fashioned.") *The Strange Case* has its documentary aspects as well. In one apparent non sequitur, Oliveira frames the house cat intently watching the landlady's canary. The shot is held until, somewhere in the vastness beyond the frame, a dog barks, humorously underscoring the cat's presumably unscripted concentration.

Playing out its dialectic between the infinite and the ephemeral, the movie ends with the song of the workers in the vineyard. The landlady draws the shutters on Isaac's window. The camera that is Isaac's room vanishes, along with Oliveira's, leaving only darkness and the sound of fading footsteps. The last living filmmaker born during the age of the nickelodeon, Oliveira told an interviewer that cinema today is "the same as it was for Lumiére, for Méliès and Max Linder. There you have realism, the fantastic, and the comic. There's nothing more to add to that, absolutely nothing." The great beauty of this love song to the medium is that Oliveira's eschewal remains absolute. It's a strange case—pictures move and time stands still.

CHAPTER THIRTY-FIVE

ONCE UPON A TIME IN ANATOLIA (NURI BILGE CEYLAN, 2011; TURKEY)

Turkey's leading filmmaker, Nuri Bilge Ceylan had several accomplished, festival-friendly evocations of urban isolation to his credit—notably the character study *Distant* (2002) and the pensive breakup not-quite-comedy *Climates* (2006)—when his *Once Upon a Time in Anatolia* had its world premiere as the last competition movie shown on the last night of the 2011 Cannes Film Festival.

In themes and style, Ceylan's earlier films are evocative of early Antonioni; *Once Upon a Time in Anatolia*, a 157-minute police procedural at once sensuous and cerebral, profane and metaphysical, "empty" and abundant, is closer to the Antonioni of *L'Avventura*, and it elevates the fifty-two-year-old director to a new level of achievement.

I first saw *Once Upon a Time* under less than optimal circumstances and it knocked me out; the movie seemed even stronger on second viewing, and left me curious to see it again. The title suggests a shaggy-dog story or a fairy tale, or you could call it an epistemological murder mystery. Like several recent Romanian movies—notably Corneliu Porumboiu's 2009 *Police, Adjective* and Cristi Puiu's 2010 *Aurora—Once Upon a Time* is a nominal genre film that, in the way that its narrative is delivered, invites the viewer to meditate on the nature of truth or the basis of knowledge.

It's also, like Ceylan's earlier films, shot on high-definition video and transferred to 35mm film, and an impeccably beautiful representation of the everyday—as demonstrated by the brief prologue, a slow, steady zoom through a service station's dirt-encrusted window into a barren room where three guys, one of whom will perhaps be killed by the other two, eat and drink under the blind gaze of a blurry black-and-white TV. Cue the distant thunder—let the investigation begin.

At once absurd road film and grand metaphor, the movie's first third is a search for meaning in the void. A convoy of official cars drive by night through the barren countryside; they have two suspects in custody and are vainly seeking the spot (by a "round" tree) where they claim to have buried the third. "How do you know it's not here?" one of the increasingly frustrated cops demands.

Everyone on this journey is a student of life. The futile quest and fruitless interrogation are paralleled by inane small talk among the various investigators as well as a series of fraught private conversations between the party's two professionals—the glib prosecuting attorney and a self-effacing young doctor riding along as a witness to pronounce the corpse dead if found. Headlights illuminate the landscape and transform it into a near-empty stage. (As much as *Once Upon a Time* concerns the problems of deductive logic, it's also a movie about the quality of the light.) Midway through, in a scene of uncanny loveliness and material visions, the group pulls into a remote village for a late-night meal at the headman's house. The night has given birth to a dream. Later, with the sky beginning to lighten over a hill as bleak as Calvary, the searchers find that for which they have been searching (perhaps) and go about creating an official report complete with detailed descriptions and photographs of … what?

"There's a reason for everything," someone says unconvincingly, once back in the car. With the mission accomplished, in a somewhat farcical fashion, the film might have ended here. There is, however, a morning after. The corpse is brought back to town so that the doctor may perform an autopsy. The night of mystery is over. The evidence can now be pondered by the dawn's dreary light. Procedure is followed. Still, however banal the daytime images, a metaphysical darkness remains—and even grows. Will the presumed widow identify the body? Can she? The autopsy begins, presenting more puzzling facts. Why is there dirt in the corpse's lungs? What is dug up must again be buried.

A grand narrative yarn spun from a number of smaller ones, *Once Upon a Time in Anatolia* demonstrates the truism that the more we know, the less we understand. Or is it vice versa? Perhaps the greater under-standing is admitting how little we can know.[1]

---

1   This appreciation of *Once Upon a Time in Anatolia* is drawn from what would be my last review for the *Village Voice*, a publication where I had written on film for over thirty years. I was pleased to have concluded my run with so great a movie; it was similarly fortunate the remainder of my page was devoted to another terrific work, Ken Jacobs's *Seeking the Monkey King* which was screening that week in support of Occupy Wall Street:

> An exhilarating audiovisual workout that simultaneously engages multiple parts of the brain, Jacobs's forty-minute movie is a sort of hal-lucinatory jeremiad. The basic imagery seems derived from close-ups of crumpled metallic foil; this material, which oscillates in color between rich amber and deep blue, is subjected to a barrage of cyclical digital manipulations and married to J. G. Thirlwell's clamorous score. The sound surges; the screen is a roiling imaginary landscape of frozen fire and burning ice. Intermittently, Jacobs superimposes the text of a caustic anti-capitalist, anti-patriotic harangue addressed to a figure he calls "The Monkey King": "Oh, mighty lord of deception, America has always kissed your hairy ass."
>
> Covering 500 years of American history, this furious beatnik analy-sis makes a people's historian like Howard Zinn seem like a Chamber of Commerce booster, particularly as delivered amid Thirlwell's indus-trial-strength rhapsodic noise drone, against the seething apocalypse of melting glaciers and crystallized lava that soon becomes an ongoing Rorschach test. Faces come out of the rain, along with paper snakes, Tibetan samurais, baleful simians, Duchamp's *Nude Descending a Staircase*, and scarab-encrusted Mayan temples. Denouncing the US as essentially fictitious, "an enlarged and empty Brillo box," Jacobs has moments of Syberbergian melancholy, evoking admired artworks (*Moby-Dick, Freaks, Greed*) and kindred artists (Max Beckmann, Maya Deren, Fats Waller) even as a tremendous energy is unleashed on the screen. This homemade slingshot has the capacity to resist and pulverize the idiotic visual aggression of a commercial behemoth like *Transformers*. It's a '60s vision happening today—beautiful, terrifying, and determined to storm the doors of perception.

INDEX